Research and Development
Project Selection Criteria

Revised Edition

Research for Business Decisions, No. 80

Richard N. Farmer, Series Editor

Professor of International Business
Indiana University

Other Titles in This Series

Research and Development
Project Selection Criteria

Revised Edition

by
Jackson E. Ramsey

U·M·I Research Press

Ann Arbor, Michigan

658.503
R18ra

Produced and distributed by
UMI Research Press
an imprint of
University Microfilms, Inc.
Ann Arbor, Michigan 48106

Library of Congress Cataloging in Publication Data

Ramsey, Jackson Eugene, 1938-
Research and development.

(Research for business decisions ; no. 80)
Revision of thesis (Ph.D.)—State University of
New York at Buffalo, 1976.
Bibliography: p.
Includes index.
1. Research, Industrial—Decision making.
2. New Products—Decision making. I. Title.
II. Series.
T175.5.R26   1986   658.5'03   86-16085
ISBN 0-8357-1708-9 (alk. paper)

Contents

1

Introduction: The R&D to
Operations Process

New Products and R&D

Research and development are important facets of the United States economy. While spending on R&D did not grow at the rate of inflation during most of the 1970s, the last six years have seen an increased emphasis on R&D investment. According to the best estimates, $93.8 billion were spent in 1984, 47% from federal government funds.[1] For 1986, estimates suggest spending levels of about $116 billion. This 1986 spending will represent about a 4% increase over 1985, continuing the trend of the 1980s.[2] Future projections predict even greater increases in R&D expenditure. Even more important than this dollar expenditure, however, has been the rate of technological change that has obsoleted many existing products. A new product "push" seems to exist resulting from three interlocking needs: to match the new product entries of competitors, to anticipate changing customer requirements and preferences, and to keep pace with fast-moving technology. As a result, the importance of new products to the future of many firms has increased substantially over the last 20 years.

A National Industrial Conference Board report of 1962 noted that 20% of the sales of companies it surveyed came from products introduced over the previous five years.[3] Seventy percent of the firms surveyed for this report predicted that they would be even more dependent on new products in the future. While updated data of this type is not available, all indications are that the National Industrial Conference Board report understated the issue; new product sales are even more vital to firms in the 1980s than predicted in the 1960s.

Knowledge of the process of generation of new products for the firm, however, has not kept pace with the importance to the firm of new products. Within large industrial organizations the process by which ideas for new classes of products or new products within existing classes are conceived, analyzed, developed, and transferred to operating divisions is only partially understood. Some process steps, such as project selection,[4] idea generation,[5] and market introduction,[6] have been investigated in detail. Others, such as strategy formulation, decision making, compliance of the process with corporate objectives, and the interaction between R&D and operations, have had little analysis.

Types of Research

Since the general R&D area encompasses a number of different types of activities, a discussion of R&D necessitates identification and definition of different types of research. Definitions of the research spectrum are by no means consistent. Hill and Granger's definitions are typical of the literature, breaking the spectrum into basic research, applied research and development, and technical service.[7]

Basic research is defined as research seeking an understanding of the universe and knowledge about it. As basic research is used in the literature, it is concerned with the generation of ideas and identification of new phenomena and activities. It is not necessarily need or product related, and frequently offers a benefit only in terms of knowledge.

For purposes of this book, research and/or development for generic material bases without specific product application (such as nylon, transistors, microwaves, and so on) are considered basic research, since the justification for expenditures and the decision criteria differ widely from those of product-oriented research.

Applied R&D is defined as the process of applying the knowledge or results of the basic research and evolving a specific device or method that has some practical use. Applied R&D is often broken in the literature into two major subsystems. The first involves maintenance and strengthening of the firm's present course of earnings, and includes areas of cost reduction, process improvement, product quality improvement, and so on. The second subsystem is applied R&D generation of specific new products for the market place.

Technical service involves research that is used almost exclusively to support present sales effort. An example of technical service research is the modification of a current product for a new customer. Technical service research is normally located within the operating division rather than at a central R&D location, and is normally a part of the operating, rather than the research, division.

Applied New Product R&D

This book is concerned only with the applied research and development area, and only with the new product development subsystem. All analysis and recommendations will focus on the new product applied R&D area, although some of the recommendations may be applicable to the basic research and technical service areas as well.

R&D is accomplished by many types of organizations for many purposes. Major areas include government, university, and industrial R&D. Not all of these areas are involved in applied new product R&D. In addition, there is no reason to assume that the R&D to operations process is the same in each of these organizational areas. Because of these differences, this book will concentrate on applied new product R&D in the industrial sector.

To provide a framework for analysis and discussion, this book assumes large, profit-oriented, technologically based manufacturing firms whose R&D organizations emphasize the generation of new products. Such organizations typically have a central R&D division serving a number of operating divisions organized along product lines. These types of firms will typically have ongoing new product development functions, with new products continually being introduced into the initial stages of the development process.

The normative recommendations of the book, however, are not limited to profit-oriented industrial research. Different objectives and decision criteria are more appropriate for governmental- and academic-oriented research.

Presentation of This Investigation

The value of applied new product development to an individual firm has been well documented. The same literature, however, indicates problem areas in the development process in identifying new products to be developed, and in the movement of new product projects through the development process and into the operations process for market introduction.

The purpose of this book is to identify the R&D to operations planning process, to identify the elements within the process that cause unsatisfactory performance and inefficiencies, and to recommend a new series of R&D to operations planning processes and decisions to improve the overall efficiency of new product introduction.

The results desired are both identification of problems in the present planning system and recommendations of solutions to overcome these problems. The recommendations will present the R&D to operations planning process as a total system, rather than a compilation of separate decisions in the operational, economic, or behavorial areas, since this system's treatment by itself will aid in solving some of the identified problems.

The approach to be taken is evaluation of the present system and conceptual recommendations of problem area solutions. The objective is to provide a conceptual framework that can be used by a wide range of firms in their applied new product development decision-making processes.

The balance of this chapter identifies the present R&D to operations process as a process flow stage model compiled by combining the various activities over the development process identified in the literature.

Chapter 2 investigates the shortcomings of present management approaches to the R&D to operations process. Two major problem areas, problems due to lack of intralevel objective and strategy interaction, and problems due to failure of individual new product projects, are identified by analysis of the literature of current and past United States industrial firm results.

Shortcomings in the intralevel objective and strategy systems from the current literature are identified and analyzed in chapter 3. Shortcomings and any literature suggestions are presented from the marketing, operations research, R&D management, and strategic planning viewpoints.

Chapter 4 identifies and analyzes the shortcomings of the present R&D to operations processes in terms of evidence of causes of failure of specific new product projects. Emphasis is given to causes of economic failure of projects, with discussion being presented from organizational, control, business analysis, and decision-making viewpoints.

The identification and analysis of the intralevel objective and strategy interactions and causes of project failures are of interest for their own sake. For this book, however, their importance is as an identifying mechanism for problems to be corrected in the normative recommendations which follow.

Chapter 5 introduces the normative frameworks that follow and provides an introduction for the way in which the frameworks are recommended and the way in which they interrelate. Chapter 5 presents short conclusions of the literature surveys of chapters 3 and 4, discusses the general methodology used for development of the frameworks, and presents an overview for and discussion of the advantages of the normative frameworks.

In chapter 6 a downward cascading set of objectives and strategies is proposed for R&D intensive firms. Starting with specific definitions at the corporate level, objectives and strategies are passed down level by level through the organization. The result is a set of objectives and strategies provided to the R&D division for its use in decision making. Decision making within these provided objectives and strategies ensures decision making consistent with objectives and strategies at higher levels in the firm. Specific corporate value objectives are suggested, with specific suggestions of subsystems for corporate performance measurement in accordance with objectives and strategies derived from the corporate value objectives.

Having provided the desired objectives and strategies to the R&D decision makers, chapter 7 presents normative recommendations for new product project selection criteria and procedures consistent with the provided objectives and strategies. Four normative decisions and their locations on the new product process stage model are identified and discussed. Decision I requires a rough screening of a product idea prior to formal business analysis. Decision IIa involves creation of a pool of potentially successful product ideas. Decision IIb involves selection of specific product ideas from the pool to begin technical development. Decisions III and IV require review of decision IIb to determine if project development should be halted due to internal or external changes in expectations.

For each decision, performance objectives and measurement techniques are provided and discussed, and examples of goal values are provided and discussed. A specific step-by-step decision flow model is provided. In addition, a decision-making organizational structure and identification of individual(s) and/or functions in the structure are recommended.

Finally, chapter 8 summarizes the advantages and disadvantages of the conceptual normative framework presented. Emphasis is given to the attempt of this normative framework to structure as many of the decision details as is possible, while recognizing that the state of the art in R&D decision making is such that completely objective decision methods cannot be used. In addition, recommendations for future research based upon areas of weakness identified in this investigation are presented.

The R&D to Operations Process Flow

In general, existing literature treats the R&D to operations planning process as a set of independent steps. The decisions to be made at each step are normally considered to be independent of decisions at other steps, as if each is to be made in a vacuum rather than in the context of an ongoing process.

It is possible, however, to develop a series of usual process flow stages so that the total R&D to operations process can be viewed as a system. Such a process stage model, identifying the usual processes by which new product ideas are conceived, developed, and transferred to operating divisions within a large, technologically based industrial firm, is shown in figure 1. Six stages are suggested in this new product development model. They are: idea generation, business analysis, technical development, prototype, pre-production, and market introduction. These six stages describe all of the steps involved in the usual R&D to operations process, although many firms combine or skip some stages.

Figure 1. The New Product Development Process Stage Model

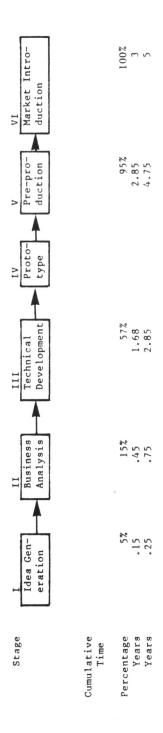

Stage	I Idea Gen- eration	II Business Analysis	III Technical Development	IV Proto- type	V Pre-pro- duction	VI Market Intro- duction
Cumulative Time						
Percentage	5%	15%	57%		95%	100%
Years	.15	.45	1.68		2.85	3
Years	.25	.75	2.85		4.75	5

In addition to identifying the stages in the model, figure 1 also maps onto the model approximate cumulative times taken by each stage in the model. These figures are based upon Booz, Allen and Hamilton studies of actual new product development projects in large, technologically based United States firms. They show a three- to five-year cycle for the completion of the total new product development system.[8] In general, the idea generation stage ranges from an approximate minimum of .15 years to an approximate maximum of .25 years, the business analysis stage .3–.5 years, and the technical development stage 1.23–2.1 years. The prototype and pre-production stages together cover 1.17–1.9 years, while the market introduction stage covers .15–.25 years.

The idea generation stage involves identification of potential new product ideas. Emphasis is given to stimulation and encouragement of individuals within and outside the firm to suggest products or product market areas for development. All functional areas within the firm are encouraged to submit product ideas, although most studies have suggested that the R&D and marketing function members are the best overall source of ideas for new products that later are successful in the marketplace.[9]

A new product idea at this stage consists of a description of the potential market and the product properties required for the potential market. The market is described in terms of expected customers, price, sales volume, market share, and so on. Desired product properties are expressed in terms of hardness, ductility, color, fragrance, appearance, strength, dimensions, and so on. The decision at the idea generation stage involves the choice of product ideas to be passed on to the business analysis stage for more formal analysis.

The business analysis stage decision involves choosing from among a group of product ideas the specific product projects to be developed technically. At this stage, technical development is assigned, and commitments made to allocate capital funds, manpower, and priorities at the prototype, pre-production, and market introduction stages. Financial decision criteria used in the business analysis stage include return on investment, discounted present value, return on sales, and so on. Marketing and technical decision criteria are also often used, including definition of the market segment to be filled, rate of sales growth, contribution to technical knowledge, and R&D personnel interests. A variety of methods for expressing and calculating various decision criteria are available.

In general, constraints on R&D manpower, R&D fund allocation, funds available for capital expenditure, and so on mean that it is not possible to technically develop all product ideas. Selection of specific products for development is generally made using various decision criteria which are based upon the subjective opinion of the decision maker or by arbitrary mathematical algorithims.

The technical development stage includes all activities required to develop a product idea with the desired properties that can be developed at the cost identified in the business analysis stage. Technical development is normally carried out by the R&D division. Decision making at the technical development stage involves specific scientific or engineering details concerned with the technical success of development, and possible halting of development if technical results appear unsatisfactory or if cost estimates are exceeded by a large amount.

The prototype stage could be included in the technical development stage. It is presented here as a separate stage to identify the area where manufacture of the product can be simulated on a scale above that of the research facility but below that of full manufacturing operation. The goal of the prototype stage is to ensure that the technically developed product can be manufactured at the appropriate cost levels in the desired quantities. Few decisions are made at the prototype stage, other than the decision to halt development if costs are much greater than anticipated.

The technically developed product is transferred to the operating division for the pre-production stage. The pre-production stage involves activities of the divisional manufacturing and marketing functions. In general, marketing must test market the product, establish advertising, pricing, and promotional policies, establish channels of distribution, provide sales personnel training, and carry out the other activities usually associated with the introduction of a new product.

At the same time the manufacturing function must modify existing equipment and install and troubleshoot new equipment for new product production. Trial quantity runs must be performed to manufacture samples for market test and to build an inventory for market introduction, as well as to verify that the new product can be produced at the desired cost, quantity, and quality levels.

While numerous minor decisions are made during the pre-production stage, the new product project usually proceeds to market introduction.

At market introduction the new product is introduced into the marketplace and made available to customers on a regular basis. Market introduction is the last stage in new product development. It is also considered in most of the literature as the first stage in the regular operating plans of an operating division. It is included in this model to provide a logical final stage. Once in this stage decisions are made as a part of the regular divisional operating plan, and the new product development process ceases to have a significant impact.

This process flow stage model is presented here as a normative recommendation and as the basis for discussion in this book. Normative recommendations as to decision content and decision locations will be mapped onto this process flow model so that their location and content can be placed in the context of the total new product R&D to operations planning system.

Summary

The importance of new product R&D to the United States economy and the economy of many firms has been well documented. This book treats the new product development planning process as a system, and presents a conceptual overview of the process with the objective of identifying weakness in the present system and providing recommendations to improve the overall R&D to operations planning process. A new product development process flow system model is formally defined to serve as a framework within which discussion can take place and normative recommendations made.

2

Problems in Present
Management Approaches

In order to identify some of the problems of the present R&D to operations planning process an extensive literature search was conducted. While this literature search covered the time period from the end of the Second World War to the start of 1986, published literature on R&D management was not spread evenly over this time period. In fact, the published work of the late 1970s and early '80s, although sparse, suggests that few changes have been made from earlier time periods.

The results of this search suggested that problems could be grouped and summarized into two major problem areas.

1. A lack of emphasis in placing the new product development process, the R&D function, and the area of individual project selection in the framework of corporate objectives and strategies.

2. An inefficient and ineffective use of resources in the new product development process as identified by a low rate of successful market introductions from products handled under the current process. (A successful market introduction is defined as a product introduced into the marketplace that generates enough sales, revenue, and profit to become an accepted part of the firm's product line.)

Lack of Intralevel Objective and Strategy Interaction

The Firm and Its Subsystems

Robert Bowie notes:

> One of the obvious means, and the first in chronological order, of achieving an effective operation is to set forth definite goals and objectives for the enterprise and to make certain that the goals and objectives of subordinate organizations are both appropriate to the function of each division, and fully integrated with the enterprise goals.[1]

Bowie then notes that although few managers disagree with this proposition in theory, few put it into practice. Corporate life is too generally strewn with "vague purposes, pious hopes, amorphous objectives, and simple omissions"[2] to expect such a strong relationship to exist among intralevel goals and objectives.

Charles Granger was among the first to formally suggest objectives within objectives—a hierarchy of objectives.[3] One of his approaches began with the overall objectives of the firm and worked downward through the various subsystem levels. His methodology suggests conceptual creation of a number of possible subobjectives and testing them against the realities of (1) consistency with internal resources, (2) consistency with environmental conditions, and (3) effective cost relationships in accomplishing the broader objectives. Note that this suggests both consistency of subobjectives with the objectives at higher levels in the system, and consistency of the subobjectives with the resources available to that particular subsystem.

Granger further points out the problems arising from the interaction between the individual and the organization, using as one example Douglas McGregor's Theory Y man, where the importance of integrating the objectives of the individual with the objectives of the organization are emphasized. Lyndall Urwick has further suggested that once an organization is formed, the individuals within the organization frequently try to substitute their personal motives for the objectives of the organization, and "often suggest that the main purpose of the undertaking which employs us is to provide us personally with a job."[4] Urwick further suggests that "every organization must be an expression of the purpose of the undertaking concern or it is meaningless and thereby redundant."[5]

In addition to theoretical arguments, Granger makes a number of practical arguments as to why subobjectives should be consistent with corporate objectives.[6] Among these are the loss of money spent on projects anywhere in the firm that may later be abandoned because they are inconsistent with broader corporate objectives, committees wasting time solving problems that are unimportant in the overall view of the organization, and vacillation on acquisition policies that upon further study are found to be inconsistent with desired objectives. Granger's practical concern, then, is about the efficient use of resources available to the firm.

The New Product Development Subsystem

The new product development function is only one of the subsystems of the firm, and the portion of the R&D subsystem dealing with new products is only one subsystem of the new product development system. As such, the duties and responsibilities of the R&D new product development subsystem, to be consistent with systems theory, should be agreed upon by both corporate management and members of the R&D subsystem (generally R&D management). After this agreement, R&D management should use the resources provided them to carry out these corporate objectives rather than for their own desires or objectives.

The problem of considering the R&D subsystem and the new product development process in the framework of system corporate goals, objectives, and strategies is most noticeable by its omission from most of the R&D process discussion. This is in part due, as Quinn notes, to the feeling prior to World War II that R&D could not be planned.[7] Planning would stifle the creativity essential to successful work, and, in any case, the uncertainty of the results was so high that planning would have no meaning. Wartime pressures, however, forced breakdown of major research programs into their elements, with substantial increased efficiency, particularly in applied research and development.

With the growth of R&D management literature, beginning in the late 1950s, most studies of R&D decision making assumed a relationship or the necessity of a relationship between the R&D decision-making process and corporate objectives. Seldom, however, were any reasons given for this relationship. Steiner notes two specific reasons why R&D decision making must be related to the financial capability, facility expansion, marketing strategies, profit plans, and so on of the overall firm.[8] Corporate management, by virtue of its function, concerns itself with the overall operation of the firm and is freer to think of various alternatives for the firm as a whole. In addition, the lack of scientific training of corporate management makes it less likely that technical research and development considerations will inhibit its thinking.

Even with renewed suggestions that R&D can be planned in a corporate framework, most planners make no attempt to tie R&D decision making to corporate objectives.[9] Others acknowledge R&D as a part of the overall firm, and suggest that R&D policies should be consistent with the firm's policies, but pass rapidly over this area into the specific topics of project selection, control, and so on.[10] In one of the few attempts to look at more specific criteria for the R&D position in corporate objectives, Rubenstein emphasizes measurement of the total results of the R&D program in meeting corporate objectives rather than the correlation of the firm's objectives with the R&D division's objectives and decision-making processes.[11] Unfortunately, Rubenstein's suggestions appear to have attracted little practical attention.

Robert Bowie makes a strong case for a detailed relationship between R&D decisions and corporate objectives with the necessity of R&D decisions carrying out corporate objectives.[12] Yet, he defends the lack of such detailed objectives in most firms noting that in an era of rapidly advancing and keenly competitive industry, it is almost impossible to provide formal written statements of policy in sufficient detail to guide the directors of research. The situation is too dynamic and too fluid. After defining these problems, Bowie admits he does not have the solution, and his only practical solution is that the R&D management should have a part in setting the corporate objectives so that they can in an informal way attempt to ensure that R&D projects are chosen consistent with corporate objectives.

In another approach, Poensgen and Hort note that the setting of goals, overall planning, and the initiation of projects should recognize the relationship of R&D and other parts of the company, but their practical suggestions deal with organizational structure, not development of R&D objectives.[13]

The only literature area in which intralevel objective interaction is not considered a problem is the R&D operations research literature. Here the objective of R&D is generally considered optimization of a single value, most frequently profitability maximization, whether applied to a single product idea or a portfolio of ideas.[14] The implicit assumption is that one single optimization objective is appropriate for both the system and each subsystem within it, including the R&D division, in both the long and short run.

Where goal programming (multiple objective) operations research techniques have been used, the result is still optimization of a group of straightforward objectives, without indicating how they are tied into corporate objectives.

Much of the recent work on R&D management has been done in terms of management of government defense-oriented work. Almost all of these authors agree that the government provides the objectives for the specific research project under consideration. Hence it is not surprising that they have not given the attention to intralevel objectives that would be necessary in other circumstances. Since much of the governmental R&D management results have been applied to private R&D, it is perhaps not surprising to find that the intralevel objectives areas have received less overall attention. Even when governmental objectives are noted in the literature there is no theoretical reason to assume that these objectives or their derivation techniques are applicable to private research and development organizations.

There have been some positive suggestions in the body of literature on corporate strategy and long-range planning. This literature, typified by Ansoff, Brandenburg, Bright, and Taylor and Wills, suggests the place that the new product function should have in a corporate framework of growth, environmental analysis, and diversification.[15] Most of this literature to date, however, has dealt with corporate strategy and corporate long-range planning where R&D new product development is only a small part of the total analysis, and as yet few details dealing with R&D and its specific place have been provided. Nevertheless the general aid that this literature provides in breaking down corporate objectives and strategies to subsystem objectives and strategies offers the potential for more specific R&D and new product development work.

The Low Rate of Successful Market Introductions

The major method of expressing the success of a firm's new product development effort is based upon evaluation of each individual product project that enters the R&D new product development process. If a high percentage of individual projects are successful in the marketplace, the total process is considered successful; if the percentage is low, the process is not considered successful. (A product is considered a "success" or a "commercial success" if it generates enough sales, revenue, and profit, and becomes an accepted part of the firm's product line. A product is considered a "technical success" if it can be developed to provide the desired properties and attributes [including unit cost] which were specified in advance of development.) Thus the measure of success of a firm's new product development effort necessitates concentration on individual projects, and most studies of project success and failure are discussed in terms of individual project selection and results.

Of the project concepts that enter the idea generation stage of the process stage model, only a very few survive to successful market introduction. By far the most comprehensive analysis of this success rate is provided by the consulting firm of Booz, Allen and Hamilton in a regularly issued report. Their most detailed report, in 1968, of 80 firms suggests that on the average only 1 out of 58 product ideas at the idea generation stage has been successfully introduced into the marketplace.[16] Using current decision techniques, 13 of these 58 ideas are given a formal business analysis, and technical development is at least initiated on 6. Translating these project numbers into dollars, about three-quarters of all applied R&D funds are spent on unsuccessful projects, with about two-thirds of these dollars spent at the technical development stage. More recent reports by Booz, Allen and Hamilton, among others, have suggested that the success rates have remained in the same general range.

These descriptions provide an obvious case for increased efficiency in the new product development process. (A more detailed analysis is provided in chapter 4.) It is interesting to note, however, that Booz, Allen and Hamilton assign the basic responsibility for the low success rate to the management and decision processes, and that they consider technical development failure to be a minor problem.

Other researchers also have identified the low success rate and inefficient use of resources in a manner similar to Booz, Allen and Hamilton. Smith studied 20 large industrial firms, and noted that fewer than 2% of the initial proposals were introduced successfully into the marketplace.[17] While the vast majority of these proposals failed to advance to the development stage, Smith notes that of the products actually developed and introduced into the marketplace, 30–90% failed to produce a satisfactory rate of return and were eventually dropped from the firm's product line.

Gerstenfeld conducted a study of 91 projects from government laboratories.[18] He concluded, without providing the specific data, that in his sample, 32% of the projects were successful, 16% failed due to technical reasons, and 52% failed due to nontechnical management causes. While it is unlikely that these results would apply to private industry new product development, they indicate the same general conclusions as other available data.

In a study of proprietary drug laboratories, Mansfield concluded that the probability of technical success of a new applied product was about 60%, while the probability of economic success was 20%.[19] While these estimates clearly reflect only that specific industry, they are also consistent with other available data.

It is surprising that the problem of a low success rate of new products has not been more clearly defined in the literature. Perhaps this is because many researchers consider the problem so obvious they feel no need to define it.[20]

Summary

A review of the R&D management literature suggests two major problems in the current R&D to operations process. The first, a lack of intralevel objective and strategy interaction, was discussed in the context of the firm as a system. In general, the interaction of corporate objectives with R&D division objectives is not discussed in the literature. When discussion was presented, it recognized the need for such interaction, but made few suggestions as to interaction methods or concepts.

Inefficient use of resources in the new product process as identified by a low rate of successful market introductions was the second major problem. In general, the literature suggested that fewer than 20% of the product ideas that began technical development were successfully introduced into the marketplace, and that about three-quarters of all applied R&D funds were spent on unsuccessful projects.

3

Analysis of Problems in
Intralevel Objective and Strategy Interaction

As noted earlier, intralevel objective and strategy interaction is most noticeable by its absence from most R&D and new product development discussion. Nevertheless, the literature available does provide a conceptual base upon which to build an interaction framework. The general subject of new product and R&D objectives and strategies and their position in the administrative framework of large, profit-oriented industrial firms has been reviewed from a number of viewpoints. To simplify analysis, this literature has been grouped into four basic topic areas: (1) marketing, (2) operations research, (3) research and development management, and (4) strategic planning. Research in these areas has not been mutually exclusive, and in many cases assignment to one category or another has been relatively arbitrary.

The works analyzed in this investigation have been chosen from the available literature which includes objective intralevel interactions. This criterion severely limits the number of works applicable from the four viewpoints under discussion and hence should not be considered representative of any field. Sources pertaining to objective intralevel interactions not included in the following discussion are included in the bibliography.

Prior to undertaking a survey of these viewpoints, it is necessary that the general field of objective and strategy discussion and interaction be narrowed so as to maintain emphasis on the R&D and new product areas. This can be done by the use of three basic assumptions.

1. Objectives and strategies of subsystems of the firm should be consistent with those of the firm as a whole. This assumption is by no means an accepted principle in general management literature or in the specialized literature relating to research and development management. Over the last 15 years, however, there has been a substantial body of systems theory and long-range planning research that has made a very strong case for the consistency of objectives at various intrafirm levels. As Mockler notes, "systems organization automatically centers attention upon the objectives for which the firm has been established and helps to generate concerted and coordinated activity toward attainment of these objectives."[1] Further, "from a systems theory viewpoint, therefore, an area of business organization can be viewed on one level as a complete, integrated, decision making system designed to achieve some specific objective."[2] Further support for this assumption is provided in chapter 2.

2. There is no single objective for a firm in either the long or short run. Stated in an alternate way, there are multiple objectives of a firm. This assumption both from a theoretical and practical viewpoint is contrary to the classical economic assumption of a rational firm with a profit maximization objective and suggests a multiple objective function with no optimization requirement. This is not meant to imply that profit or measures of profitability are not extremely important criteria in objective portfolios. Rather, the emphasis is upon the fact that profit or measures of profitability are not the only objectives of the firm.

Acceptance of the classical microeconomic assumption of a single profit maximization objective both in the long and short run has been steadily eroded. Drucker, as an example, suggests theoretical reasons for survival as the major long-range objective of the firm.[3] Ansoff suggests profitability, both because of the static nature of profit maximization and because of measurement difficulties.[4] Because of these difficulties Ansoff suggests a group of long-range proxies that can be measured with some degree of accuracy as a substitute for long-run profit maximization. These proxies are then treated as the firm's objectives.

Herbert Simon, in his "satisfice" theory, suggests a portfolio of objectives to satisfy partially the various individuals and groups who make up and interact with the firm.[5] In his framework, profit maximization would aim only at stockholder satisfaction and ignore managers, employees, customers, and so on. Further, Cyert and March suggest that a firm has no objectives, only the individuals within the firm do.[6] Since Cyert and March do not assume a rational man in the classical economic sense, it is not surprising that the implicit results of their work are recognition of both a nonoptimum objective and the potential for multiple objectives as a result of the tradeoff among individuals in the firm to develop objectives that are acceptable to a large number, if not all members of the system. This is consistent with Urwick's comments discussed in chapter 2.[7]

3. Strategic planning is an area of planning within the firm that is concerned primarily with the interaction between the firm and its environment, with particular emphasis on the product market areas the firm should be in. This is more a definition than an assumption, and is necessary because much of the management literature uses "strategy" to mean "tactics." This definition is consistent with that of Ansoff and Brandenburg, and offers aid in the translation of corporate objectives to subsystem objectives particularly in the new product and R&D areas.[8]

These assumptions, although by no means universally accepted, are widely enough used to serve as a basis both for the following analysis of intralevel goal and objective interaction and for the normative frameworks that follow in later chapters.

Marketing Viewpoint

R&D new product development is obviously a concern of the marketing function although it is not normally a responsibility of the marketing department. Even so, the place of the marketing function itself is not always clearly defined in the corporate system. In one of the few definitive statements on this subject, Norton Paley argues that marketing is an instrument of corporate policy.[9] As such, the marketing objectives and the corporate objectives are different, but the marketing objective must be only the means to the corporate objective end. Paley's emphasis is philosophical, as he goes on to note that the corporate objectives should be "a better world, a better community, and a better life."[10] No specific methods for interaction of marketing objectives with these corporate objectives are given.

Stern's emphasis is on marketing planning.[11] He also considers marketing objectives as a subset of the company's mission and goals, defining a "goal" as the end to which a plan tends and "strategy" as the technique to indicate the methods and procedures to be employed in securing the goals (strategy is thus used as tactics). As an example, Stern considers a sales objective of increasing revenue by 20% while decreasing the expense to revenue ratio to 30% as a goal, and one strategy to carry out this goal to be concentration on larger markets. He notes that several strategies will be necessary to carry out one objective.

Stern considers that the statement of company objectives provides the basic directions for all planning activity and considers some of the obvious objectives to be ensuring continued existence of the firm, minimum rate of return on investment, certain growth rates (both of sales and of revenue), and increasing shares of the market. He suggests developing strategies to aid in carrying out each of these objectives and suggests that the strategies for major objectives should be followed, the implicit assumption being that in the case of conflict those strategies aimed at carrying out major objectives should be followed over those of minor objectives. No methods are identified, however, to distinguish major from minor objectives.

Lewis Goslin's analysis of the product planning system notes that an understanding of this system requires analysis of what the firm is trying to accomplish.[12] He considers the general conditions of the corporation to include such factors as level of business activity desired, market sector, rate of business growth, variety of products available, price-quantity-reliability trade-offs, labor-management-stockholder relationships, and desired corporate image. These conditions then establish objectives such as a rate of return on investment, aggressiveness of the firm, market share, market sector, stable employment, and level of profits. Thus, he defines an objective as an intermediate operational step towards which the firm aims. In more common usage, Goslin's "conditions" are called "goals and objectives" and his "objectives" are "measurement techniques" of his "conditions."

This is of particular interest in its differentiation between the objectives of the firm as a whole, and the methods of measurement of these objectives. Goslin further notes that all of the objectives (his conditions) are not quantifiable, and that some cannot ever be measured, while the techniques he provides (his objectives) are all measurable at least in a qualitative sense. These measurement techniques do not appear to cover the full spectrum of objectives, reinforcing the opinion that not all objectives can be measured.

Much of Goslin's later description talks in terms of product planning systems enhancing profitability improvement of the firm, suggesting the need to make a profit as a strong objective of the firm. Yet in his objectives discussion above he does not include profit or profitability, and, while two measurement techniques involve profit measurements, rate of return on investment and level of profits, they are overshadowed by the marketing techniques.

Goslin then notes that product planning activities can help achieve a number of these specific techniques, but that this is dependent upon a number of factors including the varieties or kinds of products produced, the responsiveness of the firm, the customers served, and the firm's competition. He notes that a product planning system is only one method to aid in achieving the objectives of the firm although he considers it to be a particularly important method. Further discussion centers on the product planning system in terms of the product requirements necessary to satisfy a given market requirement. The development or acquisition of specific products is not discussed.

Charles Kline feels that the major concern of most businessmen is the content of their product lines, and he goes into great detail discussing numerous product policies and strategies to carry them out.[13] He treats product policies as the major objectives of the firm in their own right, although he does note that they can be used as supplemental checks on the usual profit considerations. Kline suggests internal R&D as one subset of a new product policy framework, but does not discuss R&D specifically.

Moreno considers that product policies should include in their purpose the establishment of corporate policy with respect to new products.[14] This suggests that the policies of the subsystem should formulate the policies of the corporation as a whole with respect to products, a position that reverses the systems theory assumption that goals of subsystems should be based upon system goals. A set of specific product policies is discussed: performance standards, relationship to product mix patterns, and new product policies. Performance standards include share of the market, volume, and profitability considerations (profitability standards are not further detailed), while conformance to product mix suggests new products under consideration should fit with existing products.

Edgar Pessemier considers that new product activity should be designed to locate new products that will yield the largest return from the firm's resources consistent with existing risk and organizational constraint.[15] Pessemier's major emphasis is on new product policy development from the viewpoint of the marketing manager. He stresses that products should be developed to fill market needs, but his major emphasis is on new product policy development from the viewpoint of the marketing manager. He stresses that products should be developed to fill market needs, but his major emphasis is upon market research and testing after product development is largely completed rather than on similar activities prior to technical development. Pessemier indicates return on investment as the major measurement technique of the profit objective. Hence, in addition to marketing considerations, a major portion of his work is devoted to the development of analytical methods to measure return on investment. He makes no formal connection between decision criteria and corporate objectives or between new product objectives and corporate objectives. His discussion of marketing considerations, such as market share, growth, and so on, does, however, suggest either constraints or decision criteria to meet a multiple objective function, although his major emphasis is still given to the return on investment measure.

David Uman suggests that the establishment of tentative assumptions and objectives is one of the main requirements of planning a new product program.[16] He defines assumptions as the ground rules upon which plans are based, with emphasis on future uncertainties. A statement of objectives should include a description of scope in terms of activity and range of operation, restrictions, conditions, and decision points at which selections should be made from alternatives. Uman only identifies these assumptions and strategies, but a slightly different viewpoint could suggest his "assumptions" as corporate objectives with his specific objectives being those of the new product process consistent with corporate objectives. Uman's book is of particular value because it is one of the few that suggest the timing of the project selection decision as an important consideration in both the decision-making and subsystem objective process.

An article by C. Merle Crawford integrates some of the strategy development research with new product development.[17] Crawford identifies the development of strategies for new product development as one of the set of strategies for the firm as a whole. He notes that some feel that a definite strategy may discourage innovation, but emphasizes its necessity to provide adequate direction for new product development so that the results are consistent with corporate objectives. A number of specifics that should be included in a new product strategy are suggested, including technology mix, market mix, market width, degree of innovation and imitation, price-quality ranges, competitive situation, production requirements, risk and payback considerations, minimum sales requirements, and internal or external development.

Crawford thus places internal R&D as a subset of the new product development strategy. He emphasizes that if the new product strategy is a continuing activity, then expansion of internal facilities to provide R&D offers more potential in the long run than do other methods of acquiring R&D. Crawford's overall emphasis, however, is on development of new product strategies from a marketing viewpoint and he does not emphasize the role that internal or external R&D plays in these strategies.

The vast majority of researchers publishing in the marketing and product development literature have not included analysis of the place of marketing within the framework of corporate objectives within even the limited scope suggested by the preceding analyses. An example of this literature is an article by Aubrey Wilson involving selection of new products for development.[18] In one sentence he acknowledges new product policies as a subset of general product policies of the firm, but he does not discuss this relationship or suggest any connection with corporate objectives. This perfunctory acknowledgment with no elaboration or development is true of the bulk of published material in the field.

This marketing and new product development literature review clearly indicates the lack of consideration of corporate objectives in new product development planning. While the details of any specific article may be of great value, there is little indication of any framework or description of the system in which the details of the specific article take place. Many researchers seem to assume that marketing objectives are the end objectives of the organization. While this philosophy is not restricted to marketing-oriented literature in the field of management, it is particularly noticeable in the light of the strategic and long-range planning literature.

Operations Research Viewpoint

Operations research is a discipline involving the application of mathematical techniques to problem solving. Historically, operations research has been "heavily biased towards the physical resource conversion process in the firm."[19] In addition, Simon and Newell suggest that business quantitative methods fall into the well-structured problem solving class, with primary reliance on quantitative relationships and conclusions.[20] In their definition, a well-structured problem requires that the variables be expressed in quantitative terms, that there be an objective function reducible to a scalar quantitative utility function, and that the solution be expressed in terms of an algorithm with an unambiguous computational procedure.

Although there is considerable work to suggest that the R&D decision processes, let alone the intralevel objective and strategy interaction, are not well-structured problems, there has been a substantial amount of operations research work aimed at R&D. Perhaps because much of this work was on military research and development, where objectives were provided, emphasis in operations research literature is almost completely upon project selection and almost always assumes optimization of some single value.

In 1964 Baker and Pound surveyed the R&D operations research literature.[21] After discussing the literature, they concluded that none of the techniques suggested was widely used, and that some that were used were dropped after only a short time. Baker and Pound noted that the underlying reason for selecting projects is to help the organization and its individual members achieve objectives. As long as these objectives and the relations among them are not clearly defined, they felt, it is doubtful that any R&D selection method will meet with wide approval. In spite of this comment, and in spite of the inclusion of this article as a reference by most of the later operations researchers, little additional work has been done in this area.

Another survey of R&D selection models was done in 1971 by Schroder.[22] A difference in emphasis in the development of quantitative models in terms of societies rather than firms sets this work apart from Baker and Pound's survey. Schroder defines categories of models as cost benefit, mathematical programming, and cost effectiveness analysis. He points out that in spite of their titles only a few of these models are directed specifically towards R&D project selection. The majority offer contributions toward methodological approaches with little regard for implementation. He attributes this to the fact that the field itself is in the early stages of development and also suggests this may be the reason that the models available are not widely used.

In response to the comment that these models have not been widely used, Marschak contends that the models have a very legitimate use in testing the rules of thumb used in most practical decision models, or, to "find the assumptions under which the rules of thumb are optimal."[23] Lockett and Gear further argue that mathematical tools are not available to accurately analyze portfolios of large numbers of multiple scale models in research and development.[24] They suggest use of a heuristic approach to cut down the number of potential portfolio projects so that mathematical techniques can be used, even if the results do not possess the desirable properties of optimability but only offer "good solutions to real problems."[25]

Schroder suggests that the relationship between R&D activities and objectives of the firm is a major area for investigation since existing models (1) are purely or primarily quantitative, (2) focus on decisions about the acceptance of R&D projects rather than on evaluation of the projects, and (3) attempt to optimize rather than to be satisfied with generating or searching for preferred courses of action.[26]

The vast majority of operations research articles in the R&D area completely ignore any connection between the R&D area and corporate objectives and strategies. Examples of this are the works of Mottley and Newton, Disman, Hess, Dean, Souder, Lockett and Gear, and, more recently, Mandakovic, Taylor, and Cooper.[27]

Beattie and Reader suggest that the R&D function should be consistent with corporate objectives and suggest that to overcome any gap between those responsible for the achievement of corporate objectives and the R&D functions, the R&D functions should be involved in the process of company planning and forecasting.[28]

If they are so involved, the R&D decision can be formulated and executed in direct pursuit of the corporate objectives and in light of anticipated future problems. Other than these general identifications, no analysis is provided, and they turn to optimization algorithms for project analysis and to the use of quantitative techniques to provide the most accurate numbers to use in the algorithms.

Hertz and Carlson suggest that there is a need for a starting point in selecting criteria on which to base decisions in the selection and evaluation of R&D projects, and that "we must begin with company objectives and the plans that support them."[29] They suggest two major system requirements necessary for a smooth project selection method: (1) well defined corporate objectives and (2) a smooth organizational relationship between R&D and the key functional areas of the company. They then note "we shall not concern ourselves here with corporate objectives,"[30] and do not attempt to relate their decision criteria of technical factors, economic factors, and timing factors with the long-range plans they earlier suggested or with any other manifestation of corporate objectives.

Thus, other than these few general comments the R&D operations research literature provides little insight into the intralevel goal and strategy interaction.

Research and Development Management Viewpoint

The majority of literature from the R&D management viewpoint is concerned with project selection, and is discussed in chapter 4. The literature that discusses corporate and R&D objective and strategy interaction is written almost completely from two viewpoints, the top R&D manager or the academic researcher. The backgrounds of most of these individuals, both in the industrial and academic worlds, are generally as specialists in a narrow technical sense, with those in industry reaching their position in management based upon their technical ability at lower levels in the R&D organization. This background perhaps partially explains the tendency of the literature to look at the R&D function from the top down and to largely ignore the place of the R&D function in the corporation as a whole. In addition, individuals from the R&D area are seldom appointed to other corporate level manager positions. As a result, there are few individuals at the corporate level with the background to write knowledgeably of this area.

Since this investigation is concerned only with new product development applied research, the literature analyzed represents only a portion of the total R&D management literature. For simplification, the analysis is discussed from three viewpoints: need for objectives and strategies, difficulties in objective definitions, and objective and strategy suggestions.

Need for Objectives and Strategies

Jackson and Spurlock cover the entire subject of objective and strategy interaction in one sentence, noting "the industrial manager should orient his R&D efforts into channels which will offer compound benefits to his company's overall operations."[31]

Swager suggests the framework of relationship between corporate and R&D objectives in the depth common to most of the literature.[32] He notes that the business R&D objectives of the firm, "protecting the profitability of present products and developing new sources of profits through new products, should be clearly defined and presented in detail to R&D management."[33] Unless this is done, a research program is likely to result in a number of products that contribute little towards the firm's objectives.

Peter Drucker considers the viewpoint that research needs its own scientific or technical objectives to be one of the major myths of research management.[34] He suggests that the goal of research is not scientific or technical knowledge but economic results, and hence requires business objectives as does any other portion of the firm.

"Industrial research, to be successful, must be integrated with other functions of the corporation" writes Lauren Hitchcock.[35] He notes that the firm must define what business it is in, which particular area of that business is likely to undergo rapid growth as compared to the field as a whole, the magnitude of the type of change desired consistent with available capital, and a definition of how far it wants to develop and expand away from its present product lines. Hitchcock considers answers to these questions as part of a set of strategy definitions for R&D, but does not indicate how they could be developed to serve as a framework in which specific projects can be chosen for development.

O'Donnell identifies the necessity for determining strategies for research, examples of which are such basic decisions as whether or not to engage in research and whether any research undertaken should be fundamentally defensive or offensive.[36] Once the strategies have been defined, the corporation can then set objectives to reflect the strategies. The research scientist needs the guidance of corporate objectives to develop realistic programs. The failure to provide these objectives lies more with corporate than R&D management, since corporate management and the board of directors do not recognize the necessity of providing such objectives to R&D. One specific objective he feels should be included is a decision as to whether normal plans will involve the exploitation of research results. This is necessary because many firms regard their research division as a status symbol rather than as a functional area of the firm from which tangible results are expected. O'Donnell, however, provides no suggestions as to how to translate corporate objectives to R&D objectives.

Albert Rubenstein, in looking at a model of R&D decision making in the firm, suggests that objectives and missions for R&D, as well as assigned resources and constraints, be provided by corporate management to R&D management for use in decision making.[37] The major weakness of this framework stems from the inability of corporate management to describe in other than very vague or general terms the objectives or missions for R&D, due in large part to the lack of understanding by corporate management of the capabilities and limitations of the R&D function. Rubenstein considers resources to be the means for carrying out the missions of the firm, and constraints to be the degree of resources provided to R&D. His examples consist of limitations such as a maximum total dollar expense or the number of people that can be employed, but a suggestion is also made that constraints may exist from sources other than corporate management, such as the environment, actions of competitors, state of the art, scientific knowledge, and so on.

Poensgen and Hort look at the place of R&D in the organization and the relationship between R&D and the rest of the company.[38] They suggest how return on capital can be consistent at the corporate and R&D levels, but do not discuss interaction of other objectives or goals.

Difficulties in Objective Definition

Brandenburg notes that business objectives having operational significance for some areas may not be significant for R&D.[39] As a result, managers may be frustrated in their attempts to formulate criteria functions to provide a general base for R&D decision making. An efficiency criterion for decision making is suggested, with the note that even if such a criterion can be made explicit and operational there is still the unsolved problem of more firmly including it in the framework of corporate objectives. Brandenburg also emphasizes that the inability to measure the output of most research is another problem that both makes the decision criteria difficult to set and the interrelationship with corporate objectives even more a problem.

C. Wilson Randle suggests an entirely different approach, one emphasizing that the selection of the research program, including selection of specific R&D projects, is a function of corporate management and should not be delegated.[40] The rationale for this approach is to provide a total integrated company viewpoint and a recognition that research program selection in effect involves decisions directly affecting the future course of the business, such decisions being the responsibility of the top management function. One advantage of this approach is that there is no necessity for development of R&D objectives or strategies, since corporate management will act on corporate objectives or their own desires without the necessity for objective translation.

Robert Bowie notes the difficulty of providing formal objectives to an R&D division because of the rate of change of technology and the lack of understanding of the technical specificities of the business within which the firm operates.[41] He feels these difficulties cannot be overcome, and suggests, as did Randle, that each R&D decision be made by corporate management, or that top R&D officials aid in setting corporate policy. Hence, without the need of formal mechanisms, an attempt can be made to make R&D decisions within the framework of corporate policy.

Objective and Strategy Suggestions

Most of the R&D management literature provides no details on objective and strategy interaction, and where more than the topic title is mentioned, the literature tends to be vague and general. An example is provided by Asbury, who suggests that the objectives of industrial research should be to reduce the company's overall costs, to help the company provide high quality products, and to help the company with opportunities for attractive new products.[42] He suggests the company provide guidelines for the research manager by answering such questions as: Does the company want to protect its existing position? What emphasis should be given new products or new processes? The research manager should be kept informed of such items as the availability of capital funds, the capability of manufacturing, the capability of marketing, and so on. With only this loose and inexact information the research manager can then ensure that the project selection system will be carried out according to the above objectives. Here again the emphasis is upon the research manager becoming informed and making decisions in light of that information rather than upon corporate management providing specific objectives to the R&D manager.

Hill and Granger suggest that the corporation should define a set of corporate objectives directed to research activities.[43] The objectives they suggest include profitability, market position, product leadership, productivity, balance of short- and long-range objectives, personnel development, employee attitudes, and public responsibility. The objectives of productivity and profitability are emphasized for applied research. Specific measures of profitability and market position include return on investment, dollar profit, earnings per share, increase in earnings per share, growth in dollar volume of sales, and share of the market. They are treated separately, and not integrated. Hill and Granger further note the importance of these measures in long-range planning and imply, but never actually state, that specific values for these corporate objectives should be provided to R&D management for their decision making.

Hill and Granger's article was among the first suggesting new business research activities in relationship to corporate objectives. A framework is suggested consisting of (1) determination of the extent of new business required in the corporation by internal development versus external acquisition, (2) examination of proposed new product areas in the corporate plan, (3) selection of proposed projects based upon promise, need, and empirical limitations, and (4) provision for commercialization of new business. Though Hill and Granger do not reference any of the strategic planning literature that began to appear about the same time, their framework is consistent with much of the strategic planning work and is valuable because of its application to internal product development.

The author who has done the most work in this field is James B. Quinn.[44] Quinn's emphasis is on long-range technical planning which should include: (1) establishing overall company objectives in light of expected future economic, sociological, and technical developments, (2) determining the particular technical strategy the company will use in effecting these objectives, (3) defining the specific mission of each major research and operations group in supporting the company's objectives and strategies, and (4) seeing that the research projects are ranked and balanced to best meet the company's threats and opportunities.

Quinn considers value objectives to be at the top of the corporation objective list. These are the attitudes and desires of the owners, managers, and employees of the firm, and tend to be philosophical in nature. Underneath the value objectives are the overall business objective functions, intended as targets for the firm. These business objectives are less permanent than value objectives for the firm, but, nevertheless, provide consistency for a reasonable number of years. While "reasonable" is not defined, Quinn elsewhere suggests that overall business objectives should remain stable for a sufficient time to serve as guides during the research and development lead time, approximately five to fifteen years.[45]

Overall business objectives are necessary for at least three reasons. (1) They provide criteria for judging the adequacy of individual research plans. (2) They allow self planning in organizations in that they are not constraints but suggestions as to what the organization is to accomplish, and not how the organization is to accomplish it. This is of particular importance in allowing creative individuals to select their own approaches to problem solving. (3) Objectives provide the only criteria by which actual research performance can be judged. This is of importance on a national level or on evaluating the overall results of a firm's research portfolio.

Quinn feels that overall business objectives with respect to research planning should include: (1) the kind of business the company wants to be in, (2) the method of growth, (3) the direction of growth, (4) the rate of growth, (5) the degree of dependence upon suppliers, (6) the kind of capital structure desired, (7) the degree of sales and profit stability, (8) the degree of government control, (9) price volume and profit volume markets, (10) facilities and personnel capabilities, (11) overall degree of flexibility, and (12) geographic market distribution.

Specific numbers for specific measurement techniques for each of these objectives are not provided, nor is there any suggestion of translation to R&D goals, other than their suggested use for R&D criteria as they are. Nevertheless this is the only analysis from an R&D management viewpoint that provides a specific set of corporate business objectives as they relate to the R&D division, and suggests at least a rough framework relationship.

Noting that corporate and R&D objectives as he has described them do not exist in a great many firms, Quinn discusses some of the problems in establishing such objectives. (1) Objectives change too often. Even if corporate management does not deliberately change objectives rapidly, in practice in most research programs day to day pressures of market competition are often given preference over longer-run new product development, emphasizing the rapid rate of objective change. (2) Objectives are distorted by individuals within the organization due to the communication and transmission system. As a result, the original meaning and intent are changed. Suggestions are made to improve this communication over various levels in the organization. (3) Objectives are too general in that they tend to be expressed as value objectives or in too vague or general terms. (4) Objectives can be too specific in that they serve as restraints for the research facility, and, by telling the researcher exactly what is to be done, remove a portion of the motivation for the researcher.

Quinn does not feel that every firm must have a research and development division, and suggests that a company should support a research program only if it provides the least expensive or most effective means of accomplishing the company's particular objectives. Objectives are necessary because without them research programs will drift towards studies that fascinate individual scientists, towards pet projects of key executives, or towards sales service or extremely short-run activities that bear little relationship to new product or longer-run needs.

In summary, this analysis clearly indicates the lack of work from the R&D management viewpoint or interrelationship of the objectives of R&D with the objectives and strategies of the corporation. It is particularly noteworthy that the work of Hill and Granger, and Quinn has not been followed by additional analysis, at least in part indicating the lack of concern in the field about the intralevel objective interrelationships.

Strategic Planning Viewpoint

Research and development of new products and the specific interaction of R&D objectives with corporate objectives have not been major concerns of the strategic planning area. Strategic planning research has been primarily at the corporate level, and what research has been done at the functional area levels has been primarily restricted to marketing and sales. Strategic planning is included here because what research has been done offers excellent insight into methods of translating corporate objectives to functional area objectives through the addition of strategic planning concepts between corporate and functional area objectives. Strategic planning offers special potential to the new product development area because of its emphasis on product market mix and environmental analysis.

It is not the intent of this section to discuss the field of strategic planning. Numerous authors, including Katz, Newman and Logan, Higgins and Vincze, Digman, and Thompson and Strickland, among others, have done this.[46] Some work, however, has been done in intralevel objective interaction, and in relating strategy to functional areas of the firm. Those authors whose work offers the greatest potential application to these areas are discussed.

Although a definition of corporate strategy was assumed earlier in this chapter, a brief discussion of the definitional problems is necessary. Some authors define objectives as a subset of strategy. One, Alfred Chandler, defines strategy as the determination of the basic long-term objectives of the enterprise, the adoption of courses of action, and the allocation of resources necessary to carry out these objectives.[47]

Another definition is offered by Tilles, who defines strategy as a set of objectives and major policies of the firm.[48] Tilles feels the difficulty is not in the definition of strategy, but in working out a strategy explicit enough to be of use. He suggests that corporate objectives are an indication of what the firm as a whole is trying to achieve and to become. Further, he objects to defining strategy in terms of products only since he feels that this is confining the future to a single dimension.

A more common approach is that of James Quinn, who defines strategy as a plan that determines how the organization can best achieve its desired ends in light of the opposing pressures exerted by competition and by its own limited resources.[49] He suggests that the major area of strategic planning is the use of an organization's resources so that its strengths are emphasized and its competitors' strengths minimized.

Cannon defines strategy as action decisions required in a competitive situation to accomplish the firm's objectives.[50] He suggests action strategies involving what type of business is being undertaken and the methods to undertake it, as well as definitions of products, markets, channels of distribution, product and market development, and so on. Results strategies are similar to objectives of other authors in that they involve the reasons for adopting the family of action strategies, and include profitability, technical leadership, social contribution, and so on. Commitment strategies are concerned both with the individuals and functions to carry out the strategies and with the timing of these actions.

Semantics cause a problem with Ansoff's definitions, with "strategic" having a different meaning than "strategy."[51] Ansoff breaks the decisions within the firm into three groups: strategic, administrative, and operating. Strategic decisions are concerned with the product mix of the firm. One of the strategic decisions is the choice of corporate objectives, as well as the choice of diversification, expansion, administrative, and finance strategies.

Another definition is suggested in terms of a strategy gap.[52] A set of desired objectives is identified for the firm, and the current position of the firm with respect to those objectives is diagnosed. The difference between the desired and the actual is determined, and a search is instituted for an operator (strategy) which can reduce the gap. Thus, strategy is considered to be a method to arrive at the desired objectives, or, in some ways, a subset of objectives.

A survey of the strategic planning literature is provided by Cooper and Schendel.[53] They point out that while definitions are not consistent in the literature, there are a number of common elements in most analyses. One is the acceptance of the need for basic organizational objectives. The second is an emphasis on product market mix or scope, while a third involves the deployment of major resources along a growth pattern. Based upon these elements, Cooper and Schendel then suggest that strategy be considered as the major subset of corporate objectives emphasizing interaction between the firm and its environment, with emphasis on product mix, and with policies being a subset of corporate strategy aimed at carrying out corporate strategy.

Cooper and Schendel consider that the most important function of strategy is to knit together the functional areas of the firm.

They specifically note that strategy need not spell out in advance the exact nature of new products and markets to be exploited, only that it serves as a focus for search in the area that Ansoff calls the "growth vector."[54]

As noted earlier, the assumption of strategy in this investigation as the area of planning within the firm that is concerned primarily with the interaction of the firm and its environment, with particular emphasis on what business the firm should be in, is consistent with Cooper and Schendel's and with Ansoff's definition of strategy as a method to reduce the gap between actual and desired objectives.

The strategic planning literature discussed can be broken into two groups, one discussing rudimentary R&D strategy, and the other discussing strategy that in general offers suggestions for intralevel goal and strategy interaction.

R&D Strategy

In discussing long-range planning, Collier notes that company-wide objectives are inadequate for providing direction and performance measurements required at all levels of the firm.[55] He refers to Charles Granger's hierarchy of objectives, noting that as you move down the organizational structure the objectives become more specific and have fewer long-term implications.[56] He considers acquisitions and new product development to be strategic expressions of a company's objectives. In particular, he notes the close fit between R&D and corporate objectives of many firms that are successful technical entrepreneurs, suggesting that R&D can be used as a strategy just as can acquisition or divestment.

George Steiner provides one of the more definitive frameworks of strategy development.[57] One segment of the corporate strategic plan is the corporate development plan. Two subsets of the corporation development plan are a divestment and a diversification plan while two subsets of the diversification plan are an acquisition and merger plan and an R&D plan.

Thus a descending hierarchy of plans carefully relates R&D to new product development to the corporate strategy.

Steiner also suggests that R&D planning is tied into overall comprehensive planning in the same manner as all other major functional areas. At the highest levels R&D objectives and strategies are related to financial capability, facility expansion, market strategies, profit plans, and so on. In medium-range planning more detailed R&D projects can be directly related to other functional areas. His specific examples of this medium-range planning, however, deal with cost reduction and improvement of present products rather than with the development of new products.

Steiner further notes that studies have shown that half of the successful R&D projects developed in the chemical, electronic, and drug industries were originally suggested by top management regardless of whether the managers were or were not scientifically oriented.[58] This tends to suggest control of R&D by specific project suggestions early in the research process rather than control by the use of research strategies and objectives, and perhaps offers insight into the lack of research objectives and strategies in many firms.

As far back as 1959, Hill and Granger suggested that a list of corporate objectives should include (1) profitability, in specific terms of return on investment, dollar profit, and increase of earnings per share, (2) growth in dollar volume of sales and share of the market, (3) broad product lines to be manufactured, and markets to be served, (4) marketing policies, (5) manufacturing and facilities policies, (6) organization and personnel development policies, (7) financial policies, including debt to equity ratios and dividend policies, and (8) research policies.[59] Research policies include statements of levels of expenditures for basic research, expenditures for research by broad product area within the existing product lines, and new product research.

These objectives cover both long- and short-range time periods, with different objectives applied differently to different activities of the firm in each period of time. The same corporate objectives in the short run apply to technical service to sales and manufacturing activities aimed at cost reduction and quality improvement, and broadening of present product lines. The same objectives in the long run are applied to new product development and basic research. Hill and Granger do not list suggested values for these objectives, nor do they note that long- and short-range values for the same objective can differ, although the latter can be implied from their discussion.

Corporate objectives can be translated into new business research objectives by (1) determining the extent of new business development required by the corporate plans, (2) examining the proposed new product areas in the corporate plan in terms of the contribution that external technical resources can make, (3) selecting the proposed products based upon promise, need, and empirical limits, and (4) providing for commercialization. This can be done, of course, only after the current activities of R&D have been analyzed and compared with corporate objectives, suggesting that new business objectives are set somewhat as suggested by Ansoff's "strategy gap."[60]

O'Donnell considers that the strategic premises provided by the corporation to the research division must include a decision as to whether to engage in research, and, if so, whether research will be fundamentally defensive or offensive.[61] The board of directors needs to understand the scope of the research area of interest and the time-cost-capability relationship of the scientists to contribute effectively to corporate objectives. Once this is done the firm can then define corporate objectives in light of their research strategy.

O'Donnell's approach, in which research strategies and desires assume a large role in setting corporate objectives, is not an uncommon one in R&D management-oriented literature. This is in contrast to most of the strategic planning literature in which the internal R&D role is far down the hierarchy of goals and strategies.

General Strategy

One of the most detailed objective and strategy intralevel interactions analysis has been provided by Igor Ansoff.[62] Ansoff suggests the overall purpose of the business firm is to "configure and direct the resource conversion process in such a way as to optimize the attainment of the objectives,"[63] at least implicitly suggesting the need for subsystems of the firm to use the resources provided them in an efficient, if not optimal, manner. Ansoff defines strategy as the decisions concerned with external rather than internal problems and specifically with selection of product market mix and the markets to which the firm will sell. Operating decisions are those which attempt to maximize the efficiency of the firm's resource conversion process.

Ansoff suggests that a "vector" of objectives is a more realistic model of the objectives of the firm than a single objective. In particular, the vector is normally a group of conflicting, or potentially conflicting, objectives rather than a comprehensive, consistent grouping.

In most of the literature, "objectives" and "goals" are used interchangeably. Ansoff provides separate definitions for yardsticks, goals, and objectives. The yardstick is the subset of the objective that provides the scale by which the attribute is measured, while the goal is the particular value on the yardstick scale which the firm seeks to attain. The objective itself is the attribute to be measured. This is then consistent with Hill and Granger's general business objectives rather than their value objectives.[64] As an example, Ansoff suggests an objective of optimizing return on the firm's equity with the yardstick as the average rate of return on equity over a particular time horizon.

Ansoff further analyzes in detail the return on investment objective and suggests a variety of weaknesses in it, particularly the problem of partial ignorance of the future in predicting the various pieces of information that go into the return on investment calculation.[65] While, in theory, long-term return on investment is consistent with the economists' optimization of profit, its use as a model is weak because in practice return on investment can only be estimated for a short period of time in the future. The same problems apply to capital investment theory, with the added weakness that capital investment theory assumes all of the decision alternatives can be enumerated and their outcomes measured.[66]

To overcome these problems, Ansoff suggests a group of long-range "proxy measurements" that can be used for performance reporting as well as for diagnostic analysis of the firm's performance.[67] These proxies, summarized in figure 2, are broken into three basic groups—economic objectives, noneconomic objectives, and responsibilities and constraints. Economic objectives are broken down primarily on a time frame basis, while the noneconomic objectives are viewed primarily as the views of individuals within the firm. Responsibilities and constraints also deal with value judgments of individuals within the firm, as well as financial restraints.

Strategy, according to Ansoff, should provide a broad concept of the firm's business, set forth specific guidelines by which the firm can conduct its search, and supplement the firm's objectives with decision rules which narrow the firm's selection process to the most attractive opportunities. The strategic decision-making process is on two levels, deciding what kind of business the company is in and should be in, and applying the decision rules to individual opportunities. There are two different types of decisions, those which establish yardsticks for company performance and those which define the desirable characteristics of products and markets.

Long-range objectives serve as a common yardstick to any new product market strategy which a firm may contemplate. Long-range objectives, however, are generalities and provide no indication of where a company should look for new opportunities in a broad product market field, nor any means for a final evaluation of the respective merits of the different opportunities which compete for company attention. For at least one general selection technique, Ansoff suggests that long-range objectives serve as minimum values that must be attained, and serve as constraints so that only strategies that meet the long-range objectives are permitted the final test of probable business success.

Figure 2. Long-Range Proxy Measurements

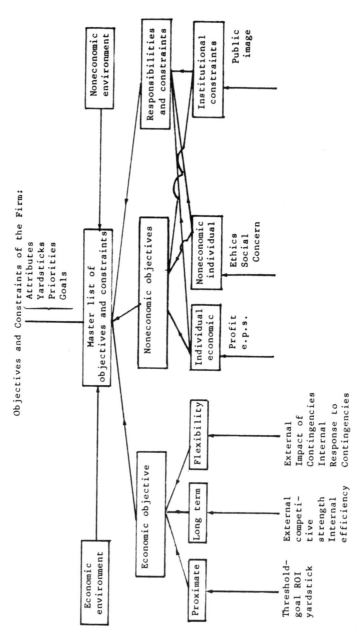

Note: Figure is based on H. Igor Ansoff, *Corporate Strategy* (New York: McGraw-Hill, 1965).

Ansoff defines a product market strategy to carry out sales objectives as a joint statement of the product line and the set of missions which the products are to fulfill. He suggests four major types of product market strategy: (1) market penetration, in which company sales are increased without departing from the original product market strategy, (2) market development, in which present products are adapted for new missions, (3) product development, in which new products are developed for present missions, and (4) diversification, where both a departure from the present product line and market structure is desired. Ansoff's interest is in diversification, and he suggests techniques for determining strategies for diversification and for analyzing the environment to identify industries, products, and markets that fit the diversification criteria.[68]

Ansoff's concern is identification, not implementation, and he does not emphasize the methods for diversification. He identifies acquisition and internal development as two methods of diversification, but relegates internal development to an operating rather than a strategic decision.

An article by Gerstner reinforces Ansoff's strategic gap theory.[69] Corporate objectives and future environmental forces determine the company's desired position. Present environmental forces, as well as the company's strengths and weaknesses, determine its present position. A comparison of the desired versus the present position indicates the gap to be filled in order to move the company to its desired position. Strategic plans are used to close the gap, although many of Gerstner's suggestions are tactical in nature.

Dalzell provides a somewhat different analysis of diversification.[70] Before a specific product is considered by the company, it is necessary to outline the corporate objectives, analyze corporate strengths and weaknesses, and set up proposed new product judgment yardsticks. Dalzell takes a hypothetical firm, suggests specific corporate objectives, identifies hypothetical strong and weak points, and suggests the major attributes a new product should have. Financial corporate goals are suggested, including a minimum 20% return on investment before taxes and production of cash flow to provide income producing investments for the owners. These goals are used directly as selection criteria for individual new product selection.

Andersen suggests that strategic planning includes: (1) planned growth rate in sales by specific product line, (2) identification of planned diversification by technologies, types of products, customers, and so on, (3) product R&D policies, and (4) planned levels of total profit, profit to investment capital ratios, earnings per share ratios, and so on.[71] Financial areas are again emphasized, with specific suggestions made for acquisition. By implication broad policies rather than specific guidelines are recommended for internal R&D.

Gilmore and Brandenburg suggest an alternate method of corporate planning with a framework consisting of four basic components: economic mission, competitive strategy, program of action, and reappraisal.[72] The economic mission is concerned with the kind of business the firm should be in and formulation of performance objectives. Competitive strategy involves determining the right product market-sales approach combination for effective accomplishment of the economic mission and the derivation of associated objectives for the various functional areas of the firm. The program of action consists of a search for efficient means of implementing the competitive strategy, while reappraisal involves determination of any need to modify earlier steps. Specific flow charts are provided to detail this framework.

Research and development is not discussed by Gilmore and Brandenburg except to include it as one area in specification of plans of action. They do suggest, however, that objectives of functional areas should be derived from competitive strategy, and that this objective derivation should be as applicable to R&D new product development as any other functional area of the firm.

A description of the strategies of growth of 53 specific companies has been provided by Gutmann.[73] The strategies that he considers most important include the choice of a general industrial field expanding more rapidly than the economy as a whole, the choice of subsectors growing more rapidly than their general field, the choice of particular subsectors at an earlier stage of economic growth than the general field, and the selection of new product policies in both old and new markets. The emphasis is on growth by acquisition rather than by internal development, although he never states that acquisition was more critical to these firms than internal R&D. Objectives of growth, sales, total profit, and profit per share are emphasized, with the strategies aimed at carrying out these objectives.

Another framework used at Hooker Chemical Corporation is identified by William Christopher, and consists of identification of mission, perspective, and management style.[74] Such a framework was needed, Christopher feels, in his highly diversified, divisionally oriented company because at the corporate level there was no articulated overall strategy, and at the divisional level there was inadequate participation in strategic planning for many years.

The concept of the firm's mission includes: (1) definition of the broad business areas in which the company will operate, (2) strategies for organizing these business areas into divisions and assignment to each division of the responsibility for developing its own business definitions, objectives, strategies, and programs, (3) definition of the relationship between the division and corporate headquarters, (4) identification to the division of specific goals for profitability, market position, public responsibility, new business, facilities, management skills, and so on, and (5) the use of planning to implement these strategic principles through all levels of operation.

Christopher suggests perspective as the method of looking at the business, both from the corporate and divisional viewpoint, and emphasizes the need for more than financial measures to control the firm as a whole. The concept of management style means a movement to human behavorial leadership, such as management by objectives, to increase interaction and planning efficiency.

Christopher shows how this framework is used at Hooker in a general way (forms and outlines) but provides few number values. In addition, his emphasis is on operating divisions (manufacturing and marketing), and he does not apply his framework specifically to Hooker's large, central R&D division.

Summary

The goal of this chapter is to analyze in depth the lack of current literature treatment of firm intralevel objective and strategy interaction. This is done by identifying the shortcomings in the intralevel treatment, and by identifying suggestions in the current literature that could aid in developing normative recommendations for problem solutions.

From the marketing viewpoint, much of the literature considers marketing objectives to be corporate objectives. It is assumed that profitable new product introductions are desired regularly, without consideration of the place of these products in a set of corporate objectives. While it is sometimes recognized that marketing objectives should be determined by corporate objectives, few specific suggestions were discovered in the literature to aid in recommending improvements in intralevel objective and strategy interaction.

In general the operations research literature assumes that the objectives at each level in the firm are the same—the optimization of some quantitatively measured function. Indeed, it is frequently assumed that the profit maximization objective holds at all levels of the firm. Thus the operations research literature offers little insight into the objective and strategy interaction problem.

From the R&D management viewpoint two opposite trends exist. The first is that R&D objectives should not be related to corporate objectives, since new product development is too unpredictable to control. The second is that R&D objectives should carry out corporate objectives, since the new product development function is a part of the firm. The latter viewpoint has gained prominence in recent years.

Even if it is accepted that R&D objectives should be derived from corporate objectives, there are no identified methods for translating corporate objectives to R&D objectives. Two practical suggestions predominate. The first is to have corporate management make all R&D decisions, eliminating the necessity for intralevel objective translation. The second is to have R&D

management aid in setting corporate objectives. Assuming these R&D managers are consistent, they will informally ensure that R&D decisions are consistent with corporate objectives, since they are committed to the corporate objectives by their part in establishing the corporate objectives.

Hill and Granger suggested that R&D objectives should include: (1) determination of the extent of new business required in the firm by internal development versus external acquisition, (2) examination of proposed new product areas in the corporate plan, (3) selection of proposed projects based upon promise, need, and empirical limitations, and (4) provision for commercialization of new business.[75] While they made no attempt to translate these upward in the firm, they do provide some suggestions for the normative recommendations of chapter 6.

In the strategic planning literature some work has been done in relating objectives and strategy, and in relating strategy to functional areas of the firm. Little specific R&D strategy work exists, other than a recognition that R&D can help carry out new product desires in product mix considerations.

In the general strategy literature, Ansoff has provided the start of a conceptual theory for more closely relating objectives and strategy.[76] Ansoff suggests a vector of objectives as a component of strategy, defining proxies in terms of economic objectives, noneconomic objectives, and responsibilities and constraints. Further, objectives are presented as descriptive attributes, with measurement yardsticks suggested for each descriptive attribute, and with goal values suggested for each measurement yardstick. (Ansoff suggests this objective breakdown conceptually, and provides details in terms of profitability measurement yardsticks and goals.)

Ansoff also provides a start in intralevel strategy interaction by suggesting product market strategies, two of which, product development and diversification, can aid in intralevel interaction for internal R&D division.

In general, this literature review has supported the identification of lack of intralevel objective and strategy interaction as a problem. It also reveals that there is little insight in the R&D literature for improving this interaction. Some of the strategy literature, particularly Ansoff's work, offers frameworks that will be used as input for the normative recommendations of chapter 6 but these frameworks are currently available only at the corporate level of the firm.

4

Analysis of Problems in Project Failure

It was noted in the discussion of objective and strategy interaction that one reason these areas were overlooked for so long was the feeling that structuring the research system would minimize output. In a similiar manner, many felt the causes of failure of R&D projects were so complex that they could not be analyzed satisfactorily. As an example, Lothrop notes that the "output of R&D is hard to measure and is usually a gamble; also it may not be successfully used for reasons too complex to discuss fully."[1]

By the early 1960s some failure cause analysis had begun. Marketing researchers had investigated the sales and field testing problems, financial analysts had become concerned with financial estimates of success, and R&D management had become concerned with the technical results of the R&D projects. This type of functional research has continued, but there has been relatively little research looking at these failure causes in terms of the overall new product development process or in terms of integrating the solutions of the various functional researchers.

The most comprehensive identification of the problem of project failure in applied R&D has suggested that only 2% of the project ideas that enter the new product development process stage model are introduced successfully into the marketplace, and that about three-fourths of the funds used in the process are used on projects that are not successful.[2]

This Booz, Allen and Hamilton report further notes that this general success and failure average differs surprisingly little among widely varying industries.[3] Since the state and rate of change of technology differ widely among industries, this identification of the relative constancy of success rate suggests that technical considerations and the state of the technical art in that industry do not play a major role in determining the new product success rate of a firm. Stated in another way, the management and decision-making aspects of new product development greatly overshadow the technical development aspects in contributing towards the success or failure of a particular project.

Booz, Allen and Hamilton surveyed companies that had been relatively successful in commercialization of new products to determine the percentage success rates. More important than this problem identification, however, was their summarized analysis of the causes of failure of the unsuccessful projects.

Fifty-five percent of all project failures were attributed to organizational type problems, particularly in coordination of various groups of individuals throughout the process, and assignment of responsibility and authority for the various steps in the new product development process.

Control and follow-up caused 12% of the problems. These tended to be mechanics of scheduling and organizing day-to-day activities. This percentage has dropped substantially from earlier Booz, Allen and Hamilton reports, and it was suggested that continued application of PERT and similar quantitative planning and control techniques should continue to lower the number of projects that failed due to control and follow-up problems.

Definition of objectives accounted for 9% of the identified failures; however 26% of the companies surveyed felt they had poorly defined corporate objectives to guide new product exploration and screening.

Business analysis accounted for 9% of the project failures, and again 26% of the firms reported this problem. Specifically, poor estimates of sales volume, total market potential, and profit were identified.

Other problems included gathering of new ideas for products, stimulation of creativity, and personnel qualifications. Regulation of idea generation and stimulation to such a minor problem area in the Booz, Allen and Hamilton report is particularly interesting since the breadth of research in idea generation and stimulation would suggest a much larger problem area.

Again, this report surveyed firms that were relatively successful in product commercialization. Other studies have suggested that problems in objective designation and business analysis were more critical in less successful firms.

Booz, Allen and Hamilton also place the project failures at various locations during the new product development process. Mapping their data onto the new product development stage model of figure 1, approximately 73% of the product ideas that started the process were dropped at the idea generation stage, 10% at the business analysis stage, 4% at the technical development stage, and 11% at the prototype, pre-production, and market introduction stages. This is again of interest in light of the volume of literature aimed at decision making during these later stages, particularly during the market testing phase of the pre-production stage.

Other researchers have identified the causes of project failure in alternate ways. Gloskey identified six major problem areas from his studies: (1) lack of interdepartmental liaison, (2) inadequate economic analysis, (3) research progressing too far before complete cost analyses were made, (4) no periodic review of project, (5) no estimate of entire project cost, and (6) lack of review by a scientist outside the project with authority to terminate it.[4]

Randle suggests that projects fail because the project concept was wrong in the first place, it was not within company fields of interest, the timing was bad, or people didn't want to buy the product.[5]

Other authors vary between Randle's unsophisticated approach to Gloskey's survey of firms, but none provides the data to suggest an order of importance among failure causes that Booz, Allen and Hamilton provide.

In addition, the problem of decision making is frequently noted, but either is not summarized or is included in other problem areas. When decision making is discussed, it is generally in terms of detailed decisions for one component of the new product process at one period of time. Almost never is decision making considered an ongoing, dynamic process in the new product development process.

The problem of objective definition is discussed in chapter 3, and a normative framework for improvement in this process is detailed in chapter 6. This chapter will analyze in depth the other causes of project failure by breaking them into the following discussion areas: (1) organizational causes, (2) control and follow-up causes, (3) business analysis causes, and (4) decision-making causes. In addition, potential solutions identified in the literature are presented to aid in establishing the normative recommendations of chapter 7.

Organizational Causes

A discussion of the organizational causes of new product failure involves considerations of R&D-marketing interactions, R&D-manufacturing interactions, and personnel promotion and control considerations, as well as the more familiar organizational structure problems. Much has been written on these areas, and only a few results are discussed here to represent the cause identifications.

In general, the marketing and R&D functions have large inputs into the early stages of the new product development process stage model, the R&D function has the major input during the development stage, and the marketing and manufacturing functions again interact heavily with R&D in the preproduction and market introduction stages. Frictions arising at the interfaces of these functional interactions are an obvious potential source of problems.

A *Research Management* journal seminar, as a typical example, describes the marketing function as an information input source to the R&D function.[6] It is suggested that a lack of coordination between the marketing and R&D functions often means that the marketing function does not provide adequate information to judge the possibility of commercial success of a project, and/or that the R&D division tends to ignore whatever information it does receive from the marketing department. The seminar suggests as a solution a clear-cut assignment of responsibility so that determination of the needs of the marketplace is a legitimate function of the marketing department, and that the R&D division use the commercial success information provided it as a major decision criterion in its project development decision.

Gerstenfeld, in a study of 91 projects, noted that 52% failed due to nontechnical causes.[7] Without providing specific data (as is common in most of the R&D literature), he feels the most prevalent explanation for these failures is "the lack of meaningful interaction between the marketing and R&D groups."[8] Two projects are discussed in detail, both of which, after successful technical development, were dropped because no market existed for the product. He attributes this to the lack of concern of the R&D management for a potential market, and the failure of the marketing function to provide accurate information to the R&D division.

Moore suggests a major failure cause in the translation of the project from the R&D division to the manufacturing division.[9] These problems are seldom technical, and are generally behavorial and managerial. Specific causes include the attitude of many R&D scientists who feel that production efforts are beneath their dignity, and the attitude of many manufacturing personnel who feel that the output of "ivory tower" scientists is not worth their efforts. Moore strongly suggests that the "not invented here" syndrome, alluding to the fact that the product was not developed in the manufacturing division, is a major problem to be overcome.

Moore makes a number of general suggestions for improvement, including allowing production personnel to have an input in R&D decision making, the creating of interdisciplinary groups to smooth the transfer, and the use of product or process managers who have working relationships with the manufacturing division. These are not unique suggestions, and some of them are included in the normative framework of chapter 7.

Another *Research Management* journal staff report before Moore's work reaches similar problem definitions and solutions.[10] While Moore's work is based upon data of one firm, and the *Research Management* report is mainly group consensus, it is interesting that the years intervening have not seen improvements in this R&D-manufacturing interaction area, and that Moore presents as current solutions the same solutions presented years earlier. While no investigations have been published in the last few years, there is no reason to assume any improvement between R&D divisions and manufacturing divisions in U.S. manufacturing companies.

Bennett has identified the promotion paths within the R&D division as an organizational problem. He notes that the best scientist is normally promoted to a managerial position, and that he makes his decisions based upon his technical expertise and background rather than upon commercial success criteria.[11] While Bennett recognizes the need for technical expertise in a R&D manager, he suggests training the scientist in financial and behavioral management techniques after he is promoted. While this solution has been widely proposed, a potential problem has been identified in the reluctance of many scientists to learn what they consider an imprecise and inexact discipline.

In their classic 1957 article Johnson and Jones identified the major causes of commercial failure of new products as the organizational structure and the interaction among the marketing, R&D, and manufacturing departments. [12]

They suggest in general terms the creation of a new products department reporting to corporate management at the same authority level as the heads of the operating and R&D divisions. Such a department, they feel, can have the responsibility for introduction of new products and the authority, by virtue of its level in the organization, to aid in this introduction. By choosing members of this new product department from the various functional areas, it can function well as a coordinating agency. In addition, its very existence indicates a greater emphasis to be given to new products in the minds of the functional managers.

In addition to these structural considerations, Johnson and Jones suggested committees made up of manufacturing, marketing, and R&D personnel to screen and approve development of new products. They also suggested for each new product proposal the need for an objective, an estimated profit, a schedule of specific activity dates, the required investment, a budget, and specific lines of project approval.

Johnson and Jones' research has stimulated much additional work, and has resulted in almost universal acceptance of the need for coordination among the R&D, manufacturing, and marketing functions. Specific results have emphasized the use of coordinating committees for decision making, the use of the project management concept, and the separation of commercial and technical project responsibility.

Numerous researchers are continuing to investigate this area, and details of implementation are becoming refined. [13] Further discussion provides little help in identifying the problems or providing background for the normative framework. Most investigators still look at organizational problems as an end in themselves and do not relate them to other failure causes in the new product development process.

The suggestions of Booz, Allen and Hamilton to solve the 55% of failures they attribute to organizational causes are consistent with the above discussions: recognition of the value of new products to the firm, a separate new product development organizational structure, and emphasis upon divisional and individual interactions. [14]

The normative decision framework of chapter 7 will include suggested solutions to organizational problems in a system combined with suggested solutions to other causes of failure.

Control and Follow-Up Causes

The definition of control is not standardized, although the term normally refers to the task of insuring that activities are producing the desired results. Activities are monitored, compared to standards, and the resultant information provided to the function or individual who can take corrective action if needed.

Control has historically been used in terms of financial and accounting budgets, and has been more recently used by organizational theorists to mean directing the efforts of subordinates.[15] Booz, Allen and Hamilton's description of this problem cause area includes both budget and subordinate direction. Their overall meaning, however, emphasizes planning and follow up of all phases of the new product development process to insure that the desired results are being accomplished.[16]

Control and follow-up are distinguished from decision making in this investigation by defining control as the comparison of actual with desired results after the decisions have been made. Nevertheless, there is substantial interaction between decision making and control, and on many detailed items the distinction is arbitrary.

The control causes of failure as identified by Booz, Allen and Hamilton are on an individual project basis. Some investigation has been given to control of the entire R&D function, either in terms of portfolio selection constraints or in terms of financial and manpower constraints in algorithmic models, but their discussion does not provide insight into the failure causes or background for the normative decision framework.

There has been little research of a theoretical nature dealing with control and follow-up in the new product process literature. Most of the literature available which deals with improving the control process are qualitative case studies of individual firms. An example is the financial budgeting follow-up during the technical development stage reported by Lindsay.[17]

His emphasis, however, is on a system to accumulate more reliable cost data rather than comparison of actual with anticipated costs. Another recent example is provided by Whitman and Landau who identified the financial budget as the single most important R&D procedure in six chemical firms they studied.[18] They note that while screening and business analysis financing may come from discretionary general purpose funds, a rigid budget is necessary to control the project from technical development to market introduction. In any case, financial control both during the development stage and during the later portions of the new product process is well documented, and is not considered a major failure cause.[19]

A number of studies have suggested that an individual's (particularly a scientist's) morale, satisfaction, and productivity may be inhibited where there is too tight control or too little autonomy or influence over technical work matters. As one example, Ansoff and Stewart were concerned with the effect of organizational structure and control upon scientists, noting that too tight control may stifle research innovation, while too loose control may mean that scientists work upon areas not directly connected with their project.[20] As another example, Randle has pointed out that R&D managers are generally technical specialists rather than trained managers, and that this general lack of expertise in managing people frequently results in misapplied technical and financial control.[21]

Souder, however, notes that R&D project output may be governed more by the nature of the technology and the orientation of the scientists towards their work than by organizational considerations.[22] This work suggests that control emphasis should be placed upon financial, scheduling, and technical content control rather than organizational control. Additional support for this de-emphasis of organizational control concerns is provided by Booz, Allen and Hamilton who note that the number of project failures due to control causes has decreased in recent years with the application of formal network planning and control models.[23] Obviously, if the actual problem was organizational in nature, it would not respond favorably to network planning methods.

Souder's study was concerned only with control at the technical development stage, and its application to other portions of the new product development process has not been verified.

Scheduling of manpower and equipment, as well as financial scheduling in terms of cash flow, is another identified failure cause area. A good summary both of the problem description and solutions by network planning methods is provided by Ashley and Austin.[24] Asbury, however, has suggested that scheduling of projects on scientific equipment is a greater problem area than has been identified, and that it has not been handled in sufficient detail in most planning models.[25]

Villers has added one other important insight in emphasizing that, if a time schedule of activities is changed, corresponding financial schedules may also need to be changed.[26] He also emphasizes that a time schedule change early in the process may necessitate changes later in the process, and that the effect of these changes on the total project outcome should be evaluated. This concern over control of the timetable is echoed by Marvin, who notes that too long a time period in development and pre-production activities may invalidate the information upon which a market was predicted.[27] He suggests that estimated times to complete these activities be a part of the marketing forecast, and that they should be closely controlled for variation from the estimated times.

Moreno specifically emphasizes the need for a periodic review of the time schedule.[28] He feels this has been neglected in favor of financial and technical success review. Again he notes that changes in time schedules can have a major effect on the market introduction date and on the commercial success of the product.

Periodic review of various aspects of a project during its life is a normal control technique. This review can vary from a casual check of the financial budget to a formal review of the time schedule, the estimates of technical success, an updating of the commercial success data, and so on. Bowie and Villers have provided two good summaries of the need for and types of both technical and business periodic reports throughout the entire new product development process.[29] It should be noted, however, that few industry studies suggest periodic updating of business analysis data in periodic reports, and failure to do so is a major reason for a product to be dropped for lack of profit after introduction into the marketplace.

Souder is concerned with the ability of R&D management to control and evaluate the day-to-day results during the development stage.[30] He investigated the validity of subjective probabilities by technical managers of technical success during the development stage at one firm. ("Technical development" means development of the desired properties of the product within the desired time period and within desired budgetary and manufacturing cost constraints.)

He undertook this study since he felt that probabilities of technical success were largely ignored in R&D decision-making processes, and that they could be valuable in this use. Using regression techniques on estimates from a number of managers within one firm's R&D division, Souder concluded that the eventual success or failure of projects can be predicted by measuring the time shape of polled probabilities of the success forecasts. In particular, he felt that the probability of success forecasting yielded more accurate advance warning indicators than several commonly used project status measures, including opinions of scientists doing the work, periodic reporting, and so on.

Business Analysis Causes

The business analysis stage of the new product development process stage model is concerned with estimating the commercial success of a proposed new product. Among other items, it requires estimates of future sales, selling price, market growth rate, total investment, useful life of facilities, manufacturing costs, marketing and distribution costs, development costs, and profit.

Gloskey has provided a comprehensive list of the various estimates of R&D, manufacturing, and marketing required for the business analysis stage.[31] One failure he has identified is the failure to routinely include all project costs in one package, with the result that the product is actually less profitable than anticipated. This is at least in part attributed to corporate accounting methods, which may not be set up to give a total development cost, and where R&D costs may either be capitalized or expensed, depending upon the firm.[32]

One obvious problem is the inability to forecast the future with the desired accuracy. While Gloskey provided a list of economic type forecasts necessary, Quinn has also identified the need to place economic forecasts in the framework of sociological and technical forecasting.[33] (Sociological forecasting is concerned with demographic structure, shifting expenditure priorities, the role of the government towards business, and so on; technical forecasting is concerned with the development of new technologies and the flow of information.) Ignoring these sociological and technical considerations may decrease the accuracy of the economic estimates substantially.

In addition to forecasting future values, Brandenburg notes that "unanticipated occurrences are characteristic of R&D activities."[34] He feels that development activities are much more uncertain than other functional activities of the firm, and that unanticipated outcomes may dominate anticipated outcomes in most cost and benefit areas.

Rubenstein has suggested that this uncertainty can be in part due to inadequate or poor quality of information.[35] He suggests specifically poor information supplied by the R&D laboratory as the major information cause. His analysis is aimed at the market testing portion of the pre-production stage, and he emphasizes that poor information from the R&D division results in poor or inadequate market testing, with the result that the product is frequently dropped. No specifics are provided, however, and in fact market testing involves much information and input outside the control of the R&D division. A generalization of Rubenstein's comments suggests that the accuracy and gathering of information is a major problem throughout the new product process.

Villers feels that the business analysis stage is too reliant upon qualitative rather than quantitative measures.[36] This does not mean that estimates of sales and profits are not provided in quantitative terms, but that the subjective probability estimates that go into them are based upon the qualitative opinions of the individuals making the estimates, with the resultant exclusion of any sensitivity or confidence interval type considerations which would provide more quantitative meaning to the estimates that are provided. Villers' suggestions, however, do not include formal sensitivity or confidence interval testing. Rather, he suggests the use of an index system that still relies heavily on the subjective probability he dislikes.

Cetron and others are concerned with the sensitivity of output data to small changes in input conditions.[37] A high degree of sensitivity in output to small changes in input is undesirable, since the output then becomes unstable in the presence of minor external changes. No specific methods of sensitivity analysis, or suggestions to overcome identified sensitivity are provided, however.

A summary of potential estimation errors and their effects upon R&D project selection has been provided by Brandenburg.[38] In addition to the summary, his distinction between errors based upon analytical models that assume a certain behavior of estimates and errors based upon the limited empirical studies of actual behavior of estimates is important.

Empirical studies of the accuracy of future estimates for new product development tend to be rather general. The normal result involves a general conclusion without specific data, like Marschal and Meckling's comment that cost estimates made early in the product development process show more variability and over-optimistic bias than estimates made later in the development process.[39]

One of the few detailed analyses of errors in estimation has been provided by Tull, who hypothesized one of the major failure causes of new products to be the variance between actual and predicted sales and profits.[40] Tull queried 200 large companies with R&D divisions, of whom 24 agreed to participate in his study. Of these 24, 16 provided meaningful data, and more than eight years' sales forecasts were obtained on 63 products and profit forecasts on 53 products. Tull attributed the major part of his difficulty in gathering data to the fact that many companies he queried did not make formal sales and profit forecasts for new products, and that many forecasts that were made were not in a form suitable for comparison with actual sales and profits.

A number of conclusions resulted from Tull's formal hypothesis testing of the available data.

1. The average error in forecasting sales and profits of new products is high. The mean relative error of sales forecasts for the 63 new products was 65% with a median error of 25%. The relative error of the profit forecast of 53 products was 128%, with a median error of 46%.

2. In general, forecasts of products with low sales tended to be optimistic, and forecasts of products with larger sales tended to approach actual sales closely.

3. Comparing industrial and consumer new products, Tull concluded that the mean relative error of sales forecasts is not significantly different, but the mean relative error for forecasts of profits is significantly lower for new consumer products than for new industrial products. This is in contrast to much of the marketing literature which tends to assume that consumer forecasting is more difficult than industrial forecasting.

4. Interestingly enough, Tull found that the mean relative error of both sales and profit forecasts of innovative products is not significantly different than for adaptive products.

5. The mean relative error of forecasts of sales and profits using primary data is not significantly different from those made using secondary data. (Primary data is information gained from consumers, industrial users, test markets, and so on. Secondary data is information obtained from company records, trade associations, government agencies, and so on.) This is of particular interest since it is assumed in the literature that primary data would produce the more accurate information, and hence generate a lower mean random error.

Tull was careful to point out that his study was exploratory in nature, and cautions against excessive generalization of his results. He also notes that this data applies only to products that were introduced into the marketplace and were successful enough to be retained in the firm's product line, and hence may be prejudiced against products that were dropped. Nevertheless, Tull's work is significant in that it supports the opinion that the errors in profit and sales forecasts can be large, suggests some general directions of error in profit and sales forecasts, and suggests that the use of primary methods of information gathering have not provided the answer to improving forecast accuracy.

Mansfield, Schnee and Wagner also attempted to verify some of Tull's results dealing with the accuracy of sales forecasts.[41] They hypothesized that four independent variables would affect sales forecast overruns: (1) the innovativeness of the new product, (2) the calendar year of the forecast, (3) the identity of the forecaster, and (4) the quantity of estimated sales. The only significant variable identified from their multiple regression model was a dummy variable identifying one of the forecasters.

While the meaning of these results is not entirely clear, they did feel that the time period in which the estimate was made was important, not in terms of the specific year, but in terms of the specific company's growth. That is, as new product development was increased, more trained individuals were hired to perform the forecasts, and the accuracy of the forecasts increased.

Mansfield, Schnee and Wagner provide one major suggestion for improving the accuracy of future forecasts—to devote more resources to the forecasting effort. No specific suggestions as to the amount or type of resources were made, nor were any examples given, but their general attitude is that quantitative tools to improve forecasts are available, and that the application of these tools by trained individuals could improve forecast accuracy.

Decision-Making Causes

While decision making during the new product development process was not identified as a failure cause per se by Booz, Allen and Hamilton, decision making and potential decision-making problems are interwoven throughout the project failure causes. Even more important, however, proposed solutions to many failure causes are expressed in terms of, or included in, the framework of a decision-making system.

In general, decision making in the new product development process involves a series of decisions made in selection and control of new product projects. The subject of individual project selection versus project selection as part of a portfolio of selections is an important concern. Quinn, among others, has noted that there is generally some financial constraint upon the R&D division as a whole, based upon some criterion such as percentage of sales, past experience, and so on.[42] It is the presence of this dollar constraint upon the R&D function as a whole that gives rise to the literature suggesting the need for a package of projects, rather than individual projects, to compare against the desired criteria. Seldom are any theoretical reasons given for such a dollar constraint. The obvious result of this constraint is that a great many projects that offer potential profit for the firm do not start the development cycle.

An example of decision-making techniques for individual projects is provided by Jackson.[43] He suggests techniques such as checklists, profile charts, scoring models that assign weights to individual criteria, benefit-cost ratio, and stochastic decision trees.

As an example of a portfolio treatment of R&D new product decision making, Mansfield and Brandenburg studied one firm to determine the success of the entire R&D function.[44] The authors portray decision making in terms of a formal mathematical model, but note that the model neglects organizational variables, risk attitudes, information flows, and the role of variables other than profit in the goal structure of the decision maker. That is, they assume a single goal of profit maximization.

Most of the portfolio selection research has been concerned with the effectiveness of the entire R&D technical development function, and is not particularly relevant to this study of the new product development process.

In 1964 Brandenburg provided a survey of the literature for the selection of R&D projects.[45] Since then much work has been done, at least some of it on problems Brandenburg identified. For ease of discussion, this work is summarized in terms of decision criteria, risk and uncertainty, the location of decisions in the process, the decision makers, operations research techniques, and decision indices.

Decision Criteria

A commercially successful product has been defined in this investigation as a product that is introduced into the marketplace and is subsequently retained in the firm's product line. While the profit consideration is major in the determination of success, there is no assumption that the profit decision criterion is the only criterion or even the major criterion. In fact, as discussed earlier, the general assumption today is of multiple objectives and strategies which in turn bring a need for multiple decision criteria to carry out the multiple objectives. Nonfinancial decision criteria are discussed in chapter 3 and are emphasized again in the normative frameworks in chapters 6 and 7. A brief review here of decision criteria in general aids an understanding of the problems in current decision making.

Pessemier feels the decision criteria are a major cause of new product failure, but he does not identify specific problem criteria.[46] He reinforces the profit-oriented objectives, suggesting that the answer to decision criteria problems is the formal use of rate of return on investment as the decision criterion. Pessemier then provides detailed comprehensive instructions on quantitative information gathering techniques to improve the rate of return on investment calculation. He further ties the rate of return on investment criterion to the business analysis stage without later review.

Ansoff was one of the first to suggest that financial decision criteria are not in themselves adequate to ensure a commercial success.[47] He noted that although rate of return on investment and risk estimates are a central portion of the decision-making process, strategic fit must also be taken into account. Ansoff suggests the use of an index number system blending financial and strategic considerations into a linear formula giving a "figure of merit" for risk and profit. Ansoff did not pursue this index system in his later work. The use of other index systems will be considered later.

Risk

There is no generally accepted concept or definition of risk. Hertz has provided a philosophical argument for risk as the concept that recognizes the inability to predict the future perfectly.[48] While attempting to reduce forecasting errors is a worthwhile objective, he notes, when "all is said and done the future is still the future."[49] Regardless of how well we can presently forecast, we are still left with the knowledge that we cannot eliminate all uncertainty about the future.

In statistics, a distinction is made between risk and uncertainty. Risk is defined as the condition where all of the potential outcomes of an event can be identified in advance, and where a probability of occurrence of each outcome can be assigned. Uncertainty is defined as the condition where all of the potential outcomes of an event can be identified in advance, but where there is no basis to assign probabilities of occurrence.

In current finance portfolio theory, risk is defined as the statistical variance associated with the average return of a portfolio of securities. Again, the assumption is that the outcomes of all events can be identified in advance.

In the capital budgeting and general business literature, the definition of risk varies more widely, from Tilles,[50] who talks of risk in terms of balancing broad product market areas, to Mayer,[51] who defines risk as the probability that a specific decision will cause the firm to go out of business in the long run.

In the specific R&D management area, different researchers use definitions from all of the above areas of discussion.

For ease of discussion, risk is presented in terms of three areas: financial portfolio risk, capital budgeting risk, and R&D project selection risk.

Risk in financial portfolios.   In 1952 Harry Markowitz suggested treating a group of common stocks as a portfolio to which statistical theory could be applied to calculate the expected value of return as a measure of return and the variance of the portfolio return as a measure of risk.[52] This approach has stimulated much additional work.

More recently, Schlarbaum and Racette have summarized this portfolio risk research.[53] They note that there is seemingly wide agreement that the risk of a security is somehow related to the *ex ante* probability distribution of return attributed to the securities by investors. Since this relationship is not clear, many researchers have suggested different proxies for it, and it is in the acceptance of these proxies that disagreement centers. Specifically they note: (1) disagreement as to what constitutes risk, (2) differences in the basic problem as identified by different researchers, (3) different assumptions about the extent of diversification in the securities market, and (4) different theories as to how individuals form expectations about *ex ante* risk.

The most common concept and definition of risk is that of the variance of the *ex ante* probability distributions of one period's portfolio returns. In general, a number of basic assumptions underlie this definition. One is that investors do attempt to maximize their wealth over a one-period time frame. Another is that the distribution of asset and portfolio returns is symmetric about the means of the respective distributions. A third is that the measure of risk can be associated in theory with any specific security, and that this risk can be identified as a contribution to the total risk of a portfolio. Other assumptions require that investors have homogeneous expectations about the future return for the risk, and that all investors can borrow and lend at the same riskless rate of interest.

These assumptions are challenged by, among others, Morton, who argues that risk is multidimensional, resulting from individual psychological characteristics and perceptions of the world which are subject to constant change.[54] In addition he argues that consideration of risk as a parameter of a probability distribution is an oversimplistic assumption. This viewpoint is supported by Joyce and Vogel, who consider variance as a measure of risk to be too ambiguous for consistent use, and question the lack of theoretical support for this definition.[55]

Schlarbaum and Racette conclude that attempts to measure risk quantitatively are "especially treacherous" unless their very stringent assumptions are met.[56] They suggest use of accounting definitions of risk, such as rate of return on net worth and the spread of rate of return on net worth. Although noting the technical problems of accounting measures of risk, they argue that, as long as risk measures are heterogeneous and confined to theoretical discussions, accounting measures are as good a risk proxy as any other measures currently available.

Machol and Lerner provide a different approach.[57] They note that portfolio investment theory assumes that: (1) under conditions of certainty the rational investor prefers the investment with the highest rate of return; (2) under uncertain future conditions, where future return is a random variable, the rational investor prefers the investment with the greatest expected value, providing all other moments of distribution of the random variable are equal; and, finally (3) under conditions of uncertainty, if the variance differs, but all other moments including expected value are equal, the rational investor prefers the investment with the smaller variance because it can be characterized as being less risky.

The problem with these assumptions is that they provide no aid in decision making when a comparison of two portfolios shows that one has both a higher expected value and a larger variance than the other. Should the portfolio selected for purchase be that portfolio with the highest expected value, that with the lowest variance, or a subjective choice based upon the perceived relative value of both the expected return and the variance?

Machol and Lerner also point out that few actual security portfolios are held for only one time period, and that many portfolios are made up of a great many stocks.[58] They further note that the law of large numbers suggests that with a large enough number of securities in a portfolio, the portfolio essentially becomes riskless in the sense that the portfolio variance becomes smaller and smaller. They conclude that, where many stocks are bought for a portfolio and where the stocks are to be held for a substantial period of time, one can ignore risk and purchase securities with the highest expected returns. Excessive attention is being paid to risk, they note, at the expense of theoretical concentration on maximization of portfolio expected returns.[59]

Even with all of the above research and discussion, however, there is no theoretical reason to assume that the portfolio theory definition of risk in terms of variance has any application to new product project selection, or even that the concept of a portfolio itself does. In particular, there is no theoretical reason to assume that the assumptions underlying portfolio theory apply to R&D project selection; in practice it is obvious that the assumptions do not apply.

Risk in capital budgeting and general business.   Bogue and Roll argue that capital budgeting and risk assignment problems are wholly insolvable for a general, unspecified objective function.[60] To support this, they note that all the research to date has involved maximizing some single value, such as market price of a security or profit. Such maximization, they argue, is so unrealistic an assumption of objectives as to be of little value.

Tilles, however, overcomes this by considering capital budgeting on a broad, product class scale.[61] He suggests controlling risk by balancing broad product market classes. An example might have some product areas with a high degree of technical ferment (such as pharmaceuticals) balanced with relatively stable technology areas (such as fluorescent lights and utilities).

Consistent with Tilles, Mayer defines risk as the probability that the firm's business activities may cease to be compensatory, and that the firm may go out of business in the long run.[62] Applying this definition to individual project selection, two results could be obtained. One is that the proposed project could result in a negative profit or cash flow; the second is that the proposed project could result in a low enough profit or cash flow as to fail to justify the investment required.

Since return on investment or similar measures of profitability are widely used as measures of return, some emphasis has been given to expressing risk in connection with return on investment. Dupont, generally credited with pioneering the return on investment concept, traditionally used a fixed minimum value for return on investment as the comparison base for proposed projects. If a proposed project exceeded this base, it was accepted. In the early 1970s, Dupont changed to a variable minimum return on investment figure to reflect the risk of the investment.[63] If a project is felt to be risky, a higher minimum is used. If the project is considered of low risk, a lower minimum is used. The determination of the amount of risk is left entirely to the subjective opinion of the decision maker.

Along similar lines, Ansoff suggests that since the available methods of providing for risk are so poorly developed, risk should be taken into account in setting the minimum values (goal threshold values) of the desired profitability criteria.[64] Again the subjective opinion of the decision maker determines the degree of risk and the changes in the minimum goal value to compensate for the risk.

Bower and Lassard, in their study of capital budgeting of seven firms, suggest a single number value for decision making. They feel that even though single number measures, usually some measure of profitability, are used for decision making without formal considerations of risk, the sophistication of the staff members who develop the measures in terms of statistical analysis and risk considerations is high, and that most of the problems anticipated from single number measures do not occur in practice.[65]

Bower and Lassard discuss a number of risk criteria for capital budgeting from the stockholder's viewpoint. They point out the theoretical and operational weaknesses of each. At least one screening method utilized in their study is of value for its conceptual insight. Rather than treating capital budgeting projects as part of a portfolio, they propose treating each one separately, and assuming a firm can borrow as necessary, suggest that a firm should carry out projects that hold unchanged or improve the return and risk position of the equity investors. Using the formula:

$$(R_p\text{-}r)/(SD_p) > (R_E\text{-}r)/(SD_e)$$

where R_p is the expected return on the project after taxes, R_E is the expected return to equity investors without the project, r is the after tax rate of risk, and SD_p and SD_e are the standard deviation of return on the project and to equity owners without the project, respectively. A project is accepted if the formula value is positive to zero, and rejected if it is negative.

The operational problems in use of this formula are obvious, particularly identifying and calculating the values to be employed. Conceptually, however, it is one of the few attempts to combine risk and return into a single measure, and to define as a comparison base the current activities of the firm. The weakness is that there is no theoretical reason to assume that new project return should exceed that of present projects, or that a new project return only slightly above existing returns should be accepted.

Risk control by expected value techniques.   The use of an expected value technique is one of the most common methods of adjusting return for risk. A typical example has been provided by Carter in terms of a profitability calculation.[66] For each factor that goes into a return on investment calculation (sales volume, price, cost, investment, and so on), a range of potential values rather than a single estimated value is selected. A probability of occurrence is assigned to each value, and, by multiplying the value by its probability and summing, an expected value can be calculated for each factor. The expected values of each factor are used in the return on investment formula, and an expected return calculated. The assignment of the probability of occurrence for each factor value is a subjective measure of the decision maker's risk estimate, and hence the expected value calculation takes into account the adjustment for risk.

While many problems, such as estimation of the future values, can be identified in the expected value method, much concern has been expressed both for and against the assignment of the subjective probabilities. Cyert, March, and Starbuck provide both theoretical and practical support for the use of subjective probability.[67] In particular, they found empirical validity in the assumption that individuals can and do modify their subjective estimates of the future to reflect their expectations about the returns associated with various possible risks. They further found that, in the case of conflict among individuals, a group estimate of subjective probability produces more accurate estimates than biased individual estimates.

One weakness uncovered in Cyert, March, and Starbuck's study was that different probabilities were assigned to the data depending upon whether the data was called sales data or cost data. This emphasizes the role that prior perceptions of the decision maker can have on the probability assignments, and hence the final measurement value.

Bogue and Roll note that for decisions to be consistent it is necessary to assume a common subjective probability belief about potential returns from all members of the stockholder or management group involved in a decision.[68] That is, it is necessary to assume that all managers think the same way and would make the same decision given the same information. While this assumption may seem reasonable given the assumptions of financial portfolio theory, it is obviously unreasonable where multiple objectives exist and where individuals have other goals than profit maximization.

Some specific descriptions of practical methods to assign subjective probabilities in R&D project selection have been provided by Marschak.[69]

Hertz has provided an excellent discussion of expected value techniques as decision criteria for capital investment.[70] He considers the major deficiency to be a single number representation without any other description of the entire picture that the data represents. He notes a number of improvements that have been made in an attempt to overcome the difficulties of a simple expected value rate of return measurement. One such improvement has been the development of more accurate forecasting methods. Yet, he notes, even if we can further improve on forecasting, our ability to predict the future will still be largely unknown.

Another improvement has been the adjustment of estimates of the future based upon the actual results of past decisions. Yet, there is no guarantee that the future will behave like the past. In addition, these adjustments tend to be relatively arbitrary.

A third method has been to raise the minimum goal value by some amount to reflect the uncertainty concerning the data used to estimate the rate of return. This is the approach suggested by Ansoff and used by Dupont.[71] The question generated by this approach is how much to raise the minimum goal value.

A fourth improvement involves estimating each factor in the rate of return formula (sales volume, price, cost, investment, and so on) at three levels, aiming at a low, medium, and high value for each factor. Rates of return are then calculated based upon combinations of the pessimistic, optimistic, and medium estimates. These results give a picture of the range of possible results, but do not tell the decision maker which estimate condition (pessimistic, medium, or optimistic) or combination of conditions is most likely to occur.

Risk handling by simulation. Use of techniques based upon simulation of the informational inputs to give a clear picture of the return of the project has been proposed by a number of authors, among them Hess and Quigley and Hertz.[72] These simulation analyses involve three steps. The first requires estimating the range of values for each of the input factors (sales volume, price, cost, investment, and so on), and assigning a probability of occurrence to each value in each factor. From this, a probability distribution for each factor can be constructed.

The second step requires selection of one value from the probability distribution of each factor. These values are combined and the rate of return (or any similar profitability measure) calculated. For example, a low price value might be chosen at random to combine with a high sales value and intermediate values for other factors.

Step three involves repetition of step two a great many times to give a long list of possible rates of return based upon many different combinations of input factor values. Since different combinations of factors may give the same rate of return, the list of rates of return will include repeated values. These calculated rates of return are then combined into a probability distribution and a mean and variance calculated. The mean can then be used as the expected return, and the variance can, if desired, be used as a measure of risk in a manner similar to portfolio theory. In addition risk can also be expressed in alternate methods such as by a confidence interval. For example, the result of the simulation could be expressed as a rate of return of 18% with a .99 confidence interval of 12.7% to 22.1%, or as an expected profit of $2.5 million with a plus or minus three standard deviation range of $1-$3.5 million.

Both Hertz, and Hess and Quigley assume that the management will make the capital investment decision based upon their subjective evaluation of this given information. They do not suggest decision criteria or comparison bases, nor do they suggest ways to choose when one project has both a higher return and a greater potential spread than another project. They do suggest that this simulation technique is a more theoretically correct method of measurement of both expected return and the risk of that return than any other method presented to date.

In an article comparing seven capital investment decision criteria techniques, Pegels has suggested use of the Baldwin rate of return rather than the more standard rate of return formula used by Hess and Quigley, and Hertz.[73] Pegels notes that with the regular rate of return formula the future receipts and payments are reduced to their present value by discounting them at the same rate as that which the proposed investment is estimated to provide.

Pegels translates Baldwin's verbal description into the formula

$$R = \left[\frac{\sum_{i=1}^{n} x_i(1+r_o)^{n-i}}{I} \right]^{\frac{1}{n+1}} -1$$

where R is the Baldwin rate of return and where r_o equals the interest or earnings rate that the organization on the average earns on its assets.[74] Only if r_o and R are the same would the standard rate of return formula give the same result as the Baldwin formula. Pegels notes that "a more accurate rate of return is provided by the Baldwin method than by the straight internal rate of return method."[75]

Simulation analysis techniques offer direct application to R&D project selection. By performing the calculations on the computer, costs can be kept low. There are few of the restrictive assumptions necessary for financial portfolio theory, nor is there any restrictive assumption about profit maximization or singularity of goals, since the expected return and risk of return are informational inputs to which the decision maker can add other subjective considerations. In addition, the calculations of profitability assume multiple future time periods. By use of a probability distribution for each factor, as well as the final return calculation, simulation techniques are less dependent on the accuracy of future data than any other technique using single point or expected value estimation. Finally, simulation techniques are consistent with the problem framework called "quasi-analytical" by Ansoff and "ill-structured" by Simon and Newell.[76]

Hertz and Hess and Quigley's work seem to have had little impact upon the work of other researchers as reflected in the literature although Hertz feels it is being used in practice in industry. Bower and Lassard note that two of the seven firms they studied used these type simulations, and were not satisfied with them, although no specific reasons for this dissatisfaction were given.[77]

Lewellen and Long note that simulation is not incorrect in measuring discounted cash flow expected value.[78] They feel it is not necessary, however, and their preferred technique is to discount back a single point expected value cash flow at a rate "properly adjusted" for risk. This adjusted rate should be based upon the yield of investments in similar lines of business. This suggestion, however, does not provide any details on how to set the adjusted rate, and ignores most of the reasons for using simulation in the first place.

Risk in R&D project selection.   There has been little research on risk from the research and development viewpoint. What work has been done generally involves applications of return and risk concepts from capital budgeting theory to R&D project selection.

Brandenburg has pointed out that the very nature of R&D new product selection means that the results of an R&D project are less certain than the results of decisions in other functional areas of the firm.[79] One result of this uncertainty, Marvin notes, is that many managers and even a number of firms would rather not introduce new products at all than take a chance on investing money in a project that fails.[80] The practical tendency is for R&D managers to decide whether or not a project is too risky to be undertaken based upon their informal, subjective opinion of the chances of both technical and commercial success.

Roussel and Little attribute risk problems to the difficulty in communication between R&D managers and other managers.[81] They suggest probabilistic estimates as a common ground among managers, and suggest that probablistic estimates can be made of technical success, costs, and commercial success.

Some emphasis in R&D research has been given to attempts to minimize the risk of a project by improving the accuracy of data that goes into calculation of the return. Brandenburg feels this can be done by increasing the level of effort put into estimating the input factors.[82] He suggests an attempt to determine how much money need be spent in advance to improve forecasting accuracy by a specified amount, followed by a determination of whether the improvement is worth the cost. He is careful to note, however, that there is probably a point of decreasing return to scale, after which additional expenses without control may not improve future estimates. He suggests market potential and cost of manufacture as two areas where increased effort can result in increased accuracy.

Brandenburg cautions, however, that the very nature of technological change and the state of the art of forecasting may mean that substantial improvement in accuracy may not be possible.[83] Roman supports this, noting that forecasting techniques such as time series or regression analysis may have little application for future new products.[84] He suggests in general terms subjective group estimates of the future as a method offering more potential, but provides no specifics.

One of the few formalized methods of handling risk in an R&D context has been provided by Beattie and Reader.[85] Using standard assignment of ranges and subjective probabilities for each input factor in a return formula, an expected value of return is calculated. From this expected return risk is taken into account by subtracting from the expected return some quantity dependent upon the potential spread of the return. The resulting value is called the "expected utility" of the project. Beattie and Reader provide no details as to the method employed to determine the amount to be subtracted to reflect risk, leaving the assumption that this quantity is determined by the subjective opinion of the decision maker.

Beattie and Reader's method is similar to that of Ansoff and Dupont discussed earlier.[86] Beattie and Reader suggest subtraction of some amount from the expected value of the project, while Ansoff and Dupont add some amount to the minimum acceptable goal values prior to comparison with the value calculated for the project. The same problems discussed for the Ansoff and Dupont methods also apply to the Beattie and Reader method.

In short, almost all of the risk considerations in the R&D project selection areas discussed above have been discussed by Hertz.[87] He argues that the problems identified invalidate almost all of the techniques used, and suggests simulation techniques as the most theoretically correct and practical tool available to handle both risk and return.

Summary.   Both the concept and definition of risk vary widely in the literature. In general, however, risk is involved with the inability to perfectly predict the future, and is often expressed as the potential spread of return for a proposed project.

In financial portfolio theory, risk is formally defined as the variance of the expected return of the portfolio. The assumptions of profit maximization and single time period, among others, make application of financial portfolio theory to other areas very difficult.

In capital budgeting theory risk is recognized but is normally not specifically handled in calculation of return. The input factors in the return formula, the calculated average return, or the decision criteria comparison value may all be adjusted for risk based upon the subjective opinion of the decision maker, but seldom are any guidelines provided to aid the decision makers in establishing their subjective opinion.

The simulation techniques appear to overcome many of the anticipated problems of other risk and reward handling techniques, but they do not appear to have been accepted to any extent in the literature. While this technique does offer the decision maker a better description of the data than any other technique to date, it still requires that the final decision be based upon the subjective opinion of the decision maker.

Risk has generally not been taken into account in a formal way in R&D project selection literature. Some concern has been expressed about ways to improve the accuracy of input factor data for return calculations, but in general, few specifics have been developed. A few attempts to consider risk in project selection have used the same techniques used for capital budgeting, with the same problems encountered.

In conclusion, there is no generally agreed upon method for identification and use of risk in overall decision making, let alone at the R&D project selection level. The simulation technique does offer potential for effective use. Further research will, however, be necessary before any definite assessment of the simulation technique can be reached. Supportive research results might also have the effect of stimulating further interest in the area of risk by other researchers in the field.

Location of Decisions

Smith has suggested conceptually the critical nature of the location of decisions in the new product process, and the need to look at each decision as part of a decision-making system.[88] Unfortunately, this is not a common concern, and the multitude of decisions identified at each stage of the new product development process are generally treated as separate and distinct entities.

Many decisions are made at each location in the new product development process. In general, however, most R&D and quantitative-oriented literature has tended to emphasize the business analysis decision location, while most marketing-oriented literature has emphasized decisions located at the market testing phase of the pre-production stage.

Decisions at the business analysis stage generally involve estimates of commercial and technical success for a project, and comparison of these estimates with other projects and standards. A decision then is made as to whether or not to proceed with technical development of the project. While the business analysis information gathering includes estimates of future market conditions, much marketing-oriented literature suggests that the final decision for actual introduction of the product into the marketplace should be reserved until the market testing stage. (This is of interest in light of Tull's data suggesting that market test information is no better than secondary information sources.[89]) Details of the business analysis stage decision location were introduced earlier in this chapter, and are further discussed in the operations research and indices sections.

Pessemier, Uman, and Schorr, among others, emphasize the location for decision making at the market testing phase.[90] Pessemier specifically emphasizes this decision-making location because the results of test marketing may be known, and because the location is so much closer to market introduction than the business analysis stage that the potential exists for much more accurate data.[91]

Schorr and Uman ignore new product development prior to the market testing phase, and hence consider problem identification here "early" in the new product process.[92] Problems they identify that cause eventual product failure are poor marketing plans, weak packaging, poor channels of distribution, inadequate sales force, and so on. They consider it to be a problem when there is no market for a developed product, but attribute this to poor market evaluation by the R&D division and hence outside their interest and control.

Marschak and others also emphasize the advantages of a decision at the market test location because of the potential to reduce the uncertainty about the market introduction outcome.[93]

There are at least three potential problems with a decision located at the market testing phase. One is that it is frequently difficult to distinguish between market testing and actual market introduction, so that a decision to drop a product after market testing may involve substantial customer problems. In addition, knowledge in advance that the formal decision will be made at the market testing phase of the pre-production stage can act as a psychological crutch to individuals gathering information for the business analysis stage, since they will feel any error can be corrected at the later stage.

Most important, however, is that by the market testing phase a large percentage of the total project cost, including capital equipment and manufacturing start-up, has been spent, and the decision to drop a project at this stage can be needlessly expensive. (Booz, Allen and Hamilton suggest that, on the average, 60-70% of the total project costs have been spent by the marketing testing phase, while Collier estimates 60-85%.)[94]

Decision Makers

The question of which individual, individuals, or functions should make the various decisions is unresolved. While much of this area was discussed earlier in this chapter with organizational causes of failure, some specific comment is of value here.

Randle considers a major cause of commercial failure to include project selection made solely by R&D managers.[95] Since these individuals do not have the training or information to handle all areas of the new product development function, he notes, it is not surprising that many of their decisions do not give proper weight to commercial considerations. On the other hand, decisions by corporate or divisional managers made solely on financial considerations often result in projects later being dropped because of incorrect attributes of the product, technical infeasibility, and so on.

Dean, and Johnson and Jones, among many others, have suggested a formal committee made up of R&D managers, operating division marketing and manufacturing personnel, and corporate staff personnel.[96] This committee then selects the specific projects for development, and takes the responsibility for the results. The advantages of such a committee are the informational input from the various functional areas, and the coordinating and interaction function it performs, as well as the commitment gained to the decision by those participating in it.

The problem with such a formal committee is the lack of individual responsibility. To overcome this, Hitchcock suggests a distinction between supplying information and other inputs, and actually making the decision.[97] He suggests that decision making should be a joint responsibility of R&D, manufacturing, sales, and financial executives, but that the R&D executive has the overall final responsibility and hence the final decision-making authority.

Finally, Dean, in a conceptual framework, notes that the decision makers at each stage of the new product development process need not be the same, and specifically suggests that the individuals who later review and evaluate the decisions should be different from the original decision makers.[98]

Operations Research Techniques

Operations research techniques for R&D project selection decision making are widespread. In 1964 Baker and Pound reviewed the published techniques, and emphasized the use of profit maximization techniques to insure consistency of decision making and most efficient use of resources.[99] They argued for additional research on models, considering that the state of the art was at the level where specific techniques could not be used. They also noted that where models have been thoroughly tested in practice they have usually been dropped after a short time because they did not describe accurately enough the actual process. They noted specifically that "the descriptive studies to date have not been adequate to permit a thorough description of the R&D project selection process. More descriptive work is required before the process is well enough understood to justify a detailed criticism of the operations research methods."[100]

In the same time period Brandenburg identified the conditions under which he felt allocation of resources among alternate projects may be carried out in a straightforward manner through ranking procedures, investment analysis, and mathematical programming.[101] These conditions required a limited number of alternatives, with outcomes clearly specified prior to the decision, and where relevant costs and benefits may be expressed in dollar terms with small errors of estimation. Only under these conditions, he noted, can mathematical models without insight into the total process be appropriate.

In spite of Baker and Pound's, and Brandenburg's comments, the trend in operations research studies has been to continue to construct algorithmic models without an understanding of the process they are attempting to model or the objectives the process is attempting to carry out.

As an example, consider a selection model developed by Cochran and others.[102] Their model is composed of a project selection component that utilizes discounted cash flow to reduce the measures of each project to a single economic index (expected net present value), and a project selection component that uses a linear programming algorithm with 0–1 variables to select the set of projects that maximizes the total expected net present value while satisfying specified budget constraints. While other authors use a different economic index number and possible alternate constraints, the use of a general profit maximum criterion and arbitrary application of mathematical models persists.[103]

In 1973 Souder provided additional overviews of the operations research R&D project selection models.[104] Souder first analyzed three expected value maximization models within five different firms performing applied R&D. He measured the utility of each model in terms of its ability to prescribe higher value portfolios than those actually implemented by R&D managers. (Value was expressed in terms of profit, return on investment, expenditures on unsuccessful efforts, and funds unexpended.) The linear expected value model was found to have higher utility in all five organizations than the existing decision techniques or than the nonlinear or piecewise models, but only two of the firms were willing to consider the models for permanent adoption. Most of the R&D and corporate managers considered these models highly irrelevant because of the maximization of the listed values, and several identified nonmonetary goals as paramount considerations. All of these managers, Souder feels, were sophisticated enough not to reject the formal models for the mathematics involved.

Souder concluded that "the classical project selection decisions, where an optimum set of projects is selected on the basis of financial criteria, may not be relevant in new market development R&D operations."[105]

Souder then analyzed a broad group of R&D selection models, with the same conclusions detailed above.[106]

In an attempt to investigate the reluctance of R&D managers to use mathematical models, Moskowitz developed an R&D management game.[107] This game was then used with a mixed class of R&D managers and quantitatively-oriented M.B.A. students. In advance, the students tended to chide the R&D managers for an intuitive approach to decision making and disinterest in a quantitative approach to management. The R&D managers expressed concern about the lack of relevance of formal models and the stress on the particular model rather than the logic built into the model.

When teams that included both R&D managers and students played the game, all exhibited significant degrees of illogical and suboptimal decision making, such as not being consistent on information processing, information acquisition, and strategy selection and behavior. Even the formal quantitative training of the students did not result in a consistent decision-making pattern in the game.

Moskowitz's article is of importance since it indicates some of the problems of heuristic practical R&D decision making, as well as the formal model problems. While the inconsistent nature of intuitive decision making has been widely recognized, it has not been well documented.

Decision Indices

There has been a great desire in the R&D decision-making literature to develop an index number system summarizing the entire value of a particular project in one number. While this may be in part based upon a desire to return to the simplicity of a single decision criterion, the arbitrary nature of many of the different components that make up an index suggests a desire to substitute an impersonal arbitrary mechanism for the logical reasoning power of the decision maker. While admittedly such a system is simple, and in fact requires no decision maker since a clerk or computer can choose a project on the basis of a simple number comparison, it is a gross oversimplification of the complexity of decision making in the new product development process.

Dean has provided a summary of many such indices, and a complete well developed index has been provided by Wilson.[108] Wilson takes each potential project and assigns weighting and ranking values to approximately 40 attributes of R&D, manufacturing, marketing, growth, and stability. The value for each attribute is summed to give a single number rating for the entire project. This number is then compared to the number for other projects, and the projects with the highest numbers developed. In addition to the theoretical problem of expressing a complicated decision by one number, Wilson's index is weak in that the assignments of weightings and ratings are relatively arbitrary, and different individuals may assign widely varying values.

Souder included decision indices with other types of quantitative decision-making models, and his conclusions that they have been little used and frequently dropped when used holds as well for decision indices as for other mathematical models.[109]

Summary

The objectives of this chapter were to analyze in depth the causes of individual new project failures in the current literature, and to identify suggestions in the current literature that could aid in developing normative recommendations for problem solutions.

The major failure cause was organizational problems in terms of coordination of a project through the different stages in the new product development process, and in assignment of authority and responsibility at the various stages. In general these marketing-R&D and manufacturing-R&D interfaces have been thoroughly studied, and the solution suggestions of interest in this investigation center on organizational structural changes, either in terms of a new product department or in terms of coordination techniques such as group decision making to improve interface interaction.

Control and follow-up failure causes were identified in terms of the need to ensure that the activities accomplished are consistent with those desired. Control problems have been decreasing with the increased use of formal techniques such as PERT. Of importance to this investigation is the continued emphasis of the recognition of need for formal control of timing, commercial success, and technical success, in addition to financial budgetary control.

Business analysis failure cause investigation centered on the inability to perfectly predict the future to estimate how well a potential product will meet the desired objectives. Information gathering and estimation improvement methods were discussed, and as a practical conclusion it was suggested that it will never be possible to predict the future perfectly, hence any decision-making concept must take an unpredictable future into account.

The major analysis of project failure causes was presented in a decision-making framework. Decision criteria emphasized exclusively financial profitability considerations, with only a few authors recognizing the need for other criteria, particularly strategic criteria. No specifics were provided to aid in normative recommendations.

Risk was considered as involved with the inability to predict perfectly the future, with a common expression technique involving the potential spread of return for a proposed project. The portfolio theory concept of risk as the variance of the expected return of a portfolio was discussed. The assumptions of profit maximization and single time period, among others, make application of portfolio risk to other areas difficult.

In capital budgeting theory risk is recognized, but is normally confined to profitability considerations like rate of return on investment. The input factors in the return formula, the calculated average return, or the goal value comparison base may all be adjusted up or down in some way based upon the subjective opinion of the decision maker, but no guidelines are provided to aid the decision maker in establishing the subjective opinion of the risk involved.

Simulation techniques do appear to offer theoretical advantages in application to profitability decision criteria for reward and risk. For each input factor in a rate of return on investment formula, a probability distribution is established based upon estimates of the future by the best available forecasting techniques. From each factor probability distribution a value is randomly chosen and a rate of return on investment calculated. Repeated calculations of return are made using randomly selected factor values, and combined to give a probability distribution of potential rate of return on investment. The average of this probability distribution is used as the expected rate of return on investment, and the variance is used as a measure of the risk of that return.

Although simulation methods offer a viable suggestion for profitability return and risk that is used in the normative recommendations of chapter 7, the literature offers no suggestions for handling risk for nonfinancial decision criteria.

The location of decisions in the product development process centered on the business analysis and market testing areas. Both were treated as decisions distinct from each other. Little consideration existed in the literature for a group of decisions or the location of decisions in the new product development process in terms of a series of decisions.

When combined and integrated, it appears that the causes of failure of new product projects have been well described, even if many quantitative studies supporting the descriptions are not available. Many potential solutions to these failure causes have been identified to aid in selecting normative recommendations. In particular, the insistence of the literature in treating each failure cause area as a separate, independent entity in itself suggests the potential for improving the success rate by recognizing the entire new product development process as an integrated system, and applying a consistent decision-making framework to the entire process.

5

The Task of the Normative Frameworks

In chapter 2, two major shortcomings in the present R&D to operations planning process are identified: (1) a lack of emphasis in placing the new product development process, the R&D function, and the area of individual project selection in the framework of corporate objectives and strategies, and (2) an inefficient and ineffective use of resources in the new product development process as identified by a low rate of successful market introductions from products handled under the current processes.

The purpose of this chapter is to introduce the need for the normative frameworks that follow and to provide an introduction for the way in which the frameworks are recommended and the way in which they interrelate. This chapter presents short conclusions of the two literature searches, discusses the general methodology used for development of the frameworks, and presents an overview for and discussion of the advantages of the two normative frameworks.

Conclusions of the Intralevel Objective and Strategy Interaction Search

Chapter 3 identifies and analyzes in depth the problems in the present R&D intralevel objective and strategy interaction literature and identified some solutions in the literature that could aid in developing normative recommendations for problems.

Neither the marketing nor operations research literature addressed the question of the place of R&D in corporate objectives or strategies. There is some agreement in the R&D management literature, however, that R&D objectives should carry out corporate objectives since, after all, the new product development function is a part of the firm.

Even if it is assumed that R&D objectives should be derived from corporate objectives, there are few identified methods for translating corporate objectives to R&D objectives. Two practical suggestions predominate in the literature. The first is to have corporate management make all R&D decisions, eliminating the necessity for intralevel objective translation. The second is to have R&D management aid in setting corporate objectives, hoping that the commitment to the corporate objectives gained by aiding in setting them will ensure R&D decisions consistent with corporate objectives.

In general, the strategic planning literature in the context of new product development has not been developed below the corporate level, although the input into corporate strategy of R&D to help identify new product market areas and to develop new products for product mix considerations is recognized.

Thus the need for R&D decisions to be consistent with corporate objectives and strategies is suggested in the literature, but no structured method has been developed to translate corporate objectives and strategies to the R&D level for product decision making.

Conclusions of the Project Failure Search

In chapter 4, an in-depth analysis of the R&D new product failure cause literature was conducted to investigate the causes of project failure and to identify potential solutions to the failure causes.

The major failure cause identified was organizational, in terms of the assignment of authority and responsibility of decision making at various stages in the development, and in terms of coordination of a project through different stages in the process. In general, these have been thoroughly discussed in terms of R&D manufacturing and R&D marketing interfaces. The use of groups of decision makers is a common solution. Group decision making offers the advantage of varied information inputs, and in commitment to the decisions of the group by individuals within the group who must carry out the decision. Organizational structure changes are also frequently recommended. Yet examples of success with a structure in one firm and failure with the same structure in another firm have suggested that structural changes per se are not enough to improve the new product success rate significantly.

It is generally assumed in the literature that profit and profit alone is the goal of a R&D project, or, at the other extreme, that multiple objectives are desired and that these objectives cannot be structured. Both of these assumptions are rejected as conclusions here. The strategic planning literature clearly identifies the need for noneconomic objectives and decision criteria. The literature has also identified many failures from intuitive decision making. Thus a framework that provided multiple objectives and decision criteria structured as much as is possible offers a potential for improvement over either of these extremes.

Much of the literature used one decision, located at the business analysis stage of the new product development process, for the new product development decision. An analysis of the existing data of the expense structure of the new product development process, however, indicated the bulk of the expenses late in the process. This suggests the potential for decisions (or decision reviews) late in the process to improve the efficiency of funds used.

When combined and integrated, it appears that the causes of many failures of new products have been described and possible solutions suggested, even if many quantitative studies supporting the descriptions and solutions are not available. Yet the emphasis in the literature for treating each failure cause independently in itself suggests the potential for improving the success rate by integrating the failure causes and suggested solutions, treating the new product development process as an integrated system, and applying a consistent decision-making framework to the entire process.

The Research Methodology

The objective of this book is to overcome the identified problems in the R&D to operations planning process by development of normative recommendations as a decision-making system. Careful analysis was given to the literature available, and elements were drawn from the literature where possible for inclusion in the normative frameworks. Where possible solutions were not suggested in the R&D literature, the author developed solutions based upon carefully reasoned analysis of the problem, his personal experiences, and research in other literature fields.

As discussed in chapter 4 (and as is discussed again in chapter 7), the R&D to operations planning process problems were classified as "quasi-analytical" problems. That is, problems where the rigid restrictions of operations research techniques were not appropriate, but where the potential for structuring of an intuitive problem definition exists.

Both Simon and Newell, and Ansoff have identified "quasi-analytical" problems.[1] In a strategic planning context, Ansoff has further conceptualized a "quasi-analytical" research methodology involving a portfolio of qualitative and quantitative decision criteria structured as much as is possible.[2] Further, Ansoff argues that quasi-analytical methods are not interim steps to be used until quantitative concepts and algorithms are developed to encompass the problems. He argues that conceptual quantitative methods ignore the problems of perception of decision needs and invention of decision alternatives that are an integral part of the quasi-analytical methodology, and that because of this the quasi-analytical method will continue to develop its own logically rigorous formulation.[3]

Additional support for quasi-analytical solutions has been provided by Anshen and Guth, again in the context of business policy formulation.[4] They note:

A number of uncoordinated exploratory studies have prepared the way for defining research strategies and programs. Structured case collections and systematic descriptions of the operating and institutional environments at the policy level are beginning to provide raw material for conceptualization and analysis. Theories and techniques from the quantitative and behavioral areas are being tentatively transferred to the world of strategic planning. What is needed at this point is a comprehensive research strategy or set of related strategies that will organize the earlier work and will guide resource commitment in future studies.[5]

Anshen and Guth's comments describe the R&D to operations planning process as well as they do the business policy process. The many R&D studies and descriptive and prescriptive reports serve as an uncoordinated base for conceptualization and analysis. The goal of the normative frameworks in this book is to draw together problem solutions that are available, to fill in the gaps in what is available, and to suggest a total rather than fragmented approach to solve the problems identified.

Anshen and Guth further note that unstructured problems often require methodology that lacks the precision of mathematical techniques. This methodology is "normative in character, presenting prescriptions and heuristics" about problem solutions and decision making.[6]

Another goal of the normative frameworks is to present a logical decision-making system for project selection that offers advantages over present decision-making methods. In the context of quasi-analytical methodology, Ansoff has suggested that before it is given tentative acceptance a new method of problem solving must be subjected to several tests.[7] These are: its relation to prior approaches to the same problem, its relation to actual experience, its potential usefulness, and its prospects for further development.

The normative frameworks to be presented are consistent with these tests. Most of the decision elements are based upon the literature search descriptions of prior approaches and actual experience. Emphasis is given to structuring these elements and to an overall methodology of decision making.

The potential usefulness of these frameworks is in decision making in large, profit-oriented R&D activities. The frameworks presented can be used and are consistent with, and extensions of, current decision-making processes. The frameworks are sufficiently well structured and operational enough to offer improvements over the traditional intuitive decision method techniques. In addition, through a combination of quantitative techniques where they are applicable and structured qualitative elements, these frameworks make possible analytical treatment of the total R&D to operations planning process rather than treatment only of some quantifiable portions.

These frameworks offer potential for further development both in the elements of the decisions and refinement of the research methodology. Future research areas are identified in chapter 8.

In the corporate strategy context, Ansoff has suggested certain requirements that a decision-making system must include to handle corporate strategy adequately.[8] A new method must: (1) include the stages of perception of need, formulation of courses of action, evaluation of alternatives, and choice of an alternate as a general problem solving sequence, (2) be able to handle allocation of resources between opportunities in hand and future opportunities under conditions of partial ignorance, (3) evaluate joint effects (synergy) resulting from the addition of new products to the firm, (4) single out opportunities with outstanding competitive advantages, (5) handle a vector of potentially antagonistic objectives, and (6) evaluate the long-term potential of projects even though cash flow projections are unreliable.

In a specific R&D context, Brandenburg has pointed out that a basic problem with most R&D project selection methods is that

> while the notion of the ranked list changing with time is conceptually useful, little or no information is given on the critical question of how to establish the boundaries, how to account for errors in existing critical variables, and how to place a variety of projects with different characteristics on a common scale according to commensurable criteria.[9]

Brandenburg notes in addition that the project selection decision requires answers to the questions of what mix of problems to attack, relative emphasis on different problems, trade-offs between expected value and risk, and a match between the research performing capabilities and the firm's research needs. Further, Brandenburg suggests that the project selection decision must deal with the relationships in the environment, handle characteristics of different markets, and take into account technology, the requirements of market entry, and the maintenance of market position.[10]

Taken together, Ansoff and Brandenburg have identified elements that must be handled in proposing a decision-making system for the R&D new product development process to include strategic considerations in a quasi-analytical framework. These element identifications served as methodological inputs into the normative frameworks. That is, care was taken to ensure that the questions asked by Ansoff and Brandenburg were included in the frameworks. Specific correlation of these questions with the normative recommendations are provided after the normative recommendations are presented in chapter 7. They are introduced here, however, to identify them as structuring elements in the methodology of development of the normative frameworks.

In summary, the methodology used in development of the normative frameworks is quasi-analytical, based upon developing a decision-making system drawing upon a closely reasoned analysis of problems and problem solutions identified in the literature.

An Overview of the Intralevel Objective and Strategy Interaction Normative Framework

The problem of ensuring that R&D decisions are made consistent with corporate objectives and strategies is complicated by the fact that definitive statements of objectives and strategies are necessary for use in decision making. That is, the objective must be relatively narrowly identified, some measurement technique suggested, and some comparison base goal value available in order to make a decision.

Yet there is no theoretical reason to assume that objectives of the firm at the corporate level need to be expressed in definitive terms for decision making. In fact, as discussed in chapter 3, philosophical value objectives offer advantages in long-run consistency, and in providing a normative framework within which definitive objectives can be developed. That is, the philosophical objectives can be treated as long-run expressions of desires that do not change frequently. Decision-making objectives, however, must be responsive to changes in social conditions, economic conditions, technology, and so on.

In order to develop a set of decision rules for the R&D to operations planning process consistent with corporate objectives and strategies, it is necessary to develop a framework of corporate objectives, so that objectives can be cascaded downward to the R&D level to use in decision making. The purpose of the intralevel objective and strategy interaction normative recommendations is to develop such a framework.

This normative framework suggests a hierarchy of objectives within an organization beginning with philosophical value objectives for the firm as a whole. Consistent with and subordinate to these value objectives a set of corporate performance objectives is recommended. These performance objectives allow expression of value objectives in measurable terms. That is, the performance objectives are definitive enough to identify a measurement technique for determining if a specific product or product market area is consistent with the value objectives. Corporate strategy is suggested as subordinate to corporate value objectives, and is looked upon as a method to carry out corporate value objectives.

There is much interaction among these three areas. Corporate strategy components can influence corporate value objectives, and can help identify performance objective measurement yardsticks. Likewise, corporate performance objective measurement yardsticks are used as measurement techniques for strategic planning as well as for value objective comparisons.

Five value objectives are recommended in chapter 6: product market identification, economic concerns, desired growth, stability considerations, and public image concerns. For each value objective, a group of performance objectives is identified, expressed as descriptive attributes, measurement yardsticks, and comparison base goal values. Corporate strategy is expressed in components of growth vector, product market scope, competitive advantage, and synergy. Finally, a conceptual framework is suggested for cascading objectives and strategies downward through the firm to use in decision making at the new product project selection level.

The intralevel objective and strategy interaction normative framework offers advantages over the present processes. First, it formally relates objectives and strategies at the corporate level, and specifically suggests measurement yardsticks for objectives and strategies. In addition, it attempts to structure as much as is possible the interaction between objectives and strategies at various levels of the firm, a structuring not well defined in the current literature.

As identified in chapter 3, most attempts to relate R&D criteria to corporate objectives have suggested allowing R&D management to aid in setting corporate objectives, hoping that the R&D manager's commitment to objectives they aided in setting will ensure decisions consistent with those objectives. While organizational behaviorists present a strong case for this reasoning, it is felt that this structuring of the normative frameworks is an advantage in that it places less reliance on subjective judgment of the R&D decision makers.

Igor Ansoff has provided support for the concept of this normative framework in his start of a conceptual theory for more closely relating objectives and strategies.[11] Ansoff suggested a vector of objectives as a component of strategy, defining proxies in terms of economic and noneconomic objectives, responsibilities, and constraints. Ansoff further suggests that objectives can be broken into descriptive attributes, with measurement yardsticks and goal values for each attribute. Ansoff, however, provides details only in terms of profitability measurement yardsticks and goal values.

This normative framework considers corporate strategy a component in carrying out corporate objectives. The interaction suggested in chapter 6 between corporate performance objectives and corporate strategy is consistent with Ansoff's vector of proxies. Particularly, this framework emphasizes that product markets should be chosen to carry out the objectives of the firm as a whole, not the objectives chosen to be consistent with the product markets the firm currently is in.

This framework is a conceptual extension of Ansoff's, and offers the advantage of being more detailed, and of providing emphasis and structure to the noneconomic aspects of the strategy components.

The intralevel objective and strategy interaction normative framework is also necessary to serve as a base for the project selection decision criteria. Given the current state of the literature, it is necessary to first develop objective and strategy interaction at the corporate level and then cascade these objectives downward through the firm to derive a set of R&D decision criteria consistent with corporate objectives and strategies. Thus the development of this normative framework was necessary prior to development of the project selection normative framework.

An Overview of the Applied New Product Development Project Selection Normative Framework

The recommended normative framework for applied new product development project selection is presented in chapter 7. This framework is presented as a series of four decisions mapped onto the new product development process flow stage model.

Decision I, at the idea generation stage, screens the product ideas available to determine those worth investigating in the formal business analysis stage.

Decision IIa involves creation of a pool of potentially successful products, and decision IIb involves choice from among the pool of product ideas to begin technical development. Decisions IIa and IIb are at the business analysis stage. The IIa decision criteria are developed from the downward cascade of objectives and strategies identified in chapter 6. Decision criteria in terms of economic growth, and stability performance objectives are recommended. The growth and stability performance objectives reflect strategic components as direct decision-making criteria. For each of the performance objectives, measurement yardstick and goal values are recommended.

Having identified the decision criteria, information about each product idea is gathered and the measurement yardstick values are calculated. The measurement yardstick values for each product are compared to the goal values, and, if satisfactory, the product is added to the pool of potentially successful products.

In decision IIb, time-related components of the firm are added to and possibly modify the decision IIa results. Product ideas are rank ordered based upon a consistent set of decision criteria, and, if satisfactory, are released to the R&D division for technical development.

Decision III, located near the end of the technical development stage, allows review of decision IIb prior to the commitment of the bulk of the total research funds. This results in improved efficiency in the use of the total R&D funds, since, if necessary, the project can be dropped and funds saved if the project is no longer satisfactory.

Decision IV, located at the pre-production stage, involves review of the market testing, marketing start-up, and manufacturing start-up activities to again determine if the future has changed enough to invalidate any of the earlier decisions.

Each of these four decisions is explained and developed in detail in chapter 7. In many cases the specific details are based upon the literature review of chapters 3 and 4. Where they are not, they are identified as original input. To further clarify original input, a section of chapter 8 summarizes the major advantages and contributions of the normative frameworks.

Finally, the project selection normative framework recommends three groups of individuals to make the required decisions.

The project selection normative framework offers a number of advantages over current processes. While they are discussed in detail in chapter 7, a few comments are appropriate here.

The organizational problems identified should be improved in this framework by the use of a consistent decision-making process that identifies clearly the responsibility for decision making and the responsibility for carrying out the decisions. In addition, the use of group decision making, the breaking of the decisions into detailed components, and the identification of the particular decision groups, aid in assigning responsibility and authority for the decision process. The tasks of each group and the individuals in each group were chosen to combine the advantages of technical expertise, of objective translation by senior R&D and corporate management, and of project selection by divisional level managers who will have to carry out the project development activities.

Another advantage of this framework is the formal inclusion of strategic planning considerations at the R&D project selection level. While the need for strategic considerations has been suggested in the literature, the depth in which the recommendations are made here and the consistency of expression in terms of attributes, measurement yardsticks, and goal values is a major improvement in both depth of analysis and the ability to coordinate such strategic considerations with other objectives.

The amount of structuring in this framework is important in minimizing and regulating the subjective judgment decisions. The identification of decision areas, decision groups, and decision content minimizes and structures subjective judgment as much as is possible given the quasi-analytical nature of the problem. It is an improvement over the current literature where the subjective judgment of the decision maker is required for almost every detail.

Finally, the treatment of the entire R&D to operations planning process as a total system integrating problem solutions and the stages of the process is an advantage in that it allows consideration of the total process rather than treatment of individual components of the process, and offers the potential for improvement in the success rate of new product market introductions.

6

Normative Framework:
Intralevel Objective and Strategy Interaction

Having lost sight of our objectives, we redoubled our efforts.
Granger, "The Hierarchy of Objectives"

This chapter presents a normative framework for the interaction between objectives and strategies at various levels of the firm. While a complete interaction framework is presented here, the details are aimed at identifying the intralevel interactions as applied to the internal R&D new product development function.

Development of a normative framework is a complicated procedure since there is no theoretical reason to assume that the objectives and strategies or the decision rules at any level of the firm are the same for each individual firm. In addition there is no reason to assume that the original objectives of a firm are completely consistent, and, in fact, practical experience indicates that conflicting objectives are normal. At least one preliminary analysis has suggested that a firm's past profitability, its prospects, and its present stage in its life cycle determine different objectives and hence different decision rules.[1]

Thus it is not possible to develop a normative framework wherein every objective and every rule is applicable to every firm. (This does not preclude some objectives and decision rules being used for every firm. In fact, some such decision rules are suggested for every firm in the normative framework of chapter 7.) For the same reason, a comprehensive list of all objectives and strategies that could apply to any firm would require volumes.

This framework provides major categories of objectives and strategies as a normative recommendation for large, profit-oriented, technologically based manufacturing firms in the United States economic system. Additional objectives and strategies may be added by the owners of a firm to meet any desires not expressed here.

It should be noted that this is a first attempt to provide a normative framework for intralevel objective and strategy interaction. Little support is available in the literature, and additional research is necessary to develop the recommendations in greater depth.

Assumptions

Three major assumptions are used as a base for this normative framework.

1. *The set of corporate objectives and strategies should be the guidelines in the decision processes at all levels of the firm.* This assumption is seldom stated in the R&D management and strategic planning literature, but is generally implied. Identification of this assumption is necessary, however, since a substantial portion of the organizational behavior literature emphasizes satisfying the human behavioral needs of the individuals within the firm, as well as, or in place of, corporate objectives. The discussion of the normative framework provides support for the subordination of personal objectives to corporate objectives, and additional support is provided in chapter 3.

2. *R&D project selection should take place within a system of corporate objectives and strategies provided to the R&D function by corporate headquarters rather than by personal involvement of corporate management in individual R&D project selection.* That is, corporate management should provide the framework within which decisions can be made rather than make the decisions themselves. Decisions should be made by the individuals and/or functions who must perform the development process, since their commitment to the success of the product development can be improved considerably by allowing them to participate in these decisions. Additional discussion of this assumption is provided in chapters 3 and 4.

3. *Objectives of the firm can be used to develop a framework without considering the methods to arrive at the objectives.* The methods of arriving at the objectives of the firm are widely discussed in decision-making literature, as noted in chapter 3. These methods vary from (1) interactions among managers defining objectives, to (2) suggestions that owners alone should provide objectives, to (3) the classical economic profit maximization objective. Among others, Ansoff has provided a comprehensive discussion of the methods to arrive at the objectives of the firm.[2]

Normative Framework—Intralevel Objective and Strategy Interaction

Figure 3 is a schematic diagram of the firm intralevel objective and strategy interaction for the applied internal R&D new product development function developed by this investigation. The base is a set of long-range corporate value objectives consisting of general descriptions of the basic purposes for existence of the firm. Subordinate to corporate value objectives, but interacting with them and with each other, are corporate strategy and corporate performance objectives.

Corporate strategy provides a more specific definition of what business the firm should be in than is provided by the corporate value objectives.

Figure 3.   Normative Framework for Intralevel Objective and Strategy Interaction
for the Internal Applied Research and Development Function

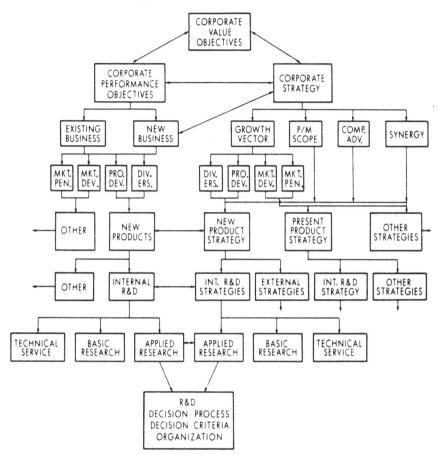

Primarily future oriented, corporate strategy is a process involving (1) analysis of the present position of the firm with respect to the corporate performance objectives, (2) identification of the future product markets of the firm with respect to future economic, sociological, and technical environments, and (3) development of a specific program to close the gap between the present position and desired objectives of the firm.

Ansoff has suggested identification of corporate strategy in terms of four components—the growth vector, the product market scope, the competitive advantage, and synergy.[3] Further, he has subdivided the growth vector into areas of diversification, product development, market development, and market penetration. This framework has been incorporated into the general normative framework (fig. 3).

Ansoff's framework for the general strategy description has been incorporated into this general normative framework for two reasons.

1. Ansoff's description, although not unique, is one of the most logical and consistent diagrams for development of a strategic plan, and fits well with the general concept of intralevel interaction shown in the general normative framework (fig. 3). In addition, its quasi-analytical approach fits more consistently with the total normative framework than does either the operations research or case study approach.

2. This investigation is designed to show the strategic interactions at various levels of the firm, not to develop an alternative description of the strategic problem.

Two of the growth vectors, diversification and product development, are particularly applicable to the development of a new product strategy. Thus, as shown, these two areas, as well as scope, competitive advantage, and synergy, contribute to the development of a specific new product strategy. Since new products can be developed in a number of ways, an internal R&D new product strategy may differ substantially from other new product strategies. In the same manner, an internal R&D new applied research product strategy may differ from internal R&D new product strategies for other types of research.

Corporate performance objectives are concerned with measurement and goal values of the specific attributes of corporate value objectives and corporate strategy. To facilitate discussion of corporate performance objectives definitions of terminology are required. Hence, for this purpose, attributes, yardsticks, and goal values are defined as follows. An attribute is the description of the corporate performance objective under consideration. The yardstick is the component of the corporate performance objective identifying the measurement technique of the attribute. The goal is the value of the attribute that is desired by the corporation on the scale of the yardstick for that attribute. As an example, consider the economic value objective. One attribute of the economic value objective is return on investment. The measurement yardstick is identified as profit divided by investment. (Definitions of "profit" and "investment" must be made for specific calculations.) The minimum goal value that is required is the marginal cost of capital to the firm.

Corporate performance yardsticks are basically the same measurement technique regardless of the level of the firm at which they are applied. The goal value for an attribute may vary depending upon the level of the firm at which it is used. The general normative framework (fig. 3) breaks down corporate performance objectives into new and existing business performance objectives. New business corporate performance objectives are then divided into components of market penetration, market development, product development, and diversification. Different attributes may be applicable for each of these growth areas. Further, when the same attribute is used for different areas, different goal values may be assigned.

From the product development and diversification components a common set of corporate value objectives is derived, since the major difference between these two components is whether the new product areas are aimed at present customers (product development) or new customers (diversification).

There is substantial interaction between corporate performance objectives and corporate strategy at many levels in this descending hierarchy. Since corporate strategy is heavily involved with new business, performance objectives for new business are directly applicable in measuring the components of strategy to determine if a specific industry or component of an industry meets the goal values desired. The same interaction applies with specific new product yardsticks and goal values and new product strategy, as well as internal R&D performance objectives and internal R&D new product strategy.

The result of this descending hierarchy is a set of corporate performance yardsticks and desired goal values available for new product project selection as an expression of the performance objectives which new projects should meet. At the same time, the descending corporate strategy hierarchy identifies potential product areas and industries meeting the value objectives and goal values of the firm after having interacted with corporate performance objectives at earlier levels in the hierarchy. These two identifications combine to provide a framework within which specific projects can be chosen for development in the R&D division. Thus, if specific R&D projects are chosen consistent with this resultant combined framework, the projects chosen will also be consistent with the corporate objectives and strategies of the firm at levels above the R&D function.

Mechanisms for translation of specific objectives, strategies, and goal values level by level through the descending hierarchy are not available. As discussed in the normative recommendations for the decision makers in chapter 7, such translation could be provided by an identified control group of corporate level managers who provide the details of the framework within which divisional level managers select specific projects for technical development. Given the lack of identified translation mechanisms available, however, such translation would probably have to be based upon the subjective judgment of the individuals involved. In any case, the purpose of this chapter is to provide an intralevel interaction normative framework in which applied internal R&D new product decisions can be made consistent with corporate objectives and strategies, not to develop decision criteria at each level. A more detailed discussion of the major components will aid in further defining the framework.

Corporate Value Objectives

Corporate value objectives are general, philosophical statements for direction and operation of the firm that serve as long-range guidelines. They are not concerned with measurement or implementation techniques.

Table 1 lists the recommended value objectives for a firm. They include: product market identification, economic concerns, desired growth, stability considerations, and public image concerns. Each firm must provide some expression of these value objectives to provide an adequate guide for the firm's actions.

Decisions involving corporate value objectives are the responsibility of those concerned with the firm in the long run: the owners of the firm, the board of directors, or, by default, the corporate management. Few guidelines are available to aid these individuals in choosing value objectives, and their choice is generally based upon their subjective judgment.

Product Market Identification

Product market identification is recommended as a corporate value objective since the owners of the firm should identify the general business area or areas in which the firm should operate. These should be expressed in terms of broad product market categories rather than in terms of specific products or specific markets. This determination should be in general terms, on the order of Levitt's classic "railroad" or "transportation" business descriptions.[4]

Originally the product market choices will probably be based upon the past history of the firm and of the value objective decision makers. These product market areas could then be revised, if the value objective decision makers agree, by formal strategic planning analysis. (Strategic planning is discussed in chapter 3. Its interaction with corporate value objectives is shown in figure 3, and is discussed later in this chapter.)

Economic Concerns

Profit as a value objective is recommended since every firm must achieve a profit in the long run to remain in business, even if maximum profit is not desired as an objective. The expression of profit or profitability should be stated in terms of the relative importance of profit considerations in the total group of value objectives rather than as identification of a specific measurement technique or goal value. (Specific measurement techniques and goal values should be suggested as corporate performance objectives.) That is, the corporate value objectives must suggest how much of the emphasis of the firm should be on achieving profits and how much should be given to the other value objectives.

Table 1.   Major Corporate Value Objectives

1. Product Marketing Identification
2. Economic Concerns
3. Desired Growth
4. Stability Considerations
5. Public Image Concerns

Assignment of the emphasis to be given the economic value objective is determined by the subjective judgment of the owners based upon the past history of the firm, the product market areas it is in, and the personal desires of the owners.

Desired Growth

Desired growth is necessary as a value objective because, in general, in the United States economy if a firm does not grow it falls behind its competitors, and because growth as an objective is a legitimate objective in itself. The firm must identify the growth that it desires, both in terms of the relative importance of growth in the value objectives, and in identification of the growth direction desired, that is, horizontal, vertical, broad band, or narrow growth in certain product market areas. A firm may also choose to grow in certain product market areas at the expense of growth in other product market areas.

The emphasis to be given the growth value objective is normally determined by the desire of the decision makers partially based upon past history. In addition elements of the corporate strategy subsystem can aid in determing the degree of emphasis.

Stability Considerations

Stability is necessary as a value objective in the long run to give recognition to the amount of risk and uncertainty the firm desires. It is particularly concerned with the ability of the firm to survive in the long run. Stability can be expressed in a number of ways, including operating stability, financial stability, management stability, and ownership stability. Specific details will be provided as corporate performance objectives. The concern of stability at the value objective level should center on the emphasis to be given stability in the context of the other value objectives.

The amount of emphasis to be given the stability value objective is normally determined by the decision makers based upon their own subjective judgment.

Public Image Concerns

A desired public image should be identified to recognize the firm-society-government interface, even if it is merely to state that no particular public image is desired. The public image value objective can be expressed in terms of public responsibility or social concern, or in terms of an image in producing quality products. It is based upon the subjective desires of the decision makers.

In addition to these recommended value objectives, other value objectives could be identified depending upon the desires of the firm. These could include such areas as allowable dependence upon suppliers, degree of centralization, synergy emphasis, and common thread emphasis.

The value objectives recommended are not mutually exclusive, and their obvious interaction suggests the need for continuity. They should be treated as a group of objectives, all of which should be followed. This is possible because in the broad expressions of the corporate value objectives, conflicts do not arise. The potential for conflict among corporate performance objectives, however, does exist, and trade-offs among performance objectives may be required.

Corporate Performance Objectives

Corporate performance objectives involve more specific descriptions of the objectives of the firm than are provided by the corporate value objectives. In this framework, a corporate performance objective is made up of three components: the attribute itself, the measurement yardstick, and the goal value. The attribute is the descriptive statement of the objective. The measurement yardstick is the scale on which the attribute is to be measured. The goal value is the statement of specific values (if any) on the yardstick scale desired by the firm.

Both the performance yardsticks and the goal values may be expressed in a number of ways, and in either quantitative or qualitative terms. There is no theoretical justification for preference of either quantitative or qualitative measures over the other. There is, however, a current practical preference towards the use of quantitative performance yardsticks because of the increase in quantitative measurement techniques available. In addition, quantitative techniques can be expressed in continuous terms while qualitative methods can generally use only a limited number of discrete comparisons.

Both quantitative and qualitative goal values can be expressed in a number of different ways. The major methods involve the expression of the goal value as a desired target value, or as a minimum or maximum goal value.

The target value has an advantage in that it provides a specific desired value that the firm desires for the attribute being measured. Its major weakness is that there is no consistent method available for arriving at a target value for most attributes important to the firm. Thus, many target goal values are arbitrary expressions of desires without adequate support, either quantitative or qualitative, for the value chosen.

The weakness of the minimum target value is that it does not provide a value at which to aim, only a floor that must be exceeded. Its advantage is that it can serve as a rejection threshold for the attribute under consideration. This is of importance in that, while a firm might desire the maximum value of a particular attribute or portfolio of attributes, it may be willing to accept a specific project if the attribute or portfolio of attributes being measured is above a certain minimum level.

To date, no method of goal expression has been generally accepted. Both target and minimum concepts will be used in this normative framework.

Table 2 identifies a set of corporate performance objectives for a firm. Under the five corporate value objectives identified earlier, a list of specific attributes is provided, each with its examples of measurement yardsticks and goal values.

While this list is quite detailed, it is unrealistic to attempt to include every potential performance objective. It is felt, however, that all major performance objectives have been recommended. In addition, each performance objective will not be applicable to every firm. While these performance objectives are as general as possible to have as wide an application as is practical, additions or deletions may be made by the owners, directors, or managers of a firm based upon their subjective judgment.

For each attribute identified, one or more measurement yardsticks have been listed. These yardsticks are not intended to be all inclusive, and, in many cases, alternate yardsticks can be developed. Those that are listed, however, are the normative recommendations of this investigation for measurement techniques.

As noted earlier, there is no assumption in this framework that all of the performance objectives can be measured. Where they can be measured, however, Ansoff has made a strong case for the use of measurement methods that utilize present data available to the firm to avoid the cost of accumulating new data for decision-making purposes.[5] Where choices among yardsticks arose, those recommended utilized existing data. In a number of cases measurement techniques are listed where there is currently no standard method available to accumulate the data necessary. Indeed, for both a number of performance objectives and yardsticks identified, there is currently no theoretical base on which to build a system to perform the measurement or set a specific goal value.

The corporate performance objectives for the economic, product market,

Table 2. Corporate Performance Objectives

ATTRIBUTES	EXAMPLES OF MEASUREMENT YARDSTICK	EXAMPLES OF GOAL VALUES
1. PRODUCT MARKET IDENTIFICATION		
a. Identification of broad product market segments	list of areas	not applicable
b. Number of market segments	number	Note 1, example – min. of 3 target of 7 max. of 10
c. Sales distribution by market segment	% of sales by product area	Note 1, example – min. of 5% target – all areas equal
d. Market share by segment	% of market by product area	Note 1, example – min. 5%
e. Product introduction position, i.e., leader, follower, etc.	qualitative judgement – comparison with actual	not applicable
f. Geographical limits or desires	% of sales by geographical region	Note 1, example – min. of 5% target – all areas equal max. 60%
g. Sales limits or desires by technology group	% of sales by technology group	Note 1
h. Sales concentrations by special groupings, i.e., civilian vs. military, etc.	% of sales by special grouping	Note 1, example – target – 30% max. to any one group

2. ECONOMIC CONCERNS		
a. Actual dollars overall	actual dollars by normal method	Note 1, example – min. $32 million target $48 million
b. Overall return on investment	profit/investment = % (definitions necessary)	Note 1, example – min. = marginal cost of capital target = 20%
c. Overall return on sales	profit/sales = %	Note 1, example – min. = 3% target = 6%
d. Earning per share	profit/number of shares of common stock outstanding	Note 1, example – min. = $ .89 target = $1.31
e. Desires of actual dollars, ROI, ROS, EPS, by product market segments	same as a–d by product market areas	Note 2

Table 2. (continued)

3.	DESIRED GROWTH		
a.	Overall sales growth rate	% of yearly increase by volume	Note 1, example – min. = 3% target = 6%
b.	Overall profit growth rate	% of yearly increase by dollars	Note 1, example – min. = 4% target = 8%
c.	Profit and sales growth rate by product market segment	same as a & b by product market segment	Note 2
d.	Market share growth rate	% of yearly increase by product market segment	Note 1, example – min. = 10% target = 30%
e.	New product area sales growth	% of total yearly growth in new product market areas	Note 1, example – min. = 10% target = 40%
f.	New product area profit growth	% of total yearly growth in new product market areas	Note 1, example – min. = 5% target = 40%

4. STABILITY CONSIDERATIONS

a. Operating Stability

1. Degree of reliability on general economy	variance in sales with general economy	Note 3
2. Seasonal sales dependence	breakdown of total sales by season	Note 1, example - target - equal split among seasons
3. Individual product or customer dependence	% of sales by product or customer	Note 1, example - max. 40%
4. Dependence on technical innovation	qualitative judgment	Note 3
5. Total product life cycle position mix	% of products at each stage of life cycle	Notes 1 & 2, example - target = equal split among stages
6. Product life cycle position mix by product market segment	% of products at each stage of life cycle	Notes 1 & 2, example - target = equal split among stages
7. Balance of "risky" and "safe" ventures	% of ventures in each category (definitions required)	Note 1, example - target = 30% risky max. = 50% risky

Table 2. (continued)

4. STABILITY CONSIDERATIONS (CONT'D)		
b. Financial Stability		
1. Liquidity measures	Current Assets/Current Liabilities Liquid Assets/Current Liabilities Fixed Assets/Total Assets	Note 1, example - target - 2.5:1 target - 1:1 target - 60%
2. Debt/Equity measure	Long-term debt/owner's equity	Note 1, example - target - .3 max. - .6
3. Desired dividends	Cash dividends/total profit	Note 1, example - target - 40%
4. Funds sources guidelines	% by source	Note 1, example - targets - stock - 70% bonds - 10% Other long-term debt - 20%
c. Management Stability		
1. Management depth	% of internal promotions; qualitative judgment	Note 1, example - target - 90%
2. Dilution of management control	Source of board members; qualitative judgment; number of compensating balances	Note 3 Note 1, example - target - 0
d. Ownership Stability		
1. Breadth of ownership	Number of stock owners; % owned by one owner	Note 1, example - target - 200,000 Note 1, example - max. - 5%
2. Dilution of stockholder control	Number of shares of voting stock % of stock sold to present stockholders	Note 1, example - target - 20,000,000 target - 80%

5. PUBLIC IMAGE CONSIDERATIONS		
a. Public service by employees	Number of employees active in community	Note 1, example – target – 10%
b. Public service image desired	Qualitative judgment	
c. Press and media coverage	Number of articles; qualitative judgment of content	Note 3

1. A specific numerical value, either expressed as a minimum, maximum, or target value, in units of the measurement yardsticks. The values listed are possible examples of values for a large, multiple product manufacturing firm in relatively mature product market areas. They are intended merely as examples of the expression technique, *not* normative values.

2. Specific numerical values as discussed in note 1, which may vary by product market area.

3. No normative recommendations, generally because there is not theoretical base available to build a measurement system or assign a goal value.

growth, and public image value objectives are largely self-explanatory. The stability performance objectives are unique in their attempt to handle business risk from the viewpoints of operating, financial, management, and ownership stability. From an operating viewpoint, establishment of measurement yardsticks and goal values for attributes like degree of reliance on the general economy, seasonal and individual product sales dependence, product life cycle mix, and so on, allow a desired operating risk attitude to be expressed in terms of a group of measurable components.

In the same way, consideration of the financial stability attributes of liquidity, debt to equity, dividends, and funds source guidelines, allows a picture of the financial risk and stability desired to be compiled from a group of financial measures. Expressing stability attributes in this way allows attributes, measurement yardsticks, and goal values to be set so that they are complementary rather than conflicting. Unfortunately, no integrating structure or methodology has as yet been developed to aid in setting such a group of complementary goal values.

Of the three components of corporate performance objectives identified in table 2, the goal value determinations require the most additional research. The goal values shown in table 2 are examples, not normative recommendations. They are integrated only in the sense that they attempt to represent a possible consistent set of goal values for a large, profit-oriented, technologically based United States manufacturing firm.

The lack of integrating mechanisms discussed is even more critical to goal value expressions than to attribute and measurement yardstick expressions. Application of this framework in its present state of development still depends on the subjective judgment of the decision makers for a consistent group of goal values.

While many of the details of these corporate performance objective recommendations require additional effort, the total framework should not be judged on the basis of any specific element within it. The major value of this normative recommendation is the concept of a group of corporate performance objectives broken down into interrelated attributes, measurement yardsticks, and goal values, and a framework that treats them as a portion of a system rather than as a separate entity.

Corporate Strategy

As noted, corporate strategy involves a definition of what business the firm should be in. Such a definition is required if the firm is to close the gap between its present and its desired position through development of a specific set of long-range plans.

The first step is to identify the present position of the firm in terms of the corporate performance yardsticks, and to compare this present position to the appropriate goal value for each attribute. Having thus determined the magnitude of the gap, a set of strategic plans can be developed to attempt to close the gap.

Techniques for the identification of the present position of a firm have been presented by a number of authors, including Ansoff and Katz.[6] Ansoff has also identified a theoretical basis for gap identification.[7] The necessity of a comparison to identify the gap means that the corporate goal values and the strategic analysis of the present position need to be expressed in terms of the same measurement yardsticks. This identifies the major interaction at the corporate level between corporate strategy and corporate performance objectives. The detailed listing of examples of corporate yardsticks in table 2 thus provides a consistent framework for expression of corporate performance objectives and for analysis of the present position of the firm.

Ansoff has suggested a breakdown of corporate strategy into components of product market scope, growth, competitive advantage, and synergy.[8] The reason for use of this breakdown was noted earlier; the components are summarized briefly here to indicate the types of considerations from which new product market strategies are derived.

Product market scope involves identification of the specific industry or subindustry for search to more carefully define the area of search for new product markets. The growth vector involves delineation of the direction of movements from the present product market position to an alternate product market position within the desired product market scope. The growth vector requires a formal search of the environment and identification of the growth methods, such as concentric, vertical, horizontal, and so on. Of the four components of the growth vector (diversification, product development, market development, and market penetration), two, diversification and product development, are particularly involved with new products and hence have substantial input to a new product strategy. Product development involves the development of new products for existing markets, while diversification involves the development of new products and new product markets for new customers.

A competitive advantage involves identification of characteristics of outstanding opportunities within the product market scope. It requires identification of particular strengths of the product market, such as patents, quality, degree of innovation, lack of competition, and so on, so that the firm will have a particular advantage in entering that product market over entering alternative product markets.

Synergy deals with techniques to be successful in the new product market entry, and involves actions internal to the firm, in contrast to the growth, scope, and competitive advantage components which deal primarily with external factors. Synergy has two basic subsets, aggressive synergy, which involves the use of the present strong points of the firm, and defensive synergy, which involves choice of a strategic plan to compensate for weak points in the present firm.

For diversification, product development, product market scope, competitive advantage, and synergy components of corporate strategy, specific substrategies appropriate for new product market areas are identified. New product market strategies are then chosen based upon comparisons of yardstick values for potential new product market strategies with the desired goal values, as schematically identified by the interaction lines at the new product strategy level in the general normative framework (fig. 3).

Once a new product market strategy has been developed a "make or buy" decision is necessary to determine whether to develop the new product market strategy internally or externally to the firm. Again a set of goal values for internal and external new product market development is identified and the values by the same yardsticks of the potential new product market strategies are compared to delineate a set of internal and external new product market strategies.

Internal strategies are normally carried out within operating divisions of the firm or by a separate internal R&D division. External strategies to acquire new product market areas or new products include purchase of a specific product or area, purchase of a going business, purchase of a license or patent, encouragement of equipment or material suppliers to perform the necessary work, hiring of knowledgeable key personnel from competitors, and industrial espionage.

The choice of an internal or external new product market development strategy is based upon the ability of each of the alternate methods to meet the corporate performance objective goal values for new product market development, including the cost and speed of obtaining the results.

Since these product market strategies are long run in nature, constraints of the R&D division do not play a part at this level except if they are expressed as part of the corporate performance objectives. (The normative framework suggestions of table 2 include no such constraints.) Constraints on internal R&D development, such as facilities restrictions, manpower, technologies, funding, and so on, are important in the selection of specific projects for internal development, however, and are discussed in chapter 7.

Having identified the desired internal product market strategies, an analysis must determine which type of research—basic, applied, or technical service—or combination of types is necessary to carry out the desired strategy. From this analysis the strategies for applied internal R&D can be identified, and provided as a base for decision making for specific development project selection.

The outcome of this descending corporate strategy hierarchy is usually expressed as a set of product market area descriptions in which new products are desired. These product market areas identified serve as the guidelines for project selection to ensure that individual product ideas chosen for development are consistent with the corporate strategy hierarchy.

No structure or mechanism has as yet been developed to identify the details of strategy development at levels below the new product strategy level shown in the normative framework of figure 3. Until such integrating methodology is developed, application of this corporate strategy framework to internal applied R&D project selection will depend upon the subjective judgment of the decision makers. (A corporate level manager control group is recommended as responsible for this area in chapter 7.)

Translation of Corporate Performance Objectives and Strategies to New Product Selection Decision Criteria

The result of this normative framework is a descending hierarchy of corporate performance objectives and strategies cascaded downward through the firm from the corporate level to the product selection level for use in R&D new product project selection. Thus, if specific new products for technical development are chosen consistent with the resultant combined frameworks, the projects chosen are consistent with the corporate objectives and strategies of the firm at levels above the R&D new product function.

As noted earlier, mechanisms for translation of specific performance objective attributes, yardsticks, and goal values, and strategic components, level by level downward through the firm have not been developed. Until such translation mechanisms can be developed, this normative framework recommends translation based upon the subjective judgment of the decision makers. (In chapter 7, it is suggested that such translation be provided by an identified control group of corporate level managers.)

Even though detailed translation mechanisms have not been developed, a set of project selection decision criteria based upon these corporate objectives and strategies is presented in the project selection normative framework of chapter 7. These decision criteria were translated from the corporate performance objectives and strategies by the author, based upon his subjective judgment supported by the literature reviews of chapters 3 and 4.

The purpose of this section is to provide an introduction to the decision criteria of the project selection normative framework of chapter 7 by showing in a theoretical, conceptual way the logical thought process where the decision criteria for new product selection are based upon and consistent with the corporate performance objectives and strategic components identified in this chapter. (The detailed corporate performance objectives were presented in table 2; the decision criteria for new product project selection will be presented later in figures 7 and 8 and tables 3 and 4.)

The corporate performance objectives of this chapter were expressed in terms of product market identification, economic concerns, desired growth, stability, and public image concerns. For the new product project selection normative framework in the next chapter, decision criteria are grouped into economic, growth, and stability performance objectives. In addition, special decision criteria allow for the addition of other operating and strategic concerns, such as R&D capacity and capability, productive capacity, and synergy. Finally, the project selection normative framework allows constraints in terms of total R&D budget, total investment, and debt limits.

To provide a conceptual identification of the relationship between the two normative frameworks, these areas are discussed in terms of the five performance objective areas identified in this chapter.

Product Market Identification

Product market identification concerns are involved with the requirements of the total product market mix of the corporation (see table 2). Under the assumptions of this book (a large, profit-oriented firm where new products are continually being added to the product line), product market identification concerns are not directly used for R&D new product selection. If a new product successfully introduced into the marketplace results in violation of the product market mix attribute goal values, a decision could be made to drop any existing product or market area (old or new) to bring the actual product mix in line with what is desired. If this is done, however, it is done for the firm as a whole, and the new product added is only one component involved in the total decision.

Recognizing that there may be special needs at certain times, the normative framework for project selection allows growth vector emphasis (diversification and product development) to be used as special decision criteria if desired by the decision maker (see chap. 7, decision IIb, step 2). In addition, if the decision makers decide that a particular product is needed for a specific operating division to change or improve a product market mix, it may also be added as a special decision criterion. Finally, a formal synergy comparison suggested by both the product market identification corporate performance objectives and the synergy component of the strategic concept is taken into account in the project selection normative framework in the review of the rate of return on investment calculation (chap. 7, decision IIb, step 4).

Economic Concerns

The economic performance objectives of this chapter are expressed as attributes of return on investment, earnings per share, actual dollars, and so on, as well as these same attributes by product market area. While these attributes of the firm as a whole are not appropriate to the project selection decision, a profitability measure can be directly translated from the corporate level to the project selection level. The profitability attribute yardstick is the internal rate of return calculation, and specific details are provided for its calculation (see chap. 7, table 3). The minimum rate of return goal value suggested in this chapter is the marginal cost of capital to the firm. This same minimum goal value is also suggested in the project selection normative framework, and specific support is provided for its use there. Thus at least one economic corporate performance objective can be directly translated to the project selection level.

Desired Growth

Desired growth is identified directly in both the corporate and new product selection normative frameworks. At the corporate level this involves identification and measurement of sales and profit growth rates, and growth rates by market segments and by product areas. At the new product selection level these are expressed in terms of desired growth rates of sales, market share, and profitability, growth potential of the same three components, and product market expansion potential. Direct translation is difficult, since a desired growth rate for the firm as a whole includes both present and new products and markets. Yet a reasonable method for total corporate growth is heavy emphasis on new product introduction. Thus, while the performance objective attributes and measurement yardsticks may be identical at both levels, the goal values may differ. For example, a minimum yearly sales growth goal value of 3% was desired for the firm as a whole (table 2). For a new product, this same goal value was set at 5% (table 3). Thus, this setting of a 5% minimum value shows the translation of goal values for the same measurement yardsticks to require a new product sales growth rate greater than that for the firm as a whole, emphasizing the importance of new products to the firm's overall sales growth rate.

It is also necessary for the new product growth rate to recognize the product life cycle and to suggest different growth rates at the early and mature stages of the life cycle. Thus, although the growth considerations at the project selection level are based upon and consistent with those at the corporate level, greater detail in attributes, measurement yardsticks and goal values is necessary at the project selection level, making a direct comparison difficult.

Stability Considerations

At the corporate level, stability considerations were intended to express risk in the long run in terms of financial, operating, management, and ownership characteristics. Of these, management and ownership stability concerns are corporate level and not germane to project selection decisions. The financial concerns of liquidity and dividends guidelines are also not important to project selection. Funds source guidelines and debt to equity measures at the corporate level are translated to a marginal approach at the product selection level, looking at the additional debt and sources of funds for the product project under consideration. These marginal considerations may be used as constraints upon the R&D activity, although this use is not recommended in the project selection normative framework (see chap. 7, decision IIb, step 5a).

The operating stability concerns of this chapter are more directly translatable into the stability performance objectives of project selection. They tend to be expressed slightly differently, stressing the product and market stability of the product under consideration rather than the position of the firm as a whole. The product stability concerns of product characteristics and life cycle in the project selection normative framework are directly derived from the life cycle technical innovation concerns of this chapter (table 2), although, of course, a new product entering the firm's product market mix is always at the start of its own product life cycle. The market stability attributes at the corporate level of seasonal sales dependence, degree of reliance on the general economy, and so on are directly used at the project selection level. The measurement yardsticks and goal values at both levels are also similar, although they need to be expressed in much greater detail for new product selection than for the firm as a whole. For example, the corporate measurement yardstick of the life cycle attribute concerns itself with the percentage of the firm's products at various stages of life cycles, while the measurement of life cycle concerns for new product selection must consider the estimated time of the total life cycle, the time until maturity, the length of maturity, and so on. Again, while the translation mechanisms cannot be presented in detail, the consistency of the attributes, measurement yardsticks, and goal values at the project selection level with those at the corporate level are clear.

Public Image Concerns

In general the public image concerns suggested for the firm as a whole are not relevant to new product decision. If it is desired that product classes or product market groups be added or not be entered into for public image reasons, they could be expressed as special decision criteria in the project selection decision (chap. 7, decision IIb, step 2). None is recommended, however, in the project selection normative framework.

Discussion

Included in the normative framework for intralevel objective and strategy interactions is a number of concepts and ideas worth special note.

Degree of Problem Structure

Two extreme approaches to general problem solving have been identified. One involves a well structured problem-solving framework, and has been called "fully analytical" by Simon and Newell.[9] This approach requires that there be an objective function, and that the objective function and all variables and relationships be expressed in quantitative terms. An opposite approach is the unstructured solution of a problem by a descriptive analysis, often attributed to the case study approach.[10]

The combination of objectives and strategies identified in the normative framework fits neither of these areas, but suggests an intermediate area where some objectives, strategies, and decision criteria may be expressed in quantitative terms, while others still remain expressed in qualitative terms. Simon and Newell describe these types as "ill structured" problems,[11] while Ansoff calls them "quasi-analytical."[12]

Thus, this normative framework presents an intermediate problem-solving formulation using a mixture of quantitative and qualitative objectives, strategies, and decision criteria.

Time Frame

Corporate value objectives, corporate strategy, and corporate performance objectives are all presented in a long-range time framework for internal applied new product development in the normative framework. Inclusion of corporate value objectives and corporate strategy in a long-run time reference is perhaps obvious; inclusion of corporate performance objectives is less clear. In general the attribute expressions of corporate performance objectives are not time related. Measurement yardsticks are also not strongly time related, although some yardsticks will require estimates of the future and subsequent concern with risk and uncertainty.

The goal value component of performance objectives may, however, be time related. For example, Hill and Granger have suggested that the same attributes may apply for both the long and short run, but that different goal values (minimums) should be used for each time frame.[13] Hill and Granger provide no theoretical support for this time frame difference in goal values, but note that practical suggestions are made in the literature that long-range goal values for attributes should be different than short-run goal values because of the greater risk and uncertainty associated with the longer time frame.

Recognition of a possible difference in goal values due, in part, to the time frame in this normative framework was implied in the earlier suggestion that different goal values may be used for present products than for new products. For internal new product applied R&D, however, both strategies and all components of performance objectives are considered long run.

There is no accepted definition of the terms long and short run. In the context of internal applied R&D, a three- to five-year period is reasonable for the time frame change. Quinn in particular has identified a five- to seven-year period as long run, considering this as a normal time range for new product development.[14]

Objectives and Constraints

In much of the literature a distinction is made between objectives and constraints. Constraints are generally defined as limiting a course of action, while objectives are the goals towards which the actions aim. In this normative framework the constraint concept fits easily within the corporate performance objective concept. A "constraint" in the general literature meaning can be the goal value of a particular attribute.

As an example, consider a new product strategy wherein the product can be obtained either from internal R&D or from external sources. If a corporate performance attribute required a continuing internal effort (for any reason), then the goal value may require that a certain minimum number of new product market strategies be developed internally to provide the base for support of a continuing R&D program. If this minimum is not being met, then the use of the goal value as a minimum constraint would require assignment of this particular new product strategy for internal development.

From another viewpoint, both informal financial analysis and formal portfolio theory suggest the need for a balancing of many items within the firm, one of which is the assignment of resources to various alternatives aimed at the firm's objectives. Use of these two concepts may also require the expression of corporate performance objective goal values in the form of constraints to carry out an implied portfolio concept. The formal portfolio concept requires a well-structured problem as discussed earlier. Since the normative framework does not fit the definition of well structured, no suggestion is made for the use of formal portfolio theory in this normative framework.

Goal Value Expressions

In general, numerical values are assigned to goals based upon currently valid and quantifiable criteria, such as earnings per share, return on investment, and so on. These, however, are generally delineated within the context of past and present performance. Future goal values which are arbitrary projections of the past, or even in part based upon present considerations, follow the implicit assumption that a projection of the past into the future is the primary strategic objective. This implicit assumption affects the development of other objectives and strategies and decreases their significance.

Recognition of this problem provides a philosophical base for this normative framework in its suggestions that goal values for new product market areas, while consistent with the corporate value objectives, should be developed separate from goal values for present product market areas. That is, while it may be realistic to measure ongoing activities in part on historical precedence, it may be extremely foolish to use the same historical base for new product market goal values. Unfortunately, as discussed earlier in this chapter, no structure exists to integrate these goals except the subjective judgment of the decision makers.

Resource Limitations

In this framework "constraints" has been used to indicate an expression of a corporate performance objective goal value used to limit actions of the firm. It is a decision internal to the firm expressed to ensure consistency of objectives and strategy through the downward cascade. Resource limitations, however, express the ability of the firm to attract and earn resources, and are hence partly external to the firm.

There is substantial disagreement in the literature on whether a decision framework should assume that decisions must be made within a framework of a limited supply of resources. As one example, Ansoff notes that regardless of how large or how small a firm is a commitment of resources to current business precludes substantial diversification, while overemphasis on diversification will lead to neglect of present products.[15] He further suggests that, given the resource limitations, a firm should use the resources available to optimize its goals and objectives. Resource limitation is also an implicit assumption of much of the operations research literature, where the normal limits on the optimization algorithm are expressed more in terms of resource limitations than constraints (as the terms are used here).

One alternative to a limited supply of resources involves a marginal approach to resource acquisition. Each specific use for additional resources is evaluated on a marginal basis, and, if acceptable, resources are acquired to carry out the project. In theory, a firm should continue to acquire resources as long as the value of the proposed project justifies the resource acquisition.

One interesting corollary to this discussion is that if resources are not limited, an optimization concept is not necessary. All alternatives with returns above the marginal cost of resource acquisition should be carried out rather than just those that optimize goals. A second conclusion is that, since the evaluation and decision among alternatives in itself uses resources, use of these resources to attempt to achieve optimization may decrease the activities of the firm as a whole, since the resources used in the optimization process cannot be applied to the alternatives themselves.

This normative framework did not consider resource limitations per se. Resource limitations can easily be handled in this framework, if desired, by translating them into performance objective goal values. Goal values as constraints, however, may be expressed for reasons other than external resource limitations.

Summary

This chapter has suggested a normative framework for corporate objective and strategy interaction at various levels of the firm. Corporate value objectives provide the long-range guides to action, while corporate performance objectives provide more detailed objectives and the desired goal values and measurement yardsticks. Corporate strategy defines plans to carry out the corporate value objectives, and interact with corporate performance objectives at various descending levels of the firm until both define a specific set of criteria in which internal applied new product development decisions can be made.

This normative framework is unique in its attempt to provide a framework in the form of a schematic diagram in which there is a consistent cascade of objectives and strategies downward through the firm. It is also one of the few attempts to formally portray interactions of objectives and strategies at various levels of the firm. Specific value objectives, performance objectives, and strategies were recommended at the corporate level. Mechanisms to translate these downward through the hierarchy to the R&D level have not been developed. Until such mechanisms can be developed, such translations must be made based upon the judgment of corporate management. Recommendations for the choice of individuals to make these translations are included in chapter 7.

7

Normative Framework:
Applied New Product Development Project Selection

This chapter presents a normative framework for the selection of specific applied new product projects to be developed and added to a firm's product line. The need for such a framework is clearly demonstrated by the high failure rate of existing decision methods as detailed in chapter 4. Chapter 4 discussion presented a framework of causes of failure, including organizational, business analysis, control and follow-up, and decision-making causes. Such a framework is useful in analyzing failure causes after the fact; it is less useful in developing a means to prevent failures from occurring.

A product has been defined as a failure if it was not retained in a firm's product line. No effort has been made to define failure in terms of profit or any other objective types of measurement. For this chapter's normative framework, however, the objective is to select products in terms of supported objectives and related decision criteria, not just to develop products that can be expected to be retained in the firm's product lines.

Thus, the framework for analysis of causes of failure used in chapter 4 is not appropriate to the recommended project selection decision process. Solutions to the causes of prior failures, however, are an integral part of the normative recommendations of this chapter. It is easy to see their application at various steps of the recommended decision process.

Since there is no theoretical justification for the assumption that the objectives, strategies, or decision rules at the project selection level of the firm are the same for each individual firm, development of this normative framework has been particularly complex. Practical experience suggests variance among firms in objectives, strategies, and decision rules and, thus, it is not possible for the normative framework to specify every objective and every decision rule for every firm. Nevertheless, the normative framework is based upon the premise that there are performance objectives and measurement yardsticks for applied new product development project selection that should be consistently used over a wide range of firms in varying circumstances and that these can be identified and analyzed.

In this framework, R&D project selection decision making is viewed as an estimation process requiring the calculation and application of expectational data that reflects the characteristics and probable outcomes of alternate project investments. While consideration is given to the sources and uses of estimates and to the methods of estimation, no new mathematical techniques are proposed. Rather emphasis is given to an evolutionary approach to developmental project selection by reviewing and evaluating estimated data over periods of time, and by formal use of a risk decision criteria which incorporates the uncertainties of future expectational data.

The chapter begins by mapping and discussing the location of each of the normative decisions on the new product process flow stage model. A number of assumptions upon which the normative framework is based are then discussed. Each of the four major decisions, at the business analysis, screening, development, and pre-production stages, is recommended, explained, and discussed. Finally, normative recommendations are made as to the individuals or functions who should make each of the decisions.

Normative Decisions and Their Locations

Normative decisions and their locations on the new product process flow stage model discussed in chapter 1 are shown in figure 4. (Detailed discussion of the content of each decision is presented later.) Decision I involves screening the project ideas available to determine those ideas worth investigating in a formal business analysis. Its purpose is to reduce the number of project ideas for business analysis, since formal business analysis is both time consuming and expensive. Decision I is located at the end of the idea generation stage just prior to the start of the business analysis stage.

Decision II involves an investigation of the formal business analysis information provided and a choice among the analyzed project ideas as to specific project ideas to begin technical development. Its purpose is to choose specific product projects to be developed. Decision II is located at the end of the business analysis stage just prior to the start of the development stage. Decisions I and II are commonly accepted in most R&D new product development process flow models.

Decision III involves a review of the decision II project information (and possible recalculation) to determine if continued effort should be expended on the project, or if enough circumstances have changed to consider dropping the project. Its location is normally near the end of the development phase.

The location of, and reason for, decision III is not common and warrants

Figure 4. Normative Decisions Located on the New Product Process Stage Model

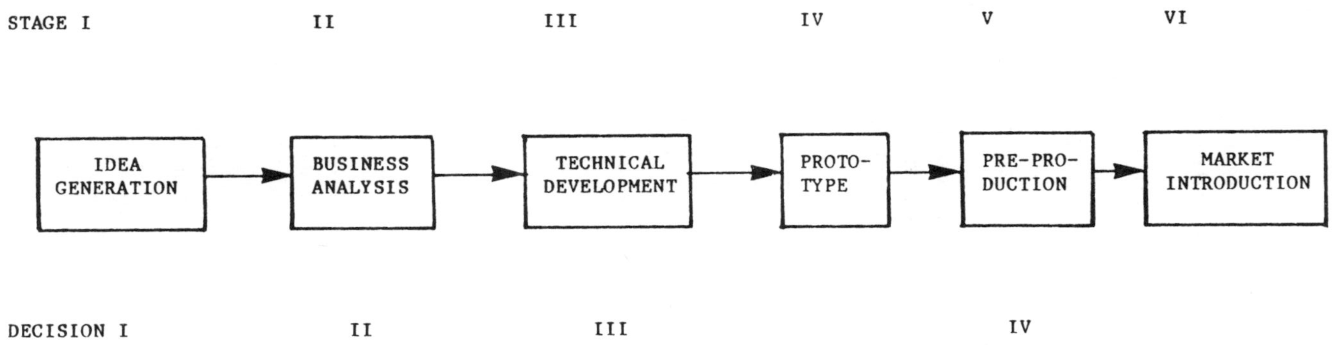

STAGE I	II	III	IV	V	VI

```
┌────────────┐    ┌────────────┐    ┌────────────┐    ┌──────────┐    ┌──────────┐    ┌──────────────┐
│    IDEA    │───▶│  BUSINESS  │───▶│ TECHNICAL  │───▶│  PROTO-  │───▶│ PRE-PRO- │───▶│   MARKET     │
│ GENERATION │    │  ANALYSIS  │    │DEVELOPMENT │    │   TYPE   │    │ DUCTION  │    │ INTRODUCTION │
└────────────┘    └────────────┘    └────────────┘    └──────────┘    └──────────┘    └──────────────┘
```

DECISION I	II	III	IV

discussion. Booz, Allen and Hamilton have noted that near the end of the development stage the probability of technical success is 80–90%.[1] Booz, Allen and Hamilton further note that approximately 40% of the total project cost (expense and capital items) have been spent or committed at that point.[2] Collier suggests 15–30% of the total expenses at this point,[3] while Mansfield's studies suggest only 17% of total cost spent prior to the prototype phase.[4] Further, the same studies suggest that most of the remaining cost is in capital equipment and working capital at the pre-production and market introduction stages. This combined information provides support for a major decision to be located where the probability of technical success is high and where a formal decision analysis can take place prior to the commitment of capital funds.

The location of decision III can be calculated for each product under development by starting at the desired market introduction date and moving back by the lead time of the capital equipment. This determines when the equipment must be ordered to have the desired production available at the desired market introduction date. While this location will vary depending upon the product and the production capacity available, interpolation of the studies just discussed, particularly the Booz, Allen and Hamilton data, suggests that this normally located the decision near the end of the development stage or very early in the prototype stage.

The calculation of the location of decision III assumed a defined market introduction date based upon estimates of the times required to complete the process stages. Although this market introduction date may vary depending on the actual activities in development, it should still be used as the base for the location of decision III. If the market introduction date changes, the time location of decision III changes as well.

There is also a frequent assumption that since the end of the development stage is located 12 to 30 months closer to market introduction than the business analysis stage, the updated information used should be more accurate than that used at the business analysis stage. Brandenburg[5] and Marschak detail examples of how data accuracy improves with time.[6] Tull, however, suggests that data gathered even later in the process flow, at market testing, is no better than secondary information sources in advance of development.[7] Tull thus suggests that this updated information is no more accurate than the information used in the business analysis stage. Decision III was located to review the product project prior to the commitment of capital funds. While the latest available information should be used, no assumption is made in the normative framework that this information is more accurate than information used earlier.

Decision IV involves a review of the market testing, market start-up, and manufacturing start-up activities to determine if any circumstances have changes beyond the limits anticipated at earlier stages. Its purpose is to determine if a project should be dropped at this stage to minimize losses. This review should be activated by adverse information during the pre-production stage.

Although decision I occurs ahead of decision II in the process flow sequence, decision I is merely an initial quick screening for decision II, and reflects the decision criteria of decision II in brief. Because of this, decision II is presented prior to decision I in this chapter.

Assumptions

The normative framework is based upon a number of assumptions. They are summarized below.

1. *There is no single objective for a firm in either the long or short run. Stated in an alternate way, each firm pursues multiple goals and objectives.* This statement was also an assumption in chapter 3 and is discussed in depth there. A note of caution of particular importance to R&D new product project selection has been sounded by Emery.[8] He notes that objectives often need to be expressed in both quantitative and qualitative measures, but that quantified objectives frequently tend to drive out qualitative objectives because of the implied accuracy in the quantified data. Care must be taken to insure that the ability to quantify an objective or the results of an objective is not alone used as an indication of the weight of that particular objective.

2. *The set of corporate objectives and strategies should be the guidelines in the decision processes at all levels of the firm.*

3. *R&D project selection should take place within a system of corporate objectives and strategies provided to the R&D function by corporate headquarters rather than by personal involvement of corporate management in individual R&D project selection.*

4. *Objectives of the firm can be used to develop a framework without consideration of the methods to arrive at the objectives.* Assumptions 2, 3, and 4 were also assumptions of the normative framework of chapter 6 and are discussed there.

5. *A monetary constraint on the total R&D function, if used at all, should be based upon objective and strategic criteria rather than upon arbitrary dollar amounts.* It appears to be common practice for the total budget of a R&D function to be based upon some arbitrary criteria, such as a percentage of sales or an arbitrary percentage change over the previous budget. Seldom is

any justification given for such practices other than ease of budgeting. Such an arbitrary constraint is rejected in this normative framework.

6. *There are normally enough ideas for new products available at the start of the new product process flow stage model so that generation of alternatives is not a major consideration of the decision process.* This assumption does not imply that idea generation is unimportant. In fact, much research has been done seeking to formalize and improve ideas for potential projects.[9] This research has been widely accepted, and the literature generally indicates a huge volume of ideas from which to choose. Current emphasis in research seems to be on improving the "quality" of ideas, or generating the "best" ideas, but the concepts of idea "quality" or "best" idea are seldom formally defined.

This normative framework emphasizes choice among alternatives assuming that many more ideas can be generated than can be developed.

7. *This normative framework was developed to select routine new product projects for development, not to handle nonroutine or special projects.* A nonroutine new product development is defined as one that requires so large a capital investment or offers such risk that unsuccessful development or unsuccessful market introduction jeopardizes the future of the firm. The term could also apply where a new product, if unsuccessful, could substantially decrease sales and profits of a number of present products of the firm.

No normative framework can be expected to handle such special cases since the information collection, the performance objectives, measurement yardsticks, and the desired goal values of objectives all require a degree of flexibility and heuristics that would defeat the very purpose of a normative framework.

The normative framework of this chapter does, however, include methods by which special projects can be identified so they are not rejected or approved inappropriately. Having been identified, they can then be treated independently of the normative framework. It is possible that much of the recommended process could be applied to these nonroutine or special projects, although different decision makers and different risk measurement techniques would be necessary. Normally, such special projects are not encountered frequently.

8. *The R&D new product development project selection problem is consistent with Simon and Newell's "ill structured" problem*[10] *and Ansoff's "quasi-analytical" problem.*[11] This assumption means that a straightforward operations research optimization technique cannot be used for project selection, because these techniques require both an optimization technique and all variables to be expressed in quantitative terms.

Brandenburg has more clearly summarized this in an R&D context, noting the conditions under which allocation of resources among alternate projects can be carried out in a straightforward manner through ranking procedures, investment analysis, and mathematical programming. These conditions include a limited number of alternatives, with outcomes clearly specified in advance, and where relevant costs and benefits may be expressed in dollar amounts with small errors of estimation.[12] Since the decisions of this normative framework do not meet Brandenburg's requirements, simple application of quantitative techniques is not appropriate.

Souder reinforces this view. Reviewing quite a number of project selection quantitative techniques and their application, he concluded that "the classical project selection decisions, where an optimum set of projects is selected on the basis of financial criteria, may not be relevant in new market development R&D operations."[13]

Shelly and Bryan note that optimality methods are not able to accommodate any concerns of variability, and hence are not appropriate for many decision classes.[14] They also suggest a long-run vulnerability of optimization techniques since the ability to gather information about the future will always be limited. Thus, from a theoretical viewpoint in the long run, it will be impossible to use optimality criteria with the desired accuracy.

Additional background for this assumption is provided in chapters 3, 4, and 6.

Decision II

Decision II involves gathering and analyzing formal business analysis information, selection of performance measurement objectives, yardsticks, and goal values, and selection from among proposed product ideas of those specific projects to begin technical development. Along with decision III it is the most important of the normative decisions, and is by far the most complex, time consuming, and expensive decision.

The second normative decision is broken into two parts. Part a (IIa) involves creation of a pool of potentially successful product ideas. Part b (IIb) involves choosing from among the pool of product ideas the specific project ideas to be developed at this time.

This split is one of the most critical innovations of this normative framework. Decision IIa involves establishment of a project pool by comparing potential product ideas to minimum values of multiple objective functions. These comparisons are made as a measure of the worth of the product idea itself, without dependence upon the conditions of the particular firm at the particular time the comparison is made. The product idea stands or falls on its own merit.

Decision IIb is theoretically necessary, however, because a product idea does not exist in a vacuum, and it is necessary to mesh the projects chosen for development with the other activities of the firm. Decision IIb thus allows the product idea to be viewed in the context of other activities of the firm at the time at which decisions for product development are made. This split in decision II allows decision IIa to be relatively static and independent of current conditions. Decision IIb maps current conditions, including strategic considerations, onto decision IIa.

The purpose of decision II is to provide as much structuring as possible so that the project selection decision can be made in a logical, consistent way. The state of the art in R&D project selection, however, is such that decisions cannot be made using completely structured formulas. It is still necessary to employ subjective judgment based on management expertise in combination with structural processes in the choice of projects. The normative recommendations, as presented, attempt to focus the subjective input needed.

Decision IIa: Creation of a Pool of Potential Product Ideas

Decision IIa involves creation of a pool of potentially successful product project ideas. For ease of presentation, the general steps in the decision IIa process flow will be presented and discussed. This is followed by presentation and analysis of the specific performance objectives recommended for the steps in decision IIa. Finally, the end product of the decision process is presented.

The decision IIa process flow steps.   The decision IIa process flow steps are shown schematically in figure 5. The recommended steps are described below.

Step 1.   For each performance objective, the descriptive attributes are determined, measurement yardsticks developed, and goal values selected. These attributes, yardsticks, and goal values are constants, and should not vary with specific product ideas.

The breakdown of the performance objectives into descriptive attributes, measurement yardsticks, and goal values was done to aid detailed expression of the decision criteria. This breakdown is consistent with that used for the corporate performance objectives in chapter 6, and was discussed there. The detailed normative recommendations for these attributes and measurement yardsticks, and examples of goal values, are presented and discussed in the next section of this chapter.

Step 2.   Steps 2 through 5 are carried out for each individual product idea.

For each measurement yardstick, the information necessary is identified, and, if not already available, is gathered, estimated, or calculated.

Figure 5. Steps in Decision IIa: Creation of a Pool of Potential Product Ideas

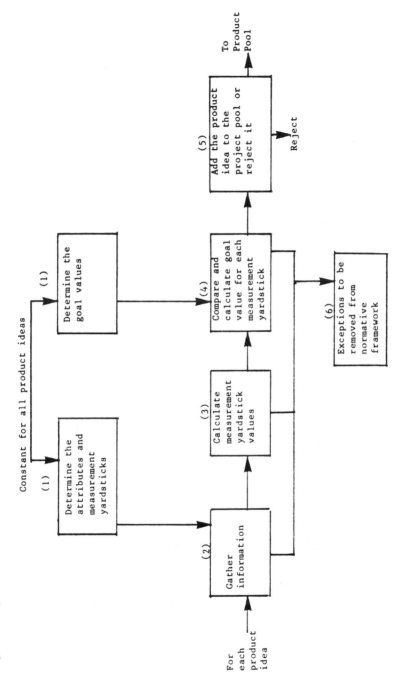

The information necessary is generally self-evident from the way the measurement yardstick is expressed. Necessary information is discussed for the specific measurement yardsticks recommended in the next section of this chapter.

Step 3.   The information generated is used to calculate the value of each measurement yardstick for each product idea.

Again, where the calculation is not self-evident from the way the measurement yardstick is expressed, it is discussed for the specific measurement yardstick recommended in the next section of this chapter.

Step 4.   The calculated value for each measurement yardstick is then compared to the goal value for the same measurement yardstick.

Step 5.   A decision is made to add the product idea to the product idea pool or to reject the product idea and not add it to the project pool as follows:

(a) If all calculated measurement yardstick values exceed their respective goal values, add the product idea to the pool.

Symbolically, let

N_e = number of economic measurement yardsticks
N_o = number of noneconomic measurement yardsticks
G_i = goal value of economic measurement yardstick i
G_j = goal value of noneconomic measurement yardstick j
$i = 1, N$
$j = 1, N$
M_{eik} = calculated economic measurement yardstick i for product k
M_{ojk} = calculated noneconomic measurement yardstick j for product k

if $(M_{eik} > G_i)$, let $E_i = 1$
if $(M_{eik} \leq G_i)$, let $E_i = 0$
if $(M_{ojk} > G_j)$, let $O_j = 1$
if $(M_{ojk} \leq G_j)$, let $O_j = 0$

if $\displaystyle\sum_{i=1}^{N_e} E_i + \sum_{j=1}^{N_o} O_j = N_e + N_o$, accept product idea.

(b) If the calculated economic measurement yardstick values are less than their respective goal values, reject the product idea.

Symbolically, if $\displaystyle\sum_{i=1}^{N_e} E_i < N_e$, reject product idea.

(c) If the majority of the noneconomic measurement yardstick calculated values are less than their respective goal values, reject the product idea.

Symbolically, if $\sum_{j=1}^{N_o} O_j \leq \dfrac{N_o}{2}$, reject product idea

(d) If the calculated economic measurement yardstick values are greater than their respective goal values, and if the majority (but not all) of the other calculated measurement yardsticks are greater than their respective goal values, add the product idea to the pool.

Symbolically,

if $\sum_{j=1}^{N_o} O_j > \dfrac{N_o}{2}$

and $\sum_{i=1}^{N_e} E_i = N_e$, accept product idea

Step 5 discussion. Step 5 requires the comparison of specific measurement yardstick calculations for each project to the respective goal values. In general, the goal values used as examples in decision IIa are expressed as minimum values. There are alternate methods to express goal values that could have been used, particularly the use of target values. The use of minimums, however, is more appropriate for a decision whose purpose is to create a pool of potentially satisfactory products rather than to select specific products for development. Ansoff has provided a thorough discussion of methods of expression of goal values that support this usage.[15]

Step 5 also requires that for the product idea to be accepted into the pool of potential projects all of the economic calculations must exceed their goal values, while only a majority of the growth and stability measurement yardsticks must exceed their goal values. Ideally, however, all of the calculated values of the measurement yardsticks for a product idea should exceed their goal values. This is currently possible for economic objectives, because economic attributes can be reduced to a few fairly well defined attributes. The state of the art in the expression of growth and stability objectives is such that a large number of attributes and measurement yardsticks must be used to adequately describe the objectives required.

Because of the large number of growth and stability yardsticks, any single yardstick does not have the same compact measurement value as an economic yardstick, and a product idea should not be dropped if it does not exceed one or a few such growth or stability yardsticks.

The choice of the majority as the minimum number of growth and stability measurement yardsticks to add a product idea to the pool is relatively arbitrary. Some alternatve value, say 75%, of the calculated measurement yardsticks for growth and stability exceeding their goal values, could also have been chosen. The choice of such a value is based upon the subjective opinion of the decision makers, and few suggestions are available to guide their choice. The specific figure is not as important as the recognition that, given the state of the art, the failure of one or a few growth or stability measurement yardsticks to exceed its goal value should not in itself be sufficient to reject the product idea. Theoretical and practical support is provided for such a value in the literature, particularly the quantitative index discussions.[16]

Step 6.   If, in generating information or in calculating values, any piece of information or result is so far removed from that of other product ideas that it is questioned, the entire product idea is removed from this normative framework and passed to senior R&D and corporate management for a separate decision.

Step 6 discussion.   Step 6 requires the removal of any product idea from this normative framework where any calculation or calculation input data is so far removed from that of other product ideas that its inclusion in this normative framework is questionable. This step is necessary to provide flexibility to remove product ideas that should not be decided on a routine basis. Such product ideas are those that could involve so large a capital investment that the future of the firm could be jeopardized or those that could result in very large changes in current product markets.

The decision to remove a product idea from the normative framework at this step is based upon the subjective judgment of the decision makers. It should be possible to identify guidelines for this step, such as a maximum capital investment size for a product idea to be handled under this normative framework, but no suggestions currently exist. A discussion of logical thought patterns for this, as well as the other subjective decisions of the decision makers, are presented when discussing recommendations for decision makers later in this chapter.

Few product ideas will fall into these special categories. Hence application of this step resulting in removal of project ideas from this normative framework should be infrequent. Competent decision makers will not look upon this step as a crutch to pass on the decision to a higher level of management.

Project selection performance objectives. The specific project selection performance objectives to be used in the application of the steps in figure 5 for creation of a pool of potential product ideas are shown in table 3. They are recommended as attributes and measurement yardsticks, with examples of goal values provided to indicate possible expression methods.

Three specific performance objective areas are recommended: economic, growth, and stability. Discussion begins by analyzing the choice of these three areas. Next the attributes, measurement yardsticks, and goal values of each area and the performance objectives as strategic considerations are discussed.

Recommendations of attributes and measurement yardsticks, and examples of goal values, are difficult to provide since there is little support in the literature. For this reason, a major contribution of this book is in the treatment of the attributes, yardsticks, and goal values as a decision-making system. Attributes, yardsticks, and goal values were chosen to complement each other and to describe a content picture. This framework should not be judged on any one attribute, yardstick, or goal value taken out of the context of the framework.

In general, selection of measurement yardsticks and goal values are based upon the subjective judgment of the decision makers. The individuals and/or functions who should make the decisions are discussed later in this chapter.

The choice of economic, stability, and growth areas. The purpose of this set of performance objectives is to ensure consistency of project selection with corporate objectives and strategies. Yet, as discussed in chapter 6, translation mechanisms are not available to translate corporate objectives and strategies to the R&D project selection level. Chapter 6 suggests the consistency of the economic, stability, and growth areas presented here with corporate objectives and strategies, but additional work is needed before the relationships can be described in more detail.

In general terms, this set of performance objectives provides the strategic planning perspective to selection of a pool of potential products. The economic performance objectives were chosen to recognize the need for a profit in the long run for the firm to remain in business. Growth was chosen to recognize different strategic concerns for a product in the early stage of its life cycle than at later stages. Stability performance objectives were identified to recognize the product market risk trade-offs at the mature stage of the product life cycle, and to attempt to express strategic proxies at the stage of the product life cycle where major contributions are made to the corporate objectives and strategies (such as cash generation) by the product.

Economic performance objectives. Two economic performance objective attributes were recommended: profitability and profitability risk.

Profitability and risk. Rate of return on investment was chosen as the profitability measurement yardstick for a number of reasons. The formula

Table 3. Normative Recommendations of Performance
Objectives, Decision IIa

ATTRIBUTES	MEASUREMENT YARDSTICKS	EXAMPLES OF GOAL VOLUES [3]
1. ECONOMIC PERFORMANCE OBJECTIVES		
a. Profitability	Rate of Return on Investment, $$I = \sum_{n=1}^{N} \frac{R_n}{(1+r_i)^n}$$ where r_i is calculated by the simulation technique (See Ch IV and Ch VII discussion) using the above formula. I is all estimated investment including, but not limited to product testing, market testing, all personnel costs, manufacturing startup costs, and capital equipment on the basis that the product can be manufactured in current plants with addition of equipment. N is the total number of years of product life n is the year of product life R_n is the estimated profit for the nth year in standard accounting terms r_i is the rate of return on the investment of project r_c is the marginal cost of capital of the firm	
b. Profitability Risk	Confidence interval about the mean of the distribution of r_i calculated by a simulation let r_{imin} = minimum value of the confidence interval	Minimum value of a .95 confidence interval above the marginal cost of capital DECISION: if $r_{imin} \geq r_c$, accept if $r_{imin} < r_c$, reject

ATTRIBUTES	MEASUREMENT YARDSTICKS	EXAMPLES OF GOAL VALUES[3]
2. GROWTH PERFORMANCE OBJECTIVES[1]		
a. Desired Growth Rates		
1. Sales volume	Increase per year in sales volume	Minimum – 5%
2. Market share	Increase per year in market share	Minimum – 1%
3. Profitability	Increase per year in rate of return on investment	Minimum – 10%
b. Growth Potential		
1. Sales volume	Total unit sales at mature stage of life cycle	Minimum – 1,000,000 units
2. Market share	% share of total market at mature stage of product life cycle	Minimum – 5%
3. Profit	Total dollar profit per year at mature stage of product life cycle	Minimum – $1 million
c. Expansion Potential		
1. Potential for product line expansion	Rating Scale 1-2-3-4-5 Poor Good	Minimum – 3 or larger
2. Potential for market scope expansion	Rating Scale 1-2-3-4-5 Poor Good	Minimum – 3 or larger

Table 3. (continued)

ATTRIBUTES	MEASUREMENT YARDSTICKS	EXAMPLES OF GOAL VALUES[3]
3. STABILITY PERFORMANCE OBJECTIVES[2]		
a. Product Stability		

1. Product characteristics	Technical Stability Rating Scale for
	Uniqueness Each Yardstick
	Difficulty of 1-2-3-4-5
	  copying Poor Good
	Quantity price
	  relationship
		Minimum - Average of 3
		              or higher

2. Life cycle	Estimated length of mature stage	Minimum - 5 years
b. Market Stability		

1. Market entry	Legal restrictions Rating Scale for
	Capital restrictions Each Yardstick
	Technology 1-2-3-4-5
	  restrictions Poor Good
		Minimum - Average of 3
		              or higher

2. Breadth of Market	Number of potential market segments Number of potential customers	Minimum - 2 Minimum - 5

3. Yearly seasonal stability	% of sales over single season	Maximum $\pm$ 20%
4. Degree of reliance on general economy	Rating scale 1-2-3-4-5 High Low	Minimum - 3 or higher
5. Individual customer dependence	% of sales to largest customer	Maximum - 40%

1. Growth objectives normally occur during the early years of a product life cycle.

2. Stability objectives are normally concerned with the mature stage of a product life cycle.

3. Goal values should be expressed, where possible, as a minimum, maximum, or target value in units of the measurement yardstick.

   The values listed are possible examples of values for a large, multiple product manufacturing firm primarily in relatively mature product market areas. They are intended as examples of the expression techniques, and are *not* normative values. Where no value is listed, no example can be provided, generally because no theoretical base exists to aid in setting a value.

lends itself very readily to variable profit for future years. This is necessary both to recognize variability in price, sales, and cost in the future, and to recognize a normal product life cycle variability. In addition, its use of total investment as a lump sum allows investment to be calculated in relatively time free considerations for decision IIa, and also allows investment to be modified readily based upon time-related conditions of decision IIb. Internal rate of return has been specifically recommended in an R&D context by Villers, Hitchcock, Scheuble, and Weston, among many others.[17]

The standard internal rate of return was chosen for use here over the Baldwin rate for two reasons.[18] (1) The Baldwin rate discounts back the future funds at the rate the organization on the average earns on its assets. Yet this use of a historical base may be inconsistent with desires to improve the rate of return by new product introduction. In addition, no theoretical base is provided for the use of the current average return on assets over any other measure of the current returns (that is, median, upper 20%, and so on). (2) The standard rate of return discounts back future funds at the rate at which the proposed investment is estimated to provide. This is consistent with the use of the marginal cost of capital as the rate of return minimum goal value to be discussed in this chapter.

One major problem with the rate of return formula is that of any other formula based upon expected future data: the inability to predict with certainty the future data that must go into the formula. Such items as future sales, prices, costs, consumer demand, etc., are all unknowns and must be estimated. While the components of profit and investment that deal with the near future can perhaps be estimated with reasonable accuracy, other longer-range components may be difficult to estimate.

Investment is assumed to have both present and future components. Estimates of future investment encounter the same problems as estimates of future profit components. For both profit and investment, methods of estimating these values for the future for the R&D project choice decision are widespread, and need not be repeated here.[19] Such areas are discussed in chapter 4.

The rate of return on investment calculation is carried out by means of a simulation analysis.[20] Simulation techniques are discussed in chapter 4 and their advantages and disadvantages summarized there. A probability distribution is created by the decision makers for each piece of data that goes into any component of the rate of return on investment formula. Drawing from these data probability distributions allows development by simulation of a probability distribution for the rate of return value itself. This is important both because any measures of central tendency desired, such as an average, can be calculated, and because it allows calculation of a risk surrogate to be discussed shortly.

The simulation technique uses as its base probability distributions for each of the component data. This requires the decision makers to express their estimates as a complete range of values, and provides more detailed estimates than use of an expected data value or a discrete set of data values (see chapter 4). Drawing from these data probability distributions to calculate the rate of return on investment thus gives a rate of return probability distribution based upon all estimated data ranges. Thus the simulation displays the resultant rate of return on investment as a probability distribution, and provided a great deal more information to the decision maker than if it were expressed as an average, expected value, or simplified range.

A risk concept, necessary because of the inability to predict the future with perfect accuracy, is handled in this normative framework by the use of a confidence interval based around the mean of the rate of return on investment figures calculated by the simulation. As noted in chapter 4, the theory of risk is ill-defined, and the use of a confidence interval as an expression of risk, while not widely identified in the literature, is a logical extension of existing theory.

Expressing the rate of return as a confidence interval allows the decision makers to view the rate of return in a form more usable for decision making than a probability distribution. It gives a potential range rather than just an average or expected rate of return.

The low end of this confidence interval is used as the calculated measurement yardstick value for comparison with the goal value. The low end of the confidence interval was chosen as the measurement yardstick to minimize the probability of the actual rate of return being lower than the value used for this comparison.

The real risk control mechanism in this profitability attribute is the determination of the width of the confidence interval. This width determination is based upon the subjective opinion of the decision makers. A .95 confidence interval was used in table 3 to reflect a conservative management philosophy that desires only a very low probability of the actual rate of return on investment dropping below the goal value. If the decision makers are willing to take a greater risk on the profitability attribute, a smaller confidence interval could be specified.

Emery also suggested the use of a confidence interval around the mean of a probability distribution as a measure of risk.[21] Apparently he was not aware of Hertz's and Hess and Quigley's work, for he notes that mathematical tools are not currently available to aid in establishing such a confidence interval. His solution was that "it is necessary to treat the world as if it were deterministic, leaving to the planner the task of compensating for uncertainty."[22]

An argument could be made for supplying a risk confidence interval around every measurement yardstick or goal value in this normative framework. This same argument could suggest use of a risk confidence interval around every component of a simulation rather than just around the final rate of return on investment figure. While this proposal may offer advantages, there is no theoretical reason to assume a more accurate end representation of risk by use of confidence intervals around individual components than by a confidence interval around the average, and mathematical tools are not available to express confidence interval data for the nonquantitative measurement yardsticks. For these reasons only a rate of return on investment confidence interval is a part of this normative framework.

The normative recommendation for the minimum goal value of rate of return on investment is the current marginal cost of capital. The current marginal cost of capital is used as the minimum goal value in decision IIa since decision IIa is intended to be as time free as is practical. The need to consider future marginal capital cost is necessary in actual project selection, and will be considered in decision IIb. Marginal cost was chosen since a company, in theory, should be able to raise money to invest in new products if the return on the new projects is greater than the cost of raising money. Henderson supports this use, noting that this net return differential on added investment is all that is really important.[23] In comparison with the average cost of capital concept, Henderson's point is important since the average cost of capital concept deals in large part with the desires of management in terms of the various methods of raising capital.

The use of the marginal cost of capital theory is consistent with the finance theory that there is no optimal cost of capital balance among the different methods of raising capital. If, however, one accepts the finance concept of an optimum mix of capital sources, then there is a limit on the amount of funds that can be raised from different sources and hence a potential constraint in terms of absolute dollars upon the total new product selection process.

Operational problems exist, however, in the use of marginal cost of capital since seldom does a firm raise money on a marginal basis for each new R&D project or indeed for a group of R&D projects. R&D capital requirements are only a part of the capital requirements for the firm as a whole, and capital is generally raised based upon the total firm's estimates of need rather than upon individual division or functional area needs. If, however, the cost of capital for the entire needed capital for a specific period of time can be treated on a net basis, then this net marginal cost of capital can be used as a minimum goal value for R&D project selection. A problem here is that R&D project development normally takes a number of years. If the projected returns from a project are near the marginal cost of capital figure, then variations among the net marginal cost of capital from time period to time period may move a project in and out of the acceptable pool.

Balancing the advantages and disadvantages of each method, this normative framework used the marginal cost of capital as its minimum goal value. Additional finance theory development is necessary before this area can be resolved.

Growth performance objectives. The growth performance objectives were split into three areas: desired growth rates, growth potential, and expansion potential. Each of these areas expresses a different component of growth. Together they provide a comprehensive consideration of growth performance objectives. Support for growth performance objectives expressed in this way (although not in the detail provided here) has been provided by Ansoff in his growth vector component,[24] and by the marketing-oriented new product literature.[25] (See also chap. 4.)

Desired growth rates. The variety among product ideas and the lack of a theoretical base precludes establishment of attributes, measurement yardsticks, and goal values for the growth vectors of sales volume, market share, and profitability at initial market introduction. Once a product is introduced, however, its sales, market share, and profit should begin increasing as it becomes accepted in the marketplace and as the increased volume lowers average unit costs. To ensure that these grow at a rapid enough rate, estimates of sales, market share, and profit per year must be provided, and a percentage increase from year to year calculated. If these percentage increases are greater than the goal values, the product idea passes these decision criteria. General support, as well as some of the suggested details, for desired growth rates are discussed by Wilson, Heyel, and Christopher, among others.[26] (See also chap. 4.)

Establishment of the goal values is a subjective judgment of the decision makers. While their thought process must recognize the variation in growth among different product ideas, they must decide on a desired momentum of growth to ensure that a product reaches its mature stage, and express minimum momentum rates as these goal values.

Growth potential. The growth potential component recognizes the need to identify in advance desired sales, market share, and profit at the mature stage of a product's life cycle to determine if the absolute size of the product market justifies its inclusion in the firm's product line. Again, sales volume, market share, and profit were chosen as vectors to be consistent with the growth rate component and to provide a complete picture of the major strategic considerations at the mature stage. The measurement yardsticks were set as an absolute value of sales volume, market share, and profit at the mature stage of the product life cycle. These values are then compared to the goal values, and, if they exceed the goal value, these decision criteria are satisfactory.

The growth potential measurement yardsticks were expressed as absolute values to recognize that a product must be a certain size to be retained in the firm's product line. Projects that return small values may not be worthwhile to the firm since there are substantial cost elements, particularly corporate management time and effort, that are not now handled by accounting theory and practice, and hence not taken into account. None of the absolute values are directly related to the amount of corporate managerial effort needed. Some minimum size should be required of each product to preclude a large number of small sales and profit products being added that could use firm efforts disproportionate to their sales and profit contributions.

Both the concept of growth potential and some of the specific attributes and measurement yardsticks of table 3 were discussed by Stern, Christopher, and Wilson, among others.[27]

The minimum goal values again must be set by the subjective judgments of the decision makers. There are no suggestions in the literature to aid them in determining a minimum size product to add to their product line.

Expansion potential.   In addition to growth in the expected markets, it may be possible to identify a potential for additional expansion of the product and expansion into different markets. If this potential could be estimated in advance it would be a part of the growth potential component. Frequently, however, additional product line and market scope expansion may appear possible, but no estimates can be prepared since such expansion is based upon the degree of success of the product idea under consideration. However, such potential should be recognized, even if estimation is not possible.

To measure these product line and market scope expansion potential attributes, two simple rating scales are recommended. These scales allow a qualitative judgment by the decision makers of the potential for expansion since estimation is not possible. These rating scales follow standard methodology, providing a 1 to 5, poor to good scale. The goal value is subjectively chosen to reflect a medium expansion potential as a minimum value. Conceptual support for the expansion potential concept was provided by Crawford and Hitchcock.[28]

Of all the growth components this expansion potential component is the most qualitative. It offers strong support to the overall corporate strategy in that it indicates potential for a product market area expansion from an individual product. It is hoped that future research will provide additional aid in estimation of these product line and market scope expansions.

Stability performance objectives.   The stability performance objectives are chosen to recognize product market risk tradeoffs and to attempt to express strategic product market proxies at the mature stage of the product life cycle. Stability is used here to express the degree of variability in the product and market components estimated for the product idea. As such, stability expresses risk informally in terms of the expected variation of a number of proxies rather than as a unique component as in the economic performance objectives. Such a handling of risk is necessary in these product market areas since there is no theoretical base to express risk for the product market area as a whole. To present stability performance objectives from the product market strategic viewpoints, the attributes are broken into product stability and market stability components.

Product stability.   Product stability attributes are expressed as product characteristics and product life cycle. Together they express the degree of variation expected due to the product. The product characteristics are measured by estimates of technical stability (the opposite of technical obsolence), the degree of patent protection, the uniquenesses of the product, the difficulty of copying, and the quantity-price-profit relationship. Together they present a picture of the ability of the product to establish and maintain a sales and profit level. For each of these measurement yardsticks a qualitative rating scale is used, since no theoretical base exists to establish alternate measurement techniques. The goal value requires a medium value of 3 or higher by the average of the rating values of the five measurement techniques to consider the attribute satisfactory. This goal value is a qualitative expression of the product stability desired by the decision makers.

The product life cycle is measured by estimating the length of the mature stage. The longer the mature stage, the more stable the product itself. The goal value is set by the decision makers as the minimum number of years they desire for the product at the mature stage.

Product stability and market stability attributes are frequently not separated in the literature. Both the concept of product stability and some of the details shown in table 3 are discussed by Stern.[29] Details are also intermingled with market stability by Heyel, Christopher, and Hitchcock.[30]

Market stability.   For the identified markets, market stability is expressed in attributes of market entry, breadth of market, degree of reliance on seasonal sales, the general economy and individual customers. Together they provide a composite picture of market stability. Market entry is measured by rating scales of legal, capital, and technology restrictions, with a subjective goal value of at least medium difficulty of entry. The breadth of the identified markets is measured by estimating the number of potential market segments and customers. Goal values are assigned as a minimum number to ensure the desired minimum number of segments and customers. As is true of all of these market stability attributes, there are no theoretical bases to aid the decision makers in their subjective judgment. Their through patterns must be aimed at identifying a general market stability desired and translating this general desire to the proxy goal values.

Desires of smooth yearly sales are measured as the variation of sales by seasons of the year. If seasonal products are not desired, a low maximum goal value figure is set. Sales of a product may move with the general trend in the economy, be counter cyclical, or remain relatively constant with changes in the economy. A qualitative rating scale is suggested for measurement, with a goal value of medium or less variance in sales with the general economy. Again a qualitative rating scale is necessary because of the lack of identification of other measurement techniques.

Individual customer dependence as measured by the percentage of sales to the largest customer is the last market stability attribute. The less the dependence on a single (or few) customer, the greater the sales stability. Hence the goal value is expressed as a maximum desired sales to any customer, and is again set by the subjective judgment of the decision makers.

Marketing stability considerations are emphasized by Wilson, and also included with product stability by Heyel, Christopher, and Hitchcock.[31]

The performance objectives as strategic considerations.   In figure 3, a framework is presented for development of a new product strategy from corporate strategy. Corporate strategy is broken into components of growth vector, product market scope, competitive advantage, and synergy. Two areas of the growth vector, diversification and product development, are shown as applicable to new product strategy, in addition to the other three corporate strategy components.

Diversification involves new products for new customers, while product development involves new products for present customers. Thus, they differ in the customer for whom the products are intended. The performance attributes of decision IIa, however, do not distinguish in measurement yardsticks or goal values between these types of customers. Thus, the attributes listed are consistent with and should be used for both diversification and product development strategies. If either diversification or product development is desired as a strategy as such, it should be called out as a special decision criteria of decision IIb, not as part of decision IIa.

The major strategic import in decision IIa is in describing the attributes and measurement yardsticks in terms of product market characteristics. This allows the product ideas in the product idea pool to be expressed in strategic terms. Thus, if special strategic conditions are required by decision IIb, the product ideas are expressed in a way so that ready selection from the pool can be made.

The profitability attribute includes both product and market considerations in its measurement yardstick, and they cannot be expressed in profitability terms separately. The same thing occurs in the desired growth rate and growth potential attributes, since the sales volume, market share, and profit considerations are dependent on both product and market characteristics. For the stability performance objectives, product and market characteristics can be separated and expressed directly as product stability and market stability.

Thus the performance objectives of decision IIa are definitely involved in and expressed as strategic product market considerations. The major strategic concerns of product market scope, competitive advantage, and synergy are a part of decision IIb. Expressing the attributes for decision IIa as was done ensures consistency with any desired special decision criteria of decision IIb.

The end product of decision IIa.   The result of a product idea IIa decision is the acceptance of the product idea into a pool of potentially successful product ideas or the rejection of the product idea for further consideration for technical development.

If a product idea is accepted, it means the product idea has been described in detail in terms of expected future activities and results and that this future information has been formally calculated and expressed as measurement yardsticks. Further, all of the economic, growth, and stability performance objectives were compared to standard goal values desired for potential product ideas, and all of the economic and more than half of the growth and stability measurement yardsticks passed the goal value comparisons. Thus the product idea, having been judged on its own intrinsic merits, has been found to offer the potential for successful market introduction.

If a product idea is rejected, it means that the product idea as estimated does not appear to offer the potential for success in the marketplace consistent with the desires of the firm.

For the new product development process as a whole, the result of decision IIa is a pool of products, that, judged on their own merits, appear to offer the potential for successful introduction in the marketplace. Yet a new product idea does not exist in a vacuum, and it is necessary to relate the individual product idea to the firm and its environment at the time at which technical development is to begin. This selection of specific products for technical development in the context of other activities of the firm is done in decision IIb.

Decision IIb—Selection of Products for Technical Development

Decision IIb involves choosing from the pool of potentially successful product ideas developed by decision IIa the specific product ideas to begin technical development. Decision IIb is necessary to relate the potential product idea to the activities and desires of the firm at the time development is to begin. This discussion begins by identifying and analyzing the steps in decision IIb. Strategic considerations are analyzed next, followed by a discussion of portfolio considerations, and the end products of the decision.

The decision IIb process steps.   Decision IIb is shown schematically in figure 6. It requires a number of specific steps.

Step 1.   Projects from the pool of product ideas are rank ordered by rate of return on investment.

Figure 6. Steps in Decision IIb: Choice of Products for Development

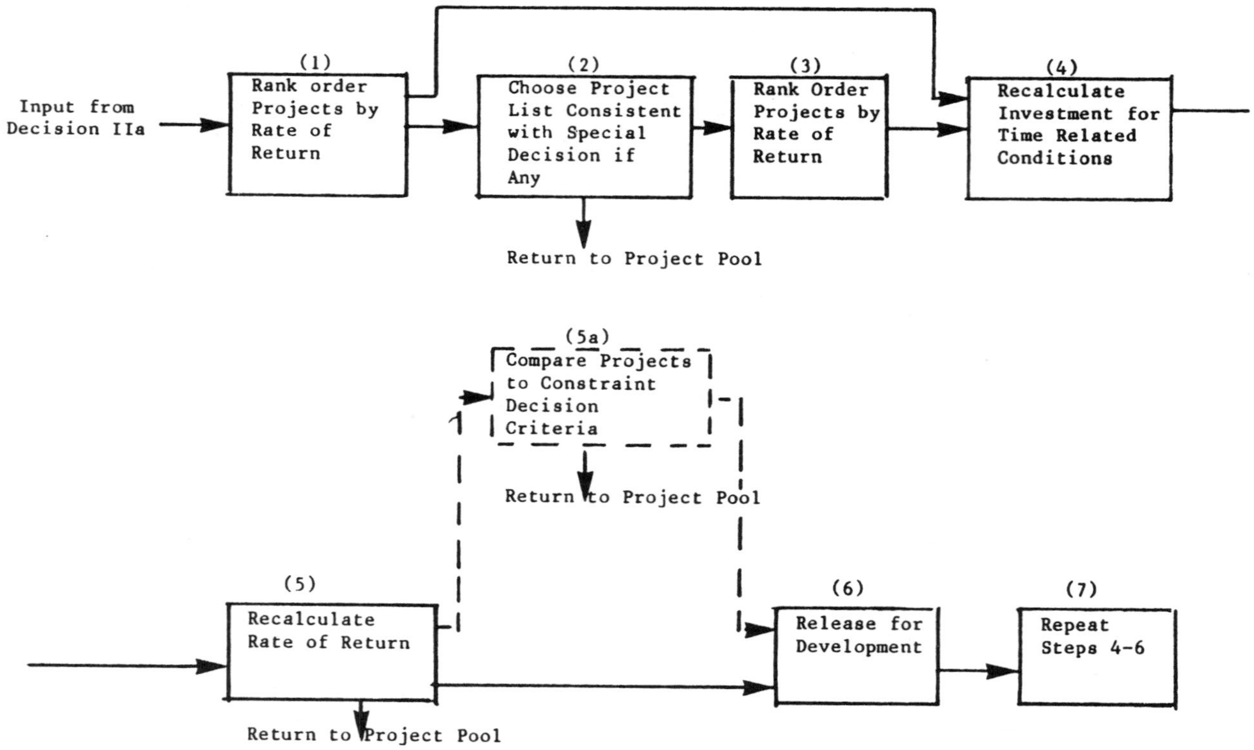

Input from
Decision IIa →

(1)
Rank order
Projects by
Rate of
Return

(2)
Choose Project
List Consistent
with Special
Decision if
Any

Return to Project Pool →

(3)
Rank Order
Projects by
Rate of
Return

(4)
Recalculate
Investment for
Time Related
Conditions

(5)
Recalculate
Rate of Return

Return to Project Pool →

(5a)
Compare Projects
to Constraint
Decision
Criteria

Return to Project Pool →

(6)
Release for
Development

(7)
Repeat
Steps 4-6

Discussion of step 1.   Ranking by rate of return on investment alone is not meant to imply that other performance objectives are not important. At present, however, there are no acceptable ranking scales available at this stage that can handle nonquantitative objectives or groups of objectives. It would be possible to handle final choice of a group of objectives by relying completely upon the subjective choice of the decision makers. This method was rejected, however, since one of the prime goals of this normative framework is to reduce reliance upon the subjective opinion of the decision makers as much as possible.

Use of the rate of return on investment as the only ranking attribute does not ignore other attributes, since to get in the pool a product idea had to have at least a majority of satisfactory growth and stability attributes in decision IIa. The use of rate of return on investment ranking in this manner is supported by Tilles, although his research was not for the R&D project selection decision.[32]

Step 2.   Special decision criteria, if any, are added. From the ranked list of step 1, projects that are consistent with any special criteria are chosen. These move to the next step. Projects that are not consistent with special needs are returned to the project pool.

Discussion of step 2.   There are no normative recommendations for special decision criteria. Special decision criteria are normally temporary conditions where it is necessary to develop new products to compensate for weaknesses in the firm due to events outside the control of the new product function, or where new products in specific product market areas are necessary to be consistent with corporate strategy.

Three examples of special decision criteria are presented and discussed in table 4. Needs of the specific operating or profit center and need to fill productive capacity are examples of special decision criteria to compensate for identified current weaknesses in the firm. Growth vector emphasis is an example of a special decision criterion to choose products for specific customer classes to carry out a corporate strategy directive. (Strategy as related to special decision criteria is discussed later in this section.)

The attributes considered as special decision criteria here are frequently included as a regular part of a decision in the current R&D management literature. They are listed as a separate step here to emphasize their temporary nature and the fact that they can change more frequently than other attributes in this project selection normative framework. The possible examples of special decision criteria detailed here are not original. Growth vector emphasis was identified by Ansoff, while the needs of operating centers and the need to fill productive capacity was identified by a number of researchers, among them Hitchcock, Stern, and Crawford.[33] (See also chap. 4.)

Step 3.   Projects compatible with the special criteria are rank ordered by rate of return on investment.

Table 4. Examples of Potential Special Decision Criteria Used in
Decision II5, Selection of Products for Development, Step 2

ATTRIBUTES	MEASUREMENT YARDSTICKS	GOAL VALUES
SPECIAL DECISION CRITERIA EXAMPLES		
A. Growth vector emphasis	Diversification (New products for new customers) Product Development (New products for existing customer)	Specific customer or customer class identified Specific customer or customer class identified
B. Need of specific operating or profit center	Detailed need Example, need to fill gap in product line; Need to keep division in existence for public image or concern objectives	Detailed identification of need
C. Need to fill productive capacity	Detailed description of equipment to be filled	Detailed description of pro-ducts that can be made on equipment

Note: Special decision criteria may sometimes be necessary to direct product selection in a particular direction for a particular time period. They are generally responses to conditions in the operating divisions of the firm that could be solved or partially solved by the addition of new products. Such special conditions should be temporary, so their regular inclusion in a product selection process is not feasible.

There are no normative recommendations for special decision criteria, and indeed, the need for their inclusion should be infrequent. No comprehensive list of special decision criteria has been developed, but three potential special criteria are discussed in the above table.

The use of special decision criteria is straightforward. For an identified special criteria attribute, the measurement yardstick is identified, and goal value is compared to the equivalent measure for the product project. If the project measure is consistent with the goal value, the project is moved to the next step. If the measure is not consistent with the goal value, the project is returned to the project pool.

Steps 1 through 3 are carried out for the entire product pool. Steps 4 through 6 require single product review starting at the top of the ranked list of step 3.

Step 4. The rate of return on investment calculation is reviewed to include the time related components of (a) R&D capacity and capability, (b) productive capacity, and (c) synergy. Details of this review are shown in figure 7. If necessary, the investment figure in the basic rate of return formula is modified as a result of this review. In general, since the investment determination in decision IIa did not take these conditions into account, any modification will result in a larger investment.

Discussion of step 4. Step 4, the most innovative feature of decision IIb, provides for review and possible recalculation of the investment figure in the rate of return on investment formula to consider the product idea in the context of the operating divisions and of the functional areas of the firm in which the product will be developed. Consideration of the time related components of R&D capacity and capability, product capacity, and synergy is recommended and discussed in figure 7. Other considerations may be added if desired by the decision makers.

The basic concept recommended here is that of adjusting individual investment components in the total investment figure to reflect added costs or cost savings from the identified time related components of development. The theory to modify the investment figure for R&D capacity and productive capacity is available in current accounting literature and is straightforward. The ability to identify investment and cost components for synergy is more complex, and little theory is available. While some recommendations for handling synergy are made in figure 7, the area has not been well developed. What is presented is only a start at developing an appropriate theory.

Step 5. If investment was modified, the rate of return on investment is recalculated using the simulation technique identified in decision IIa. In general, since the investment was larger, the modified average rate of return will be smaller than that calculated in decision IIa.

A .95 confidence interval is also calculated, and, if the minimum value is above the goal value (recommended as the marginal cost of capital), the project is passed to the next step. If the confidence interval minimum value is below the goal value, the project is returned to the project pool. Since the conditions resulting in an unacceptable rate of return are time dependent, removal of the same project from the pool at a later time could mean different modifying values and an acceptable rate of return.

Calculation of the marginal cost of capital for the goal value at this stage is not as simple as in decision IIa. E. L. Wallace has suggested that attached to each source of marginal capital are two costs: (1) the direct outlay cost of that capital when used as intended, and (2) an opportunity cost related to current use of the source which is measured by the difference between the direct cost of

Figure 7. Elements for Review of Investment Figure in Rate of
Return on Investment Formula of Decision IIb, Step 4

Introduction

In decision IIa the investment component in the rate of return on investment formula was defined as capital costs including, but not limited to, product testing, market testing, all R&D costs assuming normal internal development, manufacturing starting costs, and capital equipment on the basis that the product can be manufactured in existing facilities (perhaps with new equipment). This definition was specifically chosen to be relatively time free, so that it was not dependent upon manufacturing and R&D work loads at any one particular time.

At the time of development and market introduction, however, the investment costs will vary because of work loads and other time related factors, and it is necesary to modify the investment figure to reflect the specific time period when the product will be developed and introduced into the marketplace.

Three time related factors, (1) R&D capacity and capability, (2) productive capacity, and (3) synergy are normative recommendations of this framework. Others, of course, are also possible.

R&D Capacity and Capability

Decision IIa assumed that, for each project, scientists in the internal R&D organization have the correct technical skills, that they are available to develop the product, that necessary equipment is available, etc. If this is not true when it is decided to start development, what is necessary to develop the product must be identified, costs must be assigned, and the investment component of the rate of return formula must be adjusted accordingly.

To determine whether the assumption of decision IIa is correct it is necessary to identify for the project under consideration (1) an estimate of the length of time necessary to develop the product, (21) the technical skills of the scientists needed, and (3) the equipment needed. These can be compared to (1) the time available in the current schedule, (2) the availability of the proper scientists, and (3) the availability of equipment.

If the project needs fit those available, the assumption of decision IIa is correct, and no modification to investment is necessary. If the project needs exceed those available, a decision is necessary as to internal or external development of the project. This decision is based upon determining the lowest development cost, and adjusting the investment figure to reflect the new cost.

External development costs can be gathered by finding an external laboratory willing to develop the product, and using their contract price. (This may be adjusted for probability of technical success, delivery time, etc., by either party.)

Additional internal development costs are more complicated. It is necessary to determine the fixed and variable costs of purchasing or leasing the required equipment, hiring or training the required scientists, the opportunity costs of replacing current projects under development, etc. While accounting theory is capable of doing this, literature research revealed no specific examples.

In any case, the additional internal development cost is added to the cost calculated for the IIa decision to give a total internal cost figure under the time related conditions.

Productive Capacity

Decision IIa assumed that, for each projet, facilities were available for manufacture, even if some new equpiment or equipment modification was necessary. To determine if this assumption is correct it is necessary to identify for the project under consideration (1) the technical attributes of the equipment needed, (2) the amount of equipment necessary for anticipated sales volume, and (3) other physical facilities needed. These can then be compared to (1) the equipment available, (2) the volume of equipment available, and (3) the plant facilities available.

If the product needs fit those available, the assumption of decision IIa is correct, and no modification to investment is necessary. If the project needs exceed those available, it is necessary to define what is necessary to manufacture the product and the cost of acquiring the added capacity. These cost calculations are straightforward engineering estimates. The new cost for capital equipment (including plant and supporting facilities) is then added to the investment component in the place of the figure used in decision IIa.

Synergy

Synergy is defined here to involve a measure of the joint effects in a fit between the firm's present products and the potential new product. As noted in the normative framework of chapter 6, the purpose of this research is not to develop alternate theories of the components of strategy, such as synergy, but to use those available in a decision-making process.

Although none of the theories of synergy is well developed and widely accepted, the theory recommended here is that of H. Igor Ansoff, because it is one of the few to attempt even crude synergy measures.[1] Ansoff broke synergy into four types, sales, operating, investment, and management synergy, and defined and described each. He formalized development of a competence profile to aid in the measurement of synergy, and suggested qualitative frameworks to aid in synergy measurement.

Decision IIa made no assumption of synergy, although it may have been taken into account in individual component consideration.

Using Ansoff's framework, the synergy of the proposed project and the firm's present products is identified. A comparison is then made to determine if any synergy was assumed in decision IIa that should not have been included, or if synergy exists but was not taken into account. In the former case, the cost to develop the desired synergy is determined and added to the investment component; in the latter case, the cost of savings from the synergy is calculated and subtracted from the appropriate investment component.

One example of this modification might be an assumption in decision IIa that a current channel of distribution could be used, while a formal synergy comparison indicates that a new channel of distribution is necessary. The cost of this new channel of distribution could then be estimated and added to the marketing startup investment component.

A practical problem in use of this synergy component investment modification exists in that, while accounting theory appears capable of providing synergy costs, literature searches revealed no specific examples.

Figure 7. (continued)

Conclusion

The three factors of R&D capacity and capability, productive capacity, and synergy affect one or more components of the required potential product investment, raising or lowering the investment used in decision IIa based upon conditions in the R&D division and the remainder of the firm at the start of development, and estimates of conditions until market introduction.

No attempt has been made to provide all the details necessary to make these modifications, since in large part they are not available in the literature, and detailed development is beyond the scope of this investigation. These areas, among others, are suggested in chapter 8 as worthy of further research.

Note: H. Igor Ansoff, *Corporate Strategy* (New York: McGraw-Hill, 1965).

the immediate use of the source and the long-term cost of a combination of sources of which the source selected is but one.[34] Thus, the ability to finance a project by a low cost source does not mean that the low interest cost is the appropriate cost of capital to use. Rather the estimated cost of capital from following an optimum financing program of which the loan is one component is the appropriate cost concept. This consideration is complicated because, as discussed earlier, capital is usually raised for the firm as a whole, not just for R&D product development. Unless R&D new product capital requirements are a large part of the total firm capital requirements, new product future commitments may have little effect on changes in the marginal cost of capital for the firm as a whole.

Financial theory is not available for detailed recommendations in this area. Until theories are developed, the practical recommendation of this framework is to use the current marginal cost of capital as the goal value, and recognize in a qualitative, subjective way the opportunity costs incurred by this capital commitment.

Step 6. The product idea project is released to the R&D division for development.

Step 7. Steps 4 through 6 are repeated until all the special criteria of step 2 are met. Steps 4 through 6 are then repeated for all products in the pool.

Step 5a. The use of constraints to limit product development is not recommended in this normative framework. If, however, additional constraints are desired to assure consistency with corporate performance objectives or arbitrary financial constraints, they should be added after step 5. A brief description of such potential constraints is included in figure 8.

Discussion of step 5a. Although not recommended in this normative framework, most practical discussions of R&D decision making and theoretical considerations by operations research techniques assume some

Figure 8. Possible Corporate Constraints on the Product Selection IIb Decision, Step 5a

ATTRIBUTES	MEASUREMENT YARDSTICK	EXAMPLES OF GOAL VALUES
POSSIBLE CONSTRAINTS		
a. Total R & D Budget	DOLLAR AMOUNT. R & D Expenses for the project are added to planned and current projects. If the maximum is exceeded the project is rejected; if not the project is accepted.	$14,000,000 maximum
b. Total Investment	DOLLAR AMOUNT. Investment requirements per year for the project are added to other investments for the firm. If this causes the maximum to be exceeded, the project is rejected; if not it is accepted.	$150,000,000 maximum
c. Debt Limits (Perhaps set by Debt/Equity Ratio)	DOLLAR AMOUNT. If the source of investment capital is debt, the project amount is added to other anticipated debt. If the maximum debt is exceeded the project is rejected; if not it is accepted.	$350,000,000 maximum

Note: The use of additional overall constraints is not recommended in this normative framework. In practice, however, some constraints may be necessary to insure consistency with corporate performance objectives or with arbitrary financial constraints. Three possible constraints are listed in the above table.

Other constraints could include seasonal sales dependence, product life cycle mix, general sales mix, liquidity measure, and other funds source guidelines.

No additional details are provided since these are merely illustrative examples.

limiting constraints upon the total new product area. To add flexibility to this framework a possible constraint location is shown in this step.

Financial constraints are the usual kind suggested by the literature. As an example, Brandenburg points out the R&D resources are not fluid and interchangeable and that this necessitates a partition of overall resource allocation into subproblems according to the classes of resources available.[35] Brandenburg's comments, like most other researchers, assume a relatively short time frame for R&D project selection. In general, all of the constraints suggested can be translated rather straightforwardly into financial cost figures. Thus they can be taken into account as this normative framework suggests by modification to investment figures in decision IIb, step 4, rather than directly as arbitrary constraints.

Strategic considerations.   In general strategic considerations underlie the decision criteria of decision IIb as they did decision IIa. In decision IIb, however, they can be identified more readily. In figure 3 corporate strategy was broken into components of growth vector, product market scope, competitive advantage, and synergy. Further, diversification and product development were identified as areas of growth vector particularly applicable to new product development. Together, figure 3 suggested diversification, product development, product market scope, competitive advantage, and synergy requirements define a new product strategy.

Chapter VI presented a framework for translation of corporate strategies and objectives downward through the firm for use in R&D new product decision making. Unfortunately, there is currently no base in the literature available for this translation. In recognition of this translation difficulty, decision IIb attempts to structure as many of the strategic considerations as is possible to aid the decision makers in their subjective translation. This is particularly important since there is little theory available on strategic problems or components at the R&D level.

Strategic considerations are most influential as special decision criteria of step 2 and in recalculation of the investment components of step 4.

In step 2, the growth vector areas of diversification and product development can be applied and are discussed as special decision criteria. The decision makers identify the customer or customer classes for which new products are desired, and product ideas from the pool are selected that are aimed at these customer classes. Thus the products developed are chosen to be consistent with these strategic concerns. The choice of customer classes is made by the decision makers based upon their judgment of the needs as identified by the corporate strategy.

Product market scope, while not discussed in table 4 can also be handled if necessary as a special decision criteria of step 2. If the corporate strategy indicates products in particular product areas are necessary, the decision makers can identify these product areas as special decision criteria, and products for development can be selected in these product areas. Again, because of the lack of translation details, the necessary product areas must be selected by the decision makers based upon their judgment of the need of corporate strategy.

Synergistic effects are taken into account in the recalculation of the investment components of step 4. As discussed in figure 7, synergy effects are estimated and costs required to develop synergy (or cost savings from synergy) are added (subtracted) to the appropriate investment component.

Competitive advantage effects are included in the detailed investment review areas of R&D capacity and capability, productive capacity, and synergy in step 4. They are not handled directly, but are included with other factors in cost considerations. For example, a strong marketing competititve advantage would be reflected in lower marketing testing, channels of distribution, and so on, costs in both decision IIa and decision IIb. If reliance on a specific competitive advantage (or building up a specific area into a competitive advantage) is desired by the corporate strategy, it should be identified as a special decision criteria of step 2 and handled in that way.

Portfolio considerations. Portfolio considerations are available from a number of viewpoints. Those of possible application to this normative framework include financial portfolio theory, treatment of the entire product market mix of the firm as a portfolio, treatment of new products under development as a portfolio, and treatment of the decision II steps as a decision criteria portfolio. Each is discussed briefly.

First, formal financial portfolio theory is not appropriate because of the rigid assumptions required and the emphasis on financial reward and risk to the exclusion of all other considerations. (This was discussed in chap. 4.)

Although not usually considered as such in the literature, the product market mix of the firm as a whole could be considered as a portfolio of products and markets. As part of the strategic plan a desired product market portfolio could be identified, the present product market mix measured, and a strategic gap identified. One method to close this gap could include new product development.

The product market mix portfolio is an objective of the firm as a whole, with new product development only one method to achieve the desired results. The desire to change the present product market mix portfolio is handled in this normative framework by specification of the desired product or market areas as special decision criteria in decision IIb, step 4. The growth vector areas of diversification and product development were identified in table 4 as potential special decision criteria to reflect just such a potential concern.

Identification of desired product or market areas were included as special decision criteria of step 4 rather than as part of other steps to reflect the fact that they wil change more rapidly than other decision criteria. Hence they are more compatible with the shorter-run special decision criteria than with other more permanent decision criteria.

The concept of an R&D product portfolio itself was rejected. The concept of a group of products under development at the same time meeting certain group conditions may be of aid in judging the efficiency of the R&D function as a whole or the R&D managers. By concerning itself with the efficiency of the R&D function, the portfolio concept defeats the very concept of a decision process flow over the entire new product development process. Use of such a R&D portfolio concept could mean that decisions are made to benefit the R&D division rather than the firm as a whole. It should be noted, however, that R&D capacity and capability is taken into account in the investment review of decision IIb, step 4. This places these concerns, often included as part of the R&D portfolio concept, in a cost role, and gives them adequate weight in the decision-making process without allowing the potential for R&D objectives to replace new product objectives for the firm as a whole.

Treating a decision system as an integrated portfolio of decisions is a major objective of these normative frameworks. Thus, all decision criteria at all stages in the new product development process are part of a decision portfolio.

Finally, rejection of financial constraints on the process as a whole eliminates the need to consider a portfolio of projects within these constraints.

The end product of decision IIb. For each individual product idea the end result of decision IIb is that the product idea is considered acceptable and released to the R&D division for technical development, or it is considered unacceptable and returned to the product pool for future consideration.

If the product idea is released for technical development, it means that it is consistent with any special needs of the firm, that it has been reviewed for fit with the other activities and needs of the firm at the time technical development is to begin, and that its revised rate of return on investment is still above the minimum goal value desired.

If the product idea is returned to the product pool, it means that the product that was successful when viewed on its own merit was not satisfactory when viewed in the context of the current and desired activities of the firm. At some time in the future, however, the product idea may be satisfactory in the context of the time needs of the firm, and should be retained until that time.

Decision II—Conclusion

The goal of decision II has been to present a logical, consistent decision-making system to select products for development that offer the potential for successful introduction into the marketplace.

Igor Ansoff has suggested requirements and backgrounds for such a new method of decision making.[36] A new method must: (1) include the steps of perception of need, formulation of courses of action, evaluation of alternatives, and choice of an alternative as a generalized problem solving sequence, (2) be able to handle allocation of resources between opportunities in hand and future opportunities under conditions of partial ignorance, (3) evaluate joint effects (synergy) resulting from the addition of new products to the firm, (4) single out opportunities with outstanding competitive advantages, (5) handle a vector of potentially antagonistic objectives, and (6) evaluate the long-term potential of projects even though cash flow projections are unreliable.

Decision II fulfills all of Ansoff's requirements. The formulation of actions, evaluation of alternatives, and choice among alternatives are the heart of decisions IIa and IIb. The ability to handle future opportunities is covered by the marginal cost of capital as a minimum goal value, and by the fact that arbitrary financial constraints do not restrict the number of projects. Synergy and competitive advantage are handled directly by their effect on the investment component in the rate of return on investment calculation. Potentially antagonistic objectives are handled by the use of multiple objectives with appropriate goal values. The long-term cash flow is handled both by the use of a simulation technique and by the risk confidence interval added to it.

The basic concept of ranking projects and choosing from the top of the list is not new. Many such methods have been suggested. In terms of R&D project selection, Brandenburg has pointed out the basic problem with most suggested methods, noting that

> while the notion of the ranked list changing with time is conceptually useful, little or no information is given on the critical question of how to establish the boundaries, how to account for errors in estimating critical variables, and how to place a variety of projects with different characteristics on a common scale according to a commensurable criteria.[37]

Decisions IIa and IIb overcome these shortcomings noted by Brandenburg by recommending measurement yardsticks and appropriate goal values to establish boundaries, by a simulation method and risk confidence interval to compensate for inability to predict the future, and by the use of multiple objectives with appropriate goal values to compensate for the different characteristics desired.

Brandenburg notes in addition that the project selection decision requires answers to the questions of what mix of problems to attack, relative emphasis on different problems, trade-off between expected value and risk, past experience in relation to present project requirements, and a match between research performing capabilities and the firm's research needs.[38] It is also important to emphasize the interconnection between the R&D department and other functional areas of the firm, since the ultimate success of R&D depends upon how well the results are commercialized and how well technical results fit the financial, product market, and managerial needs of the firm.

Brandenburg also suggests that the project selection decision must deal with relationships in the environment, handle characteristics of different markets, and take into account technology, the requirements of market entry, and the maintenance of market position.

Brandenburg's questions as to trade-offs and constraints are handled by the performance objective attributes and measurement yardsticks of decision II, as is his recognition of the need for inclusion of environmental and market needs. Connection between the R&D and other functional departments is handled in this normative framework both in the generation of project ideas and in the gathering of information, as well as in the composition of the group of decision makers.

Treating decision II as a product idea selection system is thus consistent with Ansoff's requirements for a general strategic decision-making system and with Brandenburg's more specific identification for a R&D project selection decision.

Decision I

Although decision I precedes decision II in chronological order in the decision flow process, it is described after decision II to reflect the fact that it uses simplified versions of the decision II decision criteria.

Decision I involves choosing from among the large number of ideas suggested for potential development those product ideas to be formally evaluated and screened. Its purpose is to reduce the number of product ideas for business analysis, since formal business analysis is both time consuming and expensive.

Decision I Steps

Step 1. For each product idea identified, estimates of sales volume, market share, and profit at the mature stage of the product life cycle are calculated.

As identified in figure 9, the growth potential performance objective

Figure 9. Decision I Performance Objectives

ATTRIBUTES	MEASUREMENT YARDSTICKS	EXAMPLES OF GOAL VALUES[1]
PERFORMANCE OBJECTIVES		
1. Sales volume potential	Sales in units at mature stage of product life cycle (S_{mi}) (i=product i)	Minimum – 1,000,000 units (S_{min}) if $S_{mi} \geq S_{min}$, accept if $S_{mi} < S_{min}$, reject
2. Market share potential	Market share in percent at mature stage of product life cycle (MS_{mi})	Minimum – 5% (MS_{min}) if $MS_{mi} \geq MS_{min}$, accept if $MS_{mi} < MS_{min}$, reject
3. Profit potential	Actual profit at mature stage of profit life cycle (P_{mi})	Minimum – \$1,000,000 (P_{min}) if $P_{mi} \geq P_{min}$, accept if $P_{mi} < P_{min}$, reject

1. The values listed are possible examples of values for a large, multiple product manufacturing firm primarily in relatively mature product market areas. They are intended as examples of the expression technique and are *not* normative values.

attributes of decision IIa are used as the performance objective attributes of decision I. As measurement yardsticks, these attributes require estimation of sales volume, market share, and profit for the product idea at the mature stage of the product life cycle.

These attributes and yardsticks were chosen for two specific reasons. Together they provide a composite, if simplified, picture of the product potential at its mature stage. Since the desire of this entire decision system is to choose products that are retained in the firm's product line, consideration of the mature stage is a better long-run proxy than consideration of the market introduction or growth stages. In addition, these three attributes provide a simplified consideration of economic and strategic concerns.

Second, the use of only three attributes provides the simplicity desired. The values calculated can be used again at the IIa decision for the satisfactory product ideas, minimizing the work effort and cost involved. In addition, realistic methods to estimate and calculate each of the values required are readily available in the literature.

Step 2.   Goal values for each measurement yardstick are provided by the decision makers. These goal values are treated as standard, and are used as the comparison base for all product ideas.

The goal values are the same as those of the growth potential goal values in decision IIa. These goal values were chosen to ensure consistency with decision IIa.

Step 3.   The calculated value for each measurement yardstick is compared to the appropriate goal value, and a decision made to accept or reject the project as follows:

(a) If all measurement yardsticks exceed their goal values, accept the product idea.

Symbolically,

if $S_{mi} \geq S_{min}$,

$MS_{mi} \geq MS_{min}$,

$P_{mi} \geq P_{min}$,   accept the product idea

(b) If any one goal value is greater than its measurement yardstick value, reject the product idea.

The three performance attributes were chosen to present a simplified composite picture of the product idea economic and strategic considerations.

Thus it is necessary that all three measurement yardsticks exceed their respective goal values so that each of these three proxy measurements contributes towards the potential success of the product idea.

Decision I Conclusion

The end result of decision I is that each product idea is accepted and passed to the business analysis stage for more formal analysis, or rejected and removed from the new product development process.

If a product is accepted it means that estimates of sales volume, market share, and profit at the mature stage of the product life cycle have been calculated and exceed desired minimum goal values. If a product is rejected it means that at least one of these estimates did not exceed its goal value.

The performance objective attributes used in decision I are repeated as growth potential attributes in decision IIa. They are repeated in decision IIa because they are only one type of growth performance objectives in decision IIa, and their repetition is necessary to give a complete growth picture.

Decision III

Decision III, located approximately at the end of the technical development stage, is the most innovative decision in this normative framework, and, with decision II, is the most important. It involves a review of the potential project results prior to the commitment of the bulk of the total funds. Support for decision III and its approximate location has been provided by Booz, Allen and Hamilton, Collier, and Mansfield who suggest that only 15–40% of the total cost has been spent by the end of the technical development stage.[39] Hence, a decision at this approximate location allows a review of the project prior to the commitment of 60–85% of the total funds.

The basic component of decision III is a review of the special decision criteria and the return on investment formula of decision IIb and its components considering the marginal funds yet to be expended. R&D expenses and other costs incurred to date are treated as sunk costs and ignored. Decision III, however, is not as expensive or time consuming as decision IIb, since most of the necessary information is available from decision II.

A great many of the specific details of decision III, such as the use of the rate of return on investment as the measurement yardstick for profitability, the use of profitability as the performance objective, the use of a simulation technique with confidence interval as a risk surrogate, and the use of the marginal cost of capital as the minimum goal value for the rate of return on investment calculation, have already been discussed in decision II.

Decision III Steps

Step 1. Step 1 involves a specific determination of the location of decision III for the project under technical development. This is necessary since the general location of decision III at the end of the development stage is only approximate, reflecting interpolation of the results of many studies, particuarly those identified by Booz, Allen and Hamilton.[40]

The exact location determination begins with the desired market introduction date for the new product and progresses backward in the process stage model. Information gathered earlier for decision II concerning the lead time of the components of all stages after the development stage are combined into a time sequence series of activities remaining to be accomplished. These components could include the lead time to develop and fill channels of distribution, market testing, production start-up, and the lead time of necessary capital equipment, among others. (Critical path methods, for example, could be used to accomplish this on a formal basis.) By subtracting the length of the longest time series of activities from the market introduction date, a time location can be determined where the decision to proceed with development is necessary to commit the capital and expense funds required to meet the market introduction date. Subtracting from this date the time required to make the decision gives the location of the start of decision III.

It is probably not possible to assign times to future activities with a great deal of accuracy. No more accuracy is necessary for this decision location, however, than is required for any other planning. Since the funds commitment data will be based on the same activity time estimates, all that is required is that the same time data be used, to insure that decision III is made prior to the commitment of capital equipment funds and other expenses.

Step 2. Step 2 involves a review, and possible revision of the special decision criteria and the component figures in the rate of return on investment calculation adjusted for the current conditions of the firm in decision IIb, step 4. If the project under review was chosen based solely upon a special decision criterion, and the special decision criterion is no longer required by the decision makers, development should be halted at the end of technical development. This allows the technical development effort to be completed so that technical success is assured, but allows the balance of the funds that would have been spent on the project to be applied to other projects. The project on which development was halted is retained for possible use later. If the project under review was not based upon a special decision criterion, this review is not necessary.

For the rate of return on investment review, each component of investment and profit is reviewed to determine if modifications should be made to any value. Such changes could include different cost and investment figures due to additional forecasting, major internal changes in the firm, activities by competitors, and other changes in the firm's environment.

Specifically, reviews should be made of sales volume in each specific year, selling price, unit manufacturing costs, and the investment components of capital equipment, product prototype testing, market testing, and manufacturing and marketing start-up. Care must be taken to ensure that the time related components of investment such as productive capacity, technology changes, and synergy (as identified in decision IIb, fig. 7) are included in individual component review.

Having reviewed and calculated modified figures as necessary for each formula component, the revised figures are compared to the figures developed in step 4 of decision IIb. If no figures have changed, or have for all components changed in a way to increase the calculated rate of return, no additional work is necessary and development continues. If, however, any figure has changed in such a way as potentially to reduce the rate of return or increase the confidence interval about the mean rate of return, step 3 is necessary.

Step 2 involves a review of the project selection decision, decision IIb. Review of decision IIa is not appropriate here since decision IIa dealt with creating a pool of potentially successful product ideas, not selecting product ideas for development.

A frequent assumption is that since the location of decision III is normally 12 to 30 months closer to market introduction than the location of decision IIb, data about the future should be more accurate. Seldom, however, is any data available to support this assumption. Tull has suggested that data gathered as late as the market testing step of the pre-production stage is not necessarily any more accurate than estimates made in advance of development, and provides the results of a major study to support his suggestion.[41]

Decision III does not assume that there will be more accurate information available. It does assume, however, that there may be changes over the intervening time period that could affect the components of the profit and investment segments of the formula, and that it is necessary to review for potential changes even if no such changes are found.

Step 3. Step 3 requires use of the figures developed in step 2 to recalculate the rate of return on investment and a risk surrogate confidence interval using a simulation. The minimum value of the new confidence interval is then compared to the current marginal cost of capital. If the minimum value of the confidence interval is above the marginal cost of capital, development continues; if it is below the marginal cost of capital, the project is not worth additional funding and development is stopped.

The major difference between the calculations in this step and decision IIb is that only future costs are included in the investment components rather than total costs. Decision III treats all costs to date as sunk costs to be ignored, and treats the investment figure as marginal investment to complete development rather than as total investment. For most projects, if the profit remains approximately the same, the marginal investment treatment should give a larger average rate of return since, in general, the investment will be smaller.

Marginal investment is used to underscore the fact that past expenses are not relevant to decision III. By decision III the project is normally near the end of the technical development stage, and the relevant question is not whether past expenses were justified but whether the project offers enough potential return to continue with the remainder of the development process. Past costs have already been raised and expended, and if future costs are not covered by future returns, there is no purpose in throwing good money after bad.

The use of the current marginal cost of capital, rather than the marginal cost of capital of decision IIb, as the minimum rate of return on investment goal value is consistent with the use of marginal investment here, and consistent with the discussion of the use of the marginal cost of capital as the minimum goal value of decision IIb.

Decision III Conclusion

Decision III involves a review of the special decision criteria and the rate of return on investment calculation of decision IIb. As a result of this review, further development is continued on the project or development is halted. If development continues, it indicates that the product still meets the decision criteria desired. If development is halted, it indicates that the product is no longer consistent with the revised decision criteria.

Decision IV

Decision IV is a minor decision activated only if the pre-production activities (market testing, marketing start-up, manufacturing start-up, and so on) indicate any significant changes in areas that affect the profit and investment components used in decision III. If, in the subjective opinion of the decision makers, any of the component values have changed significantly, it is necessary to recalculate the rate of return on investment and compare it to the new marginal cost of capital to decide if continued development and market introduction is justified.

The profit and investment components of the rate of return on investment formula are reviewed and a new rate of return and confidence interval calculated similar to that shown in steps 2 and 3 of decision III. One major difference is that the investment figure should include capital equipment and other capital expenses even if already spent or committed if they could potentially be used for other products in the future.

As in step 3 of decision III, the minimum value of a confidence interval is calculated and compared to the current marginal cost of capital. If the confidence interval minimum value is above the current marginal cost of capital, development continues; if not, it is halted.

Thus, the major purpose of decision IV is to salvage the balance of the planned expense rather than waste money on a project that will not provide an adequate return when introduced into the marketplace.

One major difference in this review is that, while all marginal future investment is included in the recalculation, all past capital expenditures for equipment and other items that could potentially be used for other projects are included as well. Thus, the investment figure used for the formula recalculation is generally smaller than that used for decision III, and is larger than if only future investment costs were used.

This means that capital equipment and other capital expenditures that could be used on other products are not treated as sunk costs. Thus the project under consideration must provide an acceptable return on this investment as well. If the project does not provide an acceptable return, the equipment should be left idle until an acceptable product is found. (Use of this idle equipment could then become a special decision criterion of decision IIa, providing a closed loop feedback within the new product decision-making process.)

Another interpolation of Booz, Allen and Hamilton's data suggests that, at the location of decision IV, 80% of the total costs have been spent or committed, and that 10 to 24 months have elapsed since decision III.[42] Consideration of marginal future investment figures only could result in so low an investment component in the formula that the resultant large rate of return would be meaningless. Again no assumption is made that this passage of time results in more accurate data, only that there has been some change of sufficient magnitude to convince the decision makers to activate decision IV.

The location of decision IV precludes the major advantage of the review of decision III. This is due to the fact that by the time decision IV is reached, the capital equipment for production and many other costs have been incurred or have been committed. For these reasons, droping the project at the decision IV location does not offer the magnitude of cost savings as does the decision III location.

The Decision Makers

At numerous locations in the recommended normative decision-making framework a need existed for a specific individual, function, group of individuals, or group of functions to choose among alternatives in order to make a specific decision. It is necessary to identify these decision makers.

In chapters 2 and 4, the individuals or functions who make the new product decisions are identified as a major cause of the failure of products in existing decision processes. This is in large part because individuals tended to give emphasis to their own functional desires. Thus, they fail to recognize that the new product development decision requires inputs and resultant activity from a wide range of technical functions, including marketing, R&D, manufacturing, and finance. A particular criticism of existing processes is that too many decisions are made by R&D managers who make decisions based upon their own personal and technical objectives rather than upon the desires of other functional areas or of the firm as a whole.

The need for interconnection between the various functional areas of the firm has been more specifically identified by Brandenburg.[43] He notes that the ultimate success of R&D depends upon how well the results are commercialized and how well the technical results fit the product market and managerial needs of the firm. This emphasis on the fact that the success of the new product development function is judged by commercial, not technical, results argues for decision making on a broader scale than that of technical R&D management alone.

It should be noted that the operations research literature, by its use of an optimization objective function and single profit maximization function, does not call for a decision maker in the sense used here. As long as information is provided, a clerk can perform the necessary calculations and issue instructions as needed.

This investigation has demonstrated, however, that the state of the art in gathering information, in project selection, and in the handling of multiple objectives is such that optimization techniques are not appropriate. While the purpose of this normative framework is to provide as much structure to the decision processes as is possible, the state of the art is such that complete structuring is not possible. Thus, there is a definite need to identify decision makers for the unstructured decision components necessary.

The subject of organizational structures within a firm for the treatment of the entire new product development process has received considerable attention. The creation of new product departments, the creation of temporary product development teams, and methods for improving interactions among operating and staff divisions, have received the bulk of the attention. Examples of this organizational structure discussion are available in the work of Pessemier, Booz, Allen and Hamilton, and Johnson and Jones, among others.[44]

The emphasis of this investigation is on the new product development decision-making processes, not the organizational structure of the functions within the firm. Thus the normative recommendations for decision makers in this framework are applicable regardless of the new product development organizational structure used.

Discussion of the decision makers begins with an analysis of the advantages of individual versus group decision making. The types of decisions with respect to different types of decision makers are presented, followed by discussion of the recommended decision groups and their members. Finally, the decisions of each group at each of the four normative decisions are discussed.

Group versus Individual Decision Making

The concept of group decision making and its advantages over individual decision making have been widely discussed. Harrison provides a good summary.[45]

The advantages of group decision making include greater sum knowledge of information, more approaches to the problem, and the fact that participation in decision making increases general acceptance of the final choice. In addition, since communication failures are reduced, there is better comprehension of the decision and the reasons behind it.

The disadvantages of group decision making include the social pressure to conform, domination by specific individuals, a desire to win the decision, and an individual accepting the solution of another individual when the latter feels strongly about a solution and the former does not. Another disadvantage of group decisions is the lack of individual responsibility. Yet the inability to pinpoint individual responsibility in case of project failure is a small price to pay for the identified benefits of the group decision.

The major advantage of an individual decision maker is the speed with which the decision can be made and the low cost of making the decision. The major disadvantage of an individual decision maker is that the person may be too influenced by personal background and desires.

Harrison further notes that there is some consensus in the literature that group decisions tend to be more accurate than individual decisions when concerned with technical issues. Finally, Harrison notes that under certain circumstances, group decision making may be preferred to individual decision making even though superior efficiency cannot be demonstrated. This is particularly true when acceptance of the decision is important or when organizational morale is a relevant consideration.

A synergistic effect in a group of decision makers has been suggested by Hampden-Turner in the same way that product market and functional areas of the firm may have synergistic benefits.[46] On the other hand, negative synergistic effects are suggested by the old saying that a camel is a horse designed by a committee.

In the specific new product development context Johnson and Jones, and Randle, among others, discuss the advantages and disadvantages of group decision making.[47] In general their advantages of group decision making are the same as those identified by Harrison, particularly the informational inputs from various functional areas, the coordinating function, and the commitment gained to the decision by the individuals participating in it.

In summary, two major advantages of group decision making stand out. The first is the greater depth of knowledge and information available in a group than in any one individual. The second is the commitment gained to the decision by the individuals participating in it. This commitment to a decision is particularly important because if the individuals in the group are chosen correctly, conflict and friction can be minimized in the group rather than cause failures due to friction and conflict in the operating areas.

Types of Decision Activities

In general, the decision activities involved in the normative decisions fall into three activity classes. One class involves the determination of information necessary, the collection of data, and the calculation of values. The second class involves review and interpretation of the data, and actual selection of product ideas for the pool and for technical development. The third class involves determination of performance objectives, attributes, measurement yardsticks, and goal values to establish a framework within which the other two decision classes are carried out.

The type of individuals required vary for each decision class. Collecting and analyzing data requires individuals with expertise in these areas. Selecting product ideas requires individuals who are familiar with steps in the process flow and who have the technical ability to follow the product idea from stage to stage. Establishing the decision framework requires individuals who can make subjective judgments, who have the ability to look at new products from the view of the firm as a whole, and who can provide the translation from corporate objectives and strategies to a new product framework.

The Decision Groups

Since group decision making offers advantages over individual decision making, and since the decision activities fall into three distinct classes, three decision groups are recommended. The first is a new product development professional staff group to gather information and perform data calculation. The second, a project selection group, is a divisional level management group to make necessary project selection decisions. The third, the control group, is a senior management group to provide the framework and ground rules for decisions.

By using three groups, each group can concentrate on and become more expert in its type of decision activities. (Other advantages of multiple group form are discussed in the context of each group.)

The use of a number of groups to make different types of decisions, rather than one group to make all decisions, is both unique to this normative framework and a logical extension of other research. Dean, for one, has suggested that the decision makers at each stage of the new product process need not be the same.[48] He specifically suggests that the individuals who later review and evaluate the decisions should be different from the project selection decision makers.

The overall method of operation of the three decision groups in this normative framework provides the type of control suggested by Dean. The staff group is responsible for gathering information and collecting data. The staff group is reviewed by the project selection group. The control group reviews the general activities of the project selection group and exercises general control over the entire new product development function.

The control group. The new product development control group is the senior level decision-making group that bears ultimate responsibility for the total new product development function. The control group in these normative recommendations provides the framework within which the project selection and staff groups function.

If the normative recommendations for intralevel objective and strategy interaction as discussed in chapter 6 existed in detail, most of the responsibilities assigned to the control group in this section would not be necessary since the translation of objectives and strategies to the R&D new product level by the corporate planners would provide the framework for decision making. However, such translation does not exist, and the control group must assume this translation function.

Specifically, the control group must establish goal values for the attributes and measurement yardsticks recommended, set any special decision criteria desired, and resolve any product ideas removed from the normative framework. In addition the control group may add or modify performance objective attributes and measurement yardsticks. The control group should establish the decision framework and change it only as necessary.

To set the goal values, special decision criteria, and so on, the control group must use its subjective judgment. While there is no method to tell an individual how to think, a logical thought structure could involve an identification of corporate objectives and strategies, comparison of the present activities of the firm with these desires, and selection of goal values and special decision criteria to aid in closing this identified gap. Ansoff has provided a start for a detailed identification of this gap, but even if the gap can be thoroughly identified, there is no theory available to aid the control group in the next step from the gap identification to the setting of goal values and special decision criteria.[49] Again, if the intralevel objective and strategy cascade identified in chapter 6 can be developed, this subjective judgment would not be necessary.

Because of its ultimate responsibility for new product development, the control group should include the corporate vice presidents of R&D, marketing, manufacturing, and finance, and the heads of the operating divisions.[50] It should be responsible to the corporate president. The individuals at this level, in general, have greater experience and management expertise than managers at lower levels of the firm. They are generally better trained to view the necessary decisions from a total firm viewpoint rather than from a functional area viewpoint. They also deal regularly with corporate objective and strategy concerns, hence they are best qualified to translate these concerns to the new product decision-making framework because of this familiarity.

The potential for conflict does exist among individuals in the control group in setting goal values, special decision criteria, etc. The group must establish its own conflict-reducing mechanisms, such as formal votes, group consensus, compromise, etc., to gain commitment of members to the decisions. Because of the group interaction, the opportunity to present one's views, and the group decision, conflict will be much less than if one individual makes the decisions and provides them to others for execution.

The project selection group.   The new product development project selection group is responsible for creation of the pool of potentially successful projects, for choice of the specific projects for technical development, and for review of the information gathering and calculation functions of the staff. They are essentially the group responsible for decision making at the specific project selection level.

Day-to-day supervision of the progress of any individual project at any stage in the new product development process stage model is not a function of the project selection group. Control at the various stages of the model should be performed by the functional area of the firm that is carrying out that stage, that is, the R&D division at the technical development stage, the marketing sector of a specific operating division for the market testing at the pre-production stage, and so on.

The project selection group is responsible for comparing the calculated values to the goal values provided and for accepting or rejecting the project at various stages in the new product development process. It is also responsible for reviewing the activities of the professional staff group, and for providing information in technical specialties to the staff group.

The project selection group should be composed of the R&D division manager and the senior manufacturing and marketing managers in each of the operating divisions. These individuals possess both management and technical expertise. More important, however, they are the managers who will be responsible for carrying out the various stages for products under development. By allowing these managers to have an input into the decision, they become personally committed to the decision. This lessens substantially the possibility of a project failure due to lack of communication among functional areas.

As discussed in chapter 4, failure of projects due to the transfer from the R&D to operating divisions at the start of the pre-production stage is common. The major solution to this problem is this decision-making system for the total process that encompasses this interface. In addition, having both operating and R&D management on the project selection group and gaining commitment to the project further smooths transition.

The project selection group decisions are generally structured, and little subjective judgment is required. Perhaps the greatest purpose of this group is to reduce project failure by information exchange and commitment of responsible managers from the functional areas to the project. Substantial support for the concept of the project selection group as summarized here, for the individuals who should make up the group, and for the ability of such a group to overcome marketing-R&D and manufacturing-R&D interfaces are provided by Johnson and Jones, *Research Management* reports, Christopher, Disman, and Gerstenfeld, among many others.[51]

The professional staff group. The new product development staff is a small group of individuals reporting to the R&D general manager. This group is responsible for gathering information and for performing all calculations necessary for all four normative decisions. At a minimum, this new product development staff should have individuals experienced in the firm in the areas of R&D, marketing, manufacturing, and finance. The head of the staff should be an individual capable of analyzing projects from the corporate viewpoint.

The staff group, by virtue of its trained members, has the technical expertise to gather necessary information and perform required calculations in a sophisticated manner. While it may identify and gather information itself, its usual source is other functional areas of the firm. Information on new markets, competition, sales desired, etc. can be gathered from the corporate and operating division market research staffs. In fact, these groups may even collect specific data, such as estimated sales for a product idea, for the new product staff. Equivalent type data could also be gathered from the appropriate manufacturing and finance staffs.

Management theories of authority and responsibility suggest that since the staff group does not have the responsibility for carrying out the required decisions, they should not have the authority to make the decisions. Care must be taken to ensure that the staff group does not assume the authority of the project selection or control groups, either by their own forceful action or by abdication of authority by either of the other groups.

Support for the activities of such a group has been provided by Johnson and Jones, Wilson, and Randle, among others.[52]

The Decision Activities at Each Normative Decision

Decision I

At decision I, the control group establishes the goal values for the sales volume, market share, and profit attributes. The staff gathers the required information from the marketplace or the appropriate operating division for each measurement yardstick for each product idea, and calculates the measurement yardstick value. The project selection group compares the calculated values to the goal values, and, if all three values exceed their goal values, passes the product idea to the business analysis stage.

Decision IIa

Prior to the analysis of any specific project, the control group determines the goal values for each measurement yardstick identified for decision IIa in table 3, and provides the goal values required to the project selection group.

The project selection group compares the measurement yardstick calculations to the goal values (step 5 of decision IIa), and either accepts or rejects the placement of the product idea into the pool of potentially successful projects. In addition, the project selection group is responsible for determining by subjective judgment exceptional projects to be removed from the normative framework and passed to the control group for decisions (step 6 of decision IIa).

If any changes to the normative recommendations of decision IIa are desired, they should be provided by the control group to the project selection and staff groups in advance of decision IIa. Such changes could include different descriptive attributes of the performance objectives, additional measurement yardsticks, and some percentage of acceptable growth and stability measurement yardsticks in place of the majority for product idea acceptance. In addition, changes in recommended goal values, such as .95 as the range of the confidence interval and the marginal cost of capital as the minimum rate of return on investment goal value, should be provided by the control group if they are desired.

Decision IIb

Prior to the analysis of any specific project, the control group must approve the time related components of decision IIb, step 4, suggested by the staff. These time related components, once approved, should be changed infrequently. In addition, the control group must identify any special decision criteria desired. If special criteria are added as decision IIb, step 2, they should be reviewed at regular intervals (say every six months) by the control group to determine if they are still necessary. When special decision criteria are identified, they should be specified as descriptive performance objective attributes, measurement yardsticks, and goal values.

The recalculation of the rate of return on investment formula and confidence interval of step 4 of decision IIb is performed by the staff. Although no subjective opinions are required, the project selection group should review the calculations and approve the product idea for development or return it to the product pool.

If the use of constraints on the total new product development process is necessary (step 5a, decision IIb), the constraints should be provided by the control group, with the project selection group approving projects consistent with the constraints.

Decision III

After a project has begun technical development, the location of decision III is calculated by the new product development staff. When the decision III location has been reached, the staff reviews the current information on the product under development and compares the data used to that of step 4 of decision IIb. If little data has changed, and the staff head decides a rate of return recalculation is not necessary, the project selection group is so notified.

If a recalculation of the rate of return is necessary, the recalculated value and the modified data are given to the project selection group. While the decision to continue or halt development requires little subjective judgment, the decision to halt or continue development should be made by the divisional management of the project selection group rather than by the staff.

Decision IV, Pre-Production Stage

The decision to activate decision IV is made by the staff head based upon a review of available information. The project selection group identifies the capital equipment that could be used on other projects and the recalculated rate of return on investment is used by the project selection group to decide to continue or halt development. Again little subjective input is required. If the decision is to halt development, the control group should be notified so that they are aware of potentially idle capital equipment to aid them in setting special decision criteria for step 2 of decision IIb.

Of course, the halting of many projects at decision IV suggests a weakness in the decision process that the control group should identify and correct.

Conclusion

Decision maker identification is necessary because the decision system for new product development cannot be completely structured. Group rather than individual decision making was recommended because of the informational value of varied inputs, and because of the commitment to the project gained by the managers who make the decision.

Three decision-making groups are recommended. The control group is responsible for providing the framework and comparison bases within which project selection decisions are made, largely on their subjective translation of corporate objectives and strategies. The creation of a pool of potentially successful projects and the selection of specific projects for development are the functions of the project selection group. All information gathering and data calculation is performed by the staff group.

Finally, the specific decisions of each decision group at each of the four normative decisions was presented.

Summary

This chapter presents a normative framework for the selection of specific new products to be developed and added to a firm's product line.

Four normative decisions were recommended. Decision I, located at the idea generation stage, involves choosing from among the large number of product ideas suggested for potential development those project ideas to be formally evaluated at the business analysis stage. Growth potential attributes, measurement yardsticks, and goal values were recommended for a simple decision consistent with and based upon the IIa decision that follows.

Decision II, located at the business analysis stage, involves gathering and analyzing formal business analysis information, selection of performance objectives, measurement yardsticks, and goal values, creation of a pool of potentially successful products, and a selection from the pool of the specific projects to begin technical development.

Decision IIa involves selection of performance objectives, measurement yardsticks and goal values, and the creation of a pool of potentially successful products. Three performance objectives—economic, growth, and stability—are recommended. For each of these, measurement yardsticks and goal values are also recommended. As an example, the profitability attribute of the economic performance objective uses rate of return on investment as the measurement yardstick and the marginal cost of capital as the minimum goal value. If the calculated rate of return on investment exceeds the minimum goal value, the product idea passes the performance objective attribute.

To be added to the potential product pool, the calculated values for each product idea must pass all of the economic and a majority of the growth and stability performance objectives.

Discussion of decision IIa centers around reasons for specific recommendations of performance objectives, measurement yardsticks, and goal values. Emphasis is given to the concept of creating a project pool that is as time free as possible; that is, measurement calculations are used that attempt to measure the potential of a product idea without considering its fit within the firm at a specific time.

Decision IIb involves an analysis of the fit of the product idea with the other products and activities of the firm at the time development is to begin, and the selection of specific projects to begin technical development. The fit of a product with the other activities of the firm is identified by the use of the time related components of R&D capacity and capability, productive capacity, and synergy. These components modify the investment components in the rate of return on investment calculation, resulting in a different rate of return than in decision IIa. If the recalculated rate of return is above the marginal cost of capital, technical development of the product idea begins.

Discussion of decision IIb centers around the details of determining the fit of a product idea with the firm's activities and the details of recalculation of the rate of return on investment.

Decision III, generally located near the end of the technical development stage, requires a review of the rate of return on investment components of decision IIb. This is to determine if, later in the process flow model, internal conditions or conditions external to the firm have changed enough to consider halting development.

Decision III involves recalculation of the rate of return on investment using only future investment and expenses. If this calculated value exceeds the current marginal cost of capital, product development continues.

The major advantage of decision III is its location for review of the profitability performance objective attribute. Its location is selected so that a review is made prior to the commitment of funds for capital equipment. Thus, if the project is no longer worthwhile, development can be halted before the commitment of a large portion of the total project expenses.

Decision IV, at the pre-production stage, involves a review of the project if there is an indication that changing conditions could result in a rate of return on investment below the marginal cost of capital. If a recalculation of the rate of return on investment results in halting development, at least some future expenses are saved. Decision IV does not offer the advantages of decision III since by the time decision IV is activated a large portion of the total funds required for the project is already committed.

Finally, this chapter of the normative framework identifies three groups of decision makers. The professional staff group gathers information and performs all calculations. The senior management control group selects goal values for all measurement yardsticks, and identifies the subjective decision input content to provide a framework within which the projects are selected. The divisional level project selection group creates the pool of projects and selects from the pool the specific projects for development.

Discussion of the decision makers centers on the advantages of the groups recommended and the individuals who comprise the groups.

The recommendation of these decisions, their locations and contents, and the individuals who make the decisions provide a complete decision process for the new product development function of a firm.

8

Summary, Conclusions, and Uses
of the Normative Frameworks

Summary

This investigation has focused on the R&D to operations planning process in large, profit-oriented, technologically based United States firms. The R&D to operations planning process was considered as a system by developing a new product process flow stage model consisting of a series of connecting and interrelated stages: idea generation, business analysis, technical development, prototype, pre-production, and market introduction.

Idea generation involved stimulation and rough screening of potential product ideas; business analysis involved formal analysis of the potential product ideas and the choice of specific ideas to be developed. Technical development required scientific development of a product with the required properties, and prototype involved preliminary manufacturing effort to ensure that the product can be manufactured with the required properties. In general, these four stages are carried out by the firm's R&D division.

Once developed, the product is transferred to an operating division for the pre-production stage. In pre-production, marketing and manufacturing activities are conducted to prepare the product for the marketplace. Finally, in the market introduction stage the product is offered for regular sale.

In 1984, approximately 3% of the United States gross national product was spent on R&D. Yet approximately 70% of this $93 billion was spent on products that were not successfully introduced into the marketplace. This suggests opportunity for improvement in the use of funds for new product development.

This investigation began by identifying the major problems of the present management approaches to the R&D to operations planning process. Two major problems are identified. The first is the failure to place the new product development process, the R&D function, and the area of individual project selection within the framework of corporate objectives and strategies. The second is an inefficient project selection process as identified by the low rate of successful market introductions.

Prior to analyzing these problems in detail a number of assumptions were necessary to define the scope of this investigation. The major assumptions included: (1) that the objectives and strategies of the new product development function should be consistent with those of the firm as a whole, (2) that there are multiple objectives of a firm rather than a single profit maximization objective, (3) that the objectives of a firm can be used to develop frameworks without considering the methods used to arrive at the objectives, and (4) that R&D decisions should take place within the framework provided by corporate headquarters rather than by personal involvement by corporate management in individual R&D project selection.

Intralevel Objective and Strategy Interaction

Problem definition. Considerations of objectives, strategies, and interactions among them was most noticed by their omission from the R&D literature. In this book, intralevel objective and strategy interaction was investigated from the marketing, operations research, R&D management, and strategic planning viewpoints.

In general, the vast majority of marketing and product development literature has not included new product development in the framework of corporate objectives. Most of the literature seems to assume that marketing objectives are the final objectives of the organization. While a great number of specific details are available on carrying out marketing goals for new products, there is little indication of a framework or system within which the marketing of new product effort takes place.

The operations research literature assumes a profit maximization objective. There is no discussion of intralevel objective and strategy interaction since it is assumed that the R&D decision makers will function to maximize the same profit function as the corporate managers.

While the R&D management literature frequently suggests that the R&D decisions should be consistent with corporate goals, there is no general assumption among R&D managers that this should occur. In fact, the assumption often is made that development should proceed for its own sake according to the desires of the R&D managers. Many suggestions have been made for improving the intralevel objective and strategy interaction from the R&D management viewpoint. These suggestions, however, normally only suggest that corporate managers make the R&D decisions themselves, or that R&D managers make decisions based upon their own subjective opinions as to whether their decisions are consistent with corporate objectives.

Finally, the field of strategic planning has provided little insight to the problem of objective and strategy interaction. The strategic planning analysis that has been done tends to concentrate on the corporate level, and has not developed to the state where details are available to use in decision making at lower levels of the firm.

Normative recommendations. A normative framework was developed to aid in overcoming these identified intralevel objective and strategy interaction problems. This framework suggests an overall set of corporate value objectives, with subordinate subsystems of corporate performance objectives and corporate strategy. Specific corporate value objectives are recommended, including product market identification, economic concerns, desired growth, stability considerations, and public image concerns.

Corporate performance objectives for each of the five value objectives are also provided. Each performance objective is expressed in terms of a descriptive attribute, with specific measurement yardsticks provided for each attribute. When possible, quantitative measurement yardsticks are suggested. In addition, examples of goal values for the measurement yardsticks are provided, and methods suggested wherein such goal values could be determined by corporate management if alternate goal values were desired.

Desired corporate strategy, in terms of the components of growth vector, product market scope, competitive advantage, and synergy, is also presented as a subordinate subsystem of corporate value objectives. Both the performance objectives and the strategic components were cascaded downward through the growth mechanisms of diversification and product development into new product components, into internal R&D components, and then into applied R&D components.

The result of this cascade is a specific set of corporate performance objectives and corporate strategy components provided to the R&D division as the basis for R&D decisions. If the R&D management uses the measurement yardsticks and goal values provided, the decisions should automatically be consistent with the objectives and strategies of the firm as a whole.

It should be noted that this intralevel objective and strategy interaction framework is a conceptual recommendation. While much detail was provided to support the specific recommendations made, these recommendations should be viewed as a first attempt to interrelate intralevel objectives and strategies, and much additional work is needed.

Decision-Making Failure

Problem definition. In the early 1960s analysis began to show that only a small percentage of individual product ideas that entered the development process were successfully introduced into the marketplace and retained in the firm's product line. This low successful market introduction rate has continued into the 1980s. While data analysis has been scattered and frequently confined to individual firms, Booz, Allen and Hamilton have compiled a summary report suggesting that 55% of project failures could be attributed to organizational types of problems, 12% to control and follow-up problems, 9% to definition of objectives, 9% to business analysis, and the remaining 15% to many small causes.[1]

The organizational failure cause literature is concerned primarily with the interfaces among the firm's R&D, marketing, and manufacturing functions. Friction among these groups has been substantial. Many operating personnel view the R&D personnel as impractical, aloof, ivory tower scientists, while the R&D scientists feel the operating personnel do not recognize their contributions to the firm. While study has centered on determining the attributes necessary to manage engineers and scientists, little work has been done on methods to improve interface coordination. Frequent suggestions involve organization structure changes, but little practical change occurs merely because a different organization chart is issued.

An additional organizational question is the choice of individuals or functions who make the decisions at various stages in the new product development process. Suggestions have been made that coordination among different functional areas can be improved by group decision making, yet most literature suggests decisions are normally made by R&D personnel alone.

The control and follow-up literature suggests failure on the part of R&D management to ensure that products are developed with the desired properties, either because of technical or financial difficulties. Many suggestions are available for better control and follow-up, centering on detailed periodic reporting and financial budgetary controls.

Although business analysis failure causes constituted a relatively small percentage, they occurred in a large number of the firms surveyed. Two basic problems are the inaccuracies in estimates of the future, and the choice of what decision ground rules should be used in project evaluation and selection.

Given the general inability to predict the future accurately, and the uncertainty of what will occur, methods to incorporate risk and uncertainty in decision making are widespread. No accepted definition of risk exists, however, let alone theoretical conceptual frameworks that can be applied consistently.

The financial portfolio theory of risk as the variance or co-variance of a probability distribution is discussed, as are a number of alternate informal methods. Finally, simulation techniques are discussed as a method that, although not widely used in practice, offer theoretical possibilities as a measure of return to which a risk component can readily be added.[2]

Numerous failures are attributed to the decision process itself. Failure to identify the basis for decisions, inconsistent application of decision criteria, and use of oversimplified profit maximization algorithms are some of the specific areas identified.

Recognizing that profit maximization techniques may not be applicable even though they dominate the academic literature, other researchers have attempted to construct decision indices to weigh multiple objectives to provide a single number measure for project selection. Almost all of these index methods tend to be arbitrary, with little justification given for the weights assigned or the objectives used.

Few suggestions are made to aid in overcoming these business analysis and decision-making failure causes. Probably the most popular suggestion is to train the decision makers so that their subjective opinion is more consistent, and to aid them in their estimating processes.

As can be seen, the causes of individual project failure have received substantial investigation. Many varieties of methods for improvements have been suggested, although most have not been implemented.

An obvious lack in most of this failure cause literature has been the failure to investigate the new product development process as a system. Few combinations of suggestions have been tried, since most researchers tend to focus on a relatively narrow operational or organizational area. These researchers tend to assume that the solution to their particular problem area will mean a successful market introduction.

Normative recommendations. To attempt to overcome these individual project failures, normative recommendations were developed. This framework is presented in terms of individual project choices in the applied new product development process. It is further presented as a series of decisions throughout the entire new product development process flow stage model. In general, the assumptions identified for the intralevel objective and strategy interaction normative recommendations apply here. In addition, this normative framework is assumed to apply to routine new product project selection rather than to unusual projects, and assumed that R&D decision making is a quasi-analytical rather than a well-structured problem.

Four normative decisions are recommended in this framework. Decision I, at the idea generation stage, involved choice of product ideas to be formally analyzed at the business analysis stage. Decisions IIa and IIb, at the business analysis stage, involved creation of a pool of potentially successful product ideas and choice from among this pool of specific product ideas to be developed at any one time. Decisions III and IV require a review of the development of the product idea to determine if the development should continue and if capital expenditures should be made.

Decision I, at the idea generation stage, requires calculation of the growth potential performance objectives attributes of sales volume and market share, and profit for each product idea. If these calculated values exceed the recommended minimum goal values, the product idea is passed to the business analysis stage for more formal analysis.

At decision IIa, economic, growth, and stability performance objectives are identified as decision criteria for creation of a pool of potentially successful product ideas. For each of these performance objective areas, sets of descriptive attributes, measurement yardsticks, and goal values are suggested. Information about each specific idea is collected and values calculated for each of the required measurement yardsticks to compare to the goal values. If the calculated measurement yardsticks for a product idea exceeded all of the economic goal values and at least half of the growth and stability goal values, the product is added to the pool of potentially successful product ideas.

The major economic measurement yardstick is a rate of return on investment profitability attribute calculated by a simulation.[3] Risk is handled by a variance type technique by calculating a confidence interval about the mean of the rate of return simulation, and using as the product idea calculated measurement yardstick value the minimum value of this confidence interval. This minimum confidence interval value is compared to the recommended marginal cost of capital goal value, and, if it exceeded the marginal cost of capital, the product idea passed this economic measurement yardstick.

Stability performance objectives include product and market stability. Growth performance objectives are concerned with the early stages in the product life cycle, and involve desired growth rates, growth potential, and potential for expansion. For each of these performance objective attributes, specific measurement yardsticks are suggested and examples of goal values provided. Where possible, quantitative measurement yardsticks are used.

Decision IIb begins by rank ordering by rate of return on investment the product ideas in the decision IIa pool. If any special decision criteria, such as growth vector emphasis, needs of specific operating or profit centers, needs to fill productive capacity, and so on, are identified, product ideas consistent with these special decision criteria are pulled from the potential product pool and reviewed first.

Because decision IIa uses time free components to calculate the rate of return on investment, it may be necessary to recalculate for each product idea the rate of return on investment for the specific time period in which technical development will begin. Each of the specific time related components are identified (R&D capacity and capability, productive capacity, and synergy, among others), reanalyzed, and, if necessary, adjustments are made to the investment or profit figures in the rate of return on investment formula.

For example, in decision IIa the investment component did not consider the fact that necessary R&D division equipment could be in use on other projects when required for this particular product idea. Decision IIb must take this possibility into account. If it is found that required equipment is not available, additional funds must be added to the investment component in the rate of return of investment formula to purchase additional equipment or to use external facilities.

After modifying the components of the rate of return on investment formula to include all time related changes, the simultion is recalculated and a new minimum value of a confidence interval calculated. If this minimum confidence interval value is above the rate of return goal value (recommended in this normative framework as the marginal cost of capital), the product idea is released for technical development. Product ideas consistent with the special decision criteria, if any, are released first, after which other satisfactory product ideas are released.

Product ideas not satisfactory at decision IIb are returned to the product idea pool, since different time related values in the future could then make the product idea satisfactory.

Arbitrary financial constraints on the product idea selection process, such as a maximum amount of R&D or capital equipment funds, are specifically rejected in this normative framework. To improve the generality of this normative framework, it is shown how such constraints could be applied, even if they are not recommended.

Decision III, generally located near the end of the technical development stage, requires a review of decision IIb to determine if, later in the process flow model, internal conditions or conditions external to the firm have changed enough to consider halting development. Decision III involves recalculation of the rate of return on investment using only future investment and expenses. If the recalculated value exceeds the current marginal cost of capital, product development continues.

The major advantage of decision III is its location for review of the profitability performance objective attribute. Its location is selected so that a review is made prior to the commitment of funds for capital equipment. Thus, if the project is no longer worthwhile, development can be halted before the commitment of a substantial portion of the total project expenses.

Decision IV, at the pre-production stage, involves a review of the project if there is an indication that changing conditions could result in a rate of return on investment below the marginal cost of capital. If a recalculation of the rate of return on investment results in halting development, at least some future expenses are saved. Decision IV does not offer the advantages of decision III since by the time decision IV is activated a large portion of the total funds required for the project is already committed.

Finally, the normative framework identifies three groups of decision makers. The professional staff gathers information and performs all calculations. The senior management control group selects goal values for all measurement yardsticks, and identifies the subjective decision input content to provide a framework within which projects are selected. The divisional level project selection group creates the pool of projects and selects from the pool the specific projects for development. Discussion of the decision makers centers on the advantages of the groups recommended and the individuals who comprise the groups.

Conclusions

As a conceptual theoretical treatment of the R&D to operations planning process, this investigation makes a number of contributions to the R&D management, strategic planning, and systems fields. Five contributions are worth particular mention: (1) treatment of the R&D to operations planning process as a system rather than as a series of separate, disconnected decisions; (2) a comprehensive, in-depth identification of the causes of development project failure in present R&D management; and (3) treatment of the R&D to operations planning process as a quasi-analytical decision rather than as a completely structured operations research decision or as a totally unstructured judgment decision.

The major contributions, however, are in the in-depth recommendation of two normative frameworks to overcome the identified failure causes: (4) one for intralevel objective and strategy interaction, and the second (5) for applied development project selection.

Systems Treatment

Systems treatment of the R&D to operations planning process means considering as an interrelated group all of the various facets of the process. This is done by identifying a process flow model of six stages to cover the entire process, by developing interrelated activities at each of the stages, and by mapping decision locations onto the model. In addition, analysis, discussion, and normative recommendations are presented within this system framework.

While such treatment might appear obvious to individuals acquainted with systems theory, it is not the normal approach in the R&D literature. In general, the cause of a project failure is identified as a narrow, specific problem, and a narrow, specific solution proposed. For example, a solution might be proposed to an organization failure cause at the R&D to manufacturing interface. No consideration would be given to other organizational problems, other interface problems, or to alternate problem solutions. In addition, there is a tendency to generalize the solutions and to apply them to areas where they are not appropriate.

Failure Cause Identification

While Booz, Allen and Hamilton provided a summary of their consultant's experience in terms of individual project failure, there has been no attempt to analyze failure causes in terms of all of the failures together, or to develop a system that attempts to overcome all of the failure causes together.[4] Thus, the literature review in chapters 3 and 4 offers a contribution in identification of failure causes as a group, and of analysis of the problems and potential solutions in the literature for all problems combined. In addition, this structuring of the causes of project failure serves as a base for a complete decision system as presented in the normative framework.

Quasi-Analytical R&D Decisions

There is a large body of operations research literature that assumes that the R&D project selection choice is a well-structured decision in which an objective function can be identified and where the objective function and all variables and relationships can be expressed in quantitative terms. Yet the R&D management literature proves that R&D decisions are not well structured, and often suggests that given the uncertainty of the future predictions, R&D decisions can never become well structured. On the other hand, much literature assumes that decision making is an art; that R&D decisions should or must be based solely on the subjective judgment of the decision maker, and that any attempt to structure or quantify the project selection decision is doomed to failure.

This book recognizes the inapplicability of a strict operations research approach, but rejects the contention that no structuring can be done. The result in the normative frameworks is an intermediate level where some objectives, strategies, and decision rules are expressed in quantitative terms, while others of necessity remain expressed in qualitative terms. Thus the decision-making process was structured as much as possible, while recognizing that complete structuring is not possible. This intermediate type of problem structure was called "quasi-analytical" by Ansoff and "ill-structured" by Simon and Newell, and is discussed throughout the book.[5]

The Intralevel Objective and Strategy Interaction Normative Framework

This framework offers a number of theoretical contributions to the objective and strategic planning fields. Of the most value is the identification of corporate value objectives in relatively specific terms, and the identification of corporate performance objectives and corporate strategy as subordinate components of corporate value objectives interacting with corporate value objectives and with each other. A detailed identification of recommended corporate performance objectives broken down into attributes, measurement yardsticks, and goal values provides insight into a practical translation of corporate value objectives into measurement methods. In addition, this framework suggests the concept of a cascade of performance objectives and strategies downward through the firm to the new product selection level. This cascade should ensure that R&D project selection is made consistent with the objectives and strategies of the firm as a whole.

This framework attempts to provide a consistent cascade of objectives and strategies at various levels of the firm. Specific value objectives, performance objectives, and strategies are recommended at the corporate level. Mechanisms to translate these downward through the firm to the R&D level have not been developed. Until such translation mechanisms can be developed, such translations must be made based upon the subjective judgment of corporate management. Nevertheless, this framework emphasizes structuring the new product process, the R&D function, and individual project selection in the framework of corporate objectives and strategies. This is a vast improvement over treatment of R&D and corporate objectives in the current literature.

The Project Selection Normative Framework

To overcome the failure causes identified, a specific project selection normative framework was developed. Treating the planning process as a system, four decisions at various locations within the process were identified. Decisions II and III in this framework are of particular importance.

Decision II, at the business analysis stage, recognizes multiple objectives of the firm, and expresses them as economic, growth, and stability objectives. This is a substantial improvement over a single profit maximization goal, and allows expression of strategic considerations as growth and stability objectives.

The split of decision II into parts is also important. Decision IIa requires establishment of a project idea pool by comparing idea performance attributes to minimum values of multiple objective functions. These comparisons give the worth of a product idea without dependence on the conditions of the firm at the time development is to begin. The product idea stands or falls on its own merit. Decision IIb is theoretically necessary, however, because a product idea does not exist in a vacuum and it is necessary to mesh the products chosen for development with other activities of the firm. Decision IIb allows the product idea to be viewed in the context of other activities of the firm at the time when decisions for product development are made.

Of particular importance in decision II is the use of strategic objectives for decision making. Even though corporate strategy emphasizes new products and product markets, this is one of the few attempts to translate strategic decision objectives from the corporate level to use in a project selection decision system.

Decision III is located near the end of the technical development stage and allows the project to be reviewed prior to the commitment of the bulk of the total development funds. (The bulk of funds are used for capital equipment and working capital for market introduction.) If estimates or internal or external conditions have changes so that the product will no longer be satisfactory in the marketplace, development can be halted resulting in substantial cost savings.

Finally, the recommendation of decision makers as a system of three groups is a major contribution. The control group establishes the framework within which project selection decisions are made. This is done by translating corporate objectives and strategies to the R&D level by their subjective judgment, and providing them to the project selection group in the form of attributes, measurement yardsticks, goal values, special decision criteria, etc.

Within these guidelines, project selection is made by a group of divisional level managers chosen to overcome organizational interface problems. Finally, a staff group is necessary to provide technical expertise to gather information and provide data to both the project selection and control groups.

Taken together, these recommendations of decision makers express the entire decision-making function as an integrated system, and provides details of how each of these three groups functions at each of the four decisions.

Summary

This book provides a number of major conceptual contributions to the R&D to operations planning process. The most important are the treatment of the process as a system, and the specific normative framework recommendations. In most of these areas this investigation is the first attempt to portray the R&D to operations planning process in such a complete, detailed manner. Additional research is needed in most areas, and it is hoped that this investigation will serve as a base to stimulate such additional research.

Uses of the Normative Frameworks

The descriptive normative frameworks developed in this investigation can serve two general purposes. First, the results provide a base for future research in intralevel objective and strategy interaction, and in applied new product development project selection. Building upon the structuring provided here, additional research in specific framework element areas can be conducted to structure the decision system further, and to aid in a better understanding of the relationship between the parts of the new product development system.

Second, the normative frameworks offer direct application for R&D managers. Detailed insights into the decision processes, into the decision criteria, and into the contents of specific decisions offer practical suggestions for present use.

Because the state of knowledge is limited in R&D project selection, there is need for experimentation on the part of R&D managers. These normative frameworks have been used in only a few organizations; there is not a great deal of evidence to prove the superiority of these frameworks over other decision methods currently used. There is support in the literature, however, for treatment of the R&D to operations planning process as a system, and substantial proof and practical examples for many of the specific elements within the decision-making process. It is also not possible to formally compare these normative frameworks to alternate frameworks because no alternate framework has been identified that attempts to treat the entire applied new product development process in the structured depth presented here.

Thus, the two uses of these descriptive frameworks are as a basis for future research and as a practical tool for R&D project selection.

Directions for Future Research

The normative recommendations of this book are a start in developing concepts and theories to treat the new product development process as a system. While this investigation provides some structuring to a relatively unstructured area, and attempts to treat as a system a process normally treated as a series of disjointed steps, it also reveals the lack of research in many specific areas of the new product development process.

One problem exists in that many of the areas for future research are not confined to the new product development area. Many areas, such as risk theory, need substantial theoretical work on a general level, with new product development application only one application area of new theories. Nevertheless, these areas as they apply to the new product development process will be discussed.

Because of the nature of the problems identified, additional research aimed at further structuring the decision processes will still be quasi-analytical. Thus it is unlikely that hypothesis testing or such formal methods will be applicable in the future.

These normative frameworks have been made available to the R&D activities of firms with whom the author has worked and is continuing to work. To date, four firms have adopted the concept of these frameworks as a system, although specific elements are different for each firm. The author is continuing field research in this area.

The areas of needed future research for these normative framework recommendations fall generally into the areas of intralevel objective and strategy interaction and of new product decision making.

Research in intralevel objective and strategy interaction. There is no theoretical reason to assume that the objectives of different firms are the same. While some objectives may occur in most firms, much work is needed to define value objectives for different classes of firms. While the five general types of value objectives recommended here should have universal applicability, details of expression of each type will vary from firm to firm and need to be investigated in more detail.

Having defined a firm's value objectives, research can be conducted to define the firm's performance objectives, develop measurement yardsticks for each attribute, and establish goal values for each measurement yardstick. This performance objective research cannot, however, be accomplished until a theoretical conceptual framework such as that presented in this normative recommendation is accepted, because corporate performance objectives must be considered in the context of other firm measures such as corporate value objectives and corporate strategy.

The normative framework for intralevel objective and strategy interaction recommends a cascading system downward through the firm from the corporate level to the R&D division for objectives and strategies. Theoretical effort is necessary on the concept of a cascading system. In addition, effort is needed to distinguish specific performance objectives for new business from those for existing business, and additional details of performance objectives for product development and diversification as distinct from those for market penetration and market development are needed. Emphasis must also be given to research on the difference between internal and external R&D, and to the ability to distinguish between the objectives for applied R&D, technical service, and basic research.

Finally, this normative framework looked at intralevel objective and strategy interaction in terms of a system assuming that the objectives and strategies at lower levels within the firm should be consistent with those of the firm as a whole. This assumption itself requires more theoretical support and development.

Research in new product development decision making.   Research is needed on the basic concept of treating the new product development process as a system. The new product development process flow stage model to express the decision system needs additional research both to develop the details of the stages and to strengthen interaction mechanisms between the stages. While the normative recommendations in terms of organizational and human behavorial considerations are a substantial improvement over the present process of interaction among stages, a more structured decision integration approach could offer even more advantages.

At the idea generation stage, decision I, more effort is needed to develop rough, simple measurement yardsticks. While the measurement yardsticks recommended in this book are adequate, more emphasis needs to be given to evaluation rather than merely stimulation of product ideas.

In decision IIa, recommendations of performance objectives, attributes, measurement yardsticks, and goal values are provided to use in creating a pool of potentially successful product ideas. Research is needed to support the premise that similar economic, growth, and stability performance objectives should apply to each firm. Research is also needed to refine the descriptive attributes of the performance objectives, and of the measurement yardsticks needed to measure the descriptive attributes. Finally, substantial research is needed both conceptually and in detailed calculations on setting the goal values to be used as comparison bases for individual product ideas.

The concept of a control decision group to select and provide these attributes, yardsticks, and goal values to a project selection group is an important recommendation. More effort is needed to determine how this control group should set these attributes, yardsticks, and goal values to ensure their consistency with corporate objectives and strategies. While the need for subjective decisions by the control group is recognized in the normative framework, every effort should be made to continue structuring these decisions as much as future improvements in theory and research methodology allow.

Specific financial theory research also is required. Major areas include theories and calculations for risk, additional theories for acceptable minimum goal values for profitability, and resolution of problems such as listing equipment in terms of book values.

For stability and growth performance objectives, more research is required on the measurement yardsticks and goal values than on the descriptive attributes. Measurement yardsticks must be specified in more detail so that quantitative details can be developed. Goal values must be developed that can be coordinated with the goal values of other measurement yardsticks.

Decision IIa assumes multiple objectives and uses rate of return on investment as only one of the objectives. Decision IIb assumes that, given the product idea is satisfactory at decision IIa, the final decision for technical development should be based upon the profitability objective of rate of return on investment. While this concept is consistent with both the recognition of multiple objectives and the need for a profit in the long run, thought must be given to the possibility of other decision criteria at decision IIb.

The normative recommendations of decision IIb add a special decision criteria classification so that temporary needs of the firm can receive priority if deemed necessary by the control group. Additional work is necessary to refine these recommended special criteria, to identify additional special criteria, to establish a control procedure to periodically review them in light of changes in the overall conditions of the firm, and to further consider a decision portfolio concept.

Additional research is needed on the concept of recalculating the components in the rate of return formula based upon the specific time frame in which the product is to be developed. Most existing frameworks try to include these time related components in a one-step project selection decision. The advantage of the recommended two-step procedure is that decision IIa can provide a measure of the value of the product idea itself, while decision IIb can modify the decision IIa rate on return on investment to allow the technical development to be made in the context of current and expected conditions of the firm. This dual decision framework offers advantages in simplification of calculation and decision making. Research is needed to identify additional time related components (in addition to the components of R&D capacity and capability, productive capacity, and synergy, defined in these recommendations), and on identifying changes in the future that should be taken into account in formula component modification.

In decision III research is necessary to refine the location of the decision. This framework notes that the location can be determined by starting with the market introduction date and working backwards by the lead time of the capital equipment. Effort is still needed to identify the accuracy of the information required, and to ensure that the correct lead time is allowed to locate decision III as late as is possible in the process flow stage model, but still prior to the commitment of capital funds.

Three groups of decision makers were recommended. While group decision making is common, the concept of a control group providing the framework with which project selection choices can be made by a project selection group is new. Research is needed for additional theoretical support to determine the composition of the control and project selection groups, and to identify mechanisms to integrate these groups with the formal organizational structure of the R&D division, operating divisions, and corporate headquarters.

Implementation of the Normative Frameworks

In spite of the additional theoretical research needed, it would be possible to implement these frameworks as they now exist in an individual firm. The advantages gained from implementation have been emphasized throughout this book.

The degree of difficulty in implementation of any new system depends in large part upon the system currently in use. This investigation is aimed at large, profit-oriented, technologically based United States manufacturing firms that normally perform applied R&D and introduce new products. As such, implementation of these frameworks would mean replacement of a present decision process rather than creation of an entire new decision system.

Implementation of a new decision system would involve specific problems related to these normative frameworks, but general methods of implementation of planned change with a minimum amount of disruption are available in the organizational development literature and need not be discussed here.[6]

Human behavioral implementation problems. There are a number of human behavioral areas where potential problems could exist in implementing these normative frameworks.

For example, the normative frameworks assume an ability and willingness to define corporate value objectives, corporate performance objectives, and corporate strategy. Yet, as Cyert and March have suggested, there is argument that the objectives of the firm vary with the attitudes of managers within the firm. This is often expressed as a comment that a firm has no objectives, only individuals within the firm do.[7] While this may be true in some firms, this book argues that this should not be and that the owners of the firm should provide long-run objectives for management direction. Nevertheless, there may be reluctance on the part of management to accept a system that requires them to define and write down objectives and strategies, since this may limit their future courses of action.

The purpose of the normative frameworks is to structure as much as is possible new product decision making. This structuring may be resented by practicing managers who have been used to free-wheeling intuitive decision making and who may object to the restrictions proposed by these frameworks.

There may also be reluctance at the divisional level to accept treatment of the new product development process as a system. The marketing, manufacturing, and R&D managers may be reluctant to give up a portion of their decision-making authority to the decision groups recommended in these frameworks. In this context, the R&D managers surrender more of their responsibility and authority to the decision groups that do the other functional areas. They may be particularly reluctant to lower their status in the organization by this loss of power.

These frameworks require that the R&D objectives for applied product development be consistent with corporate objectives. This is not necessarily true for basic research. Where both basic and applied research is carried out in the same division, R&D management may be reluctant to accept this consistency need even for applied development. In addition, there is considerable suggestion in the literature that the engineers and scientists who manage and perform the applied development tasks may be more influenced by peer group rather than organizational control.[8] This may add to the reluctance of R&D scientists to accept corporate objectives as guidelines rather than personal or scientific objectives.

It should be noted that many of these potential human behavorial implementation problems are described as project selection failure causes in the literature reviews. Thus the frameworks were developed to minimize subjective and intuitive decision making that had been identified as causing project failures. It was recognized that many individuals would be reluctant to implement this type of system because of the loss of personal decision-making authority. Nevertheless, it is felt that the structured decisions offer enough advantages so that they should be implemented in spite of these potential problems.

The cost of the frameworks.   The normative frameworks as presented would involve costs to the firm. Determining objectives and strategies, translating them to the R&D level, determining decision criteria, gathering data, and calculating the required information all require resources. In particular, developing and staffing the decision groups require identifiable costs. Finally, the review of a great many projects at the idea generation stage (decision I), the formal two-part business analysis stage decision (decision II), and the decision reviews (decisions III and IV), all are activities involving time and effort. These, of course, are probably not added costs to the firm, since many similar activities are part of the firm's present decision system and present costs.

Ideally, a firm could estimate the cost of this system, compare it to the cost of its present system, and compare the difference in costs to the benefits expected from this system. (It is assumed that this recommended system would cost more, since it is more detailed than the systems of most firms.) In practice, the accounting systems do not normally allow a comparison of decision-making costs.

Thus, although the recommended frameworks probably require added costs, such added costs cannot be readily identified. It would be necessary to implement the system, accurately measure both the benefits and added costs, and determine subjectively if the benefits of the system were worth the added cost for a cost analysis to have any meaning.

Decision criteria implementation problems.   In general, the specific details of decision criteria and information gathering are major problems in implementing any new system. Thus, in these frameworks, the details of descriptive attributes, measurement yardsticks, and goal values could be expected to be major problems. They are not, however, because the frameworks themselves recognize that specific details may not be applicable to every firm, and assign to the control group the responsibility of selecting decision criteria appropriate to the individual firm. The control group can then, if they desire, use current decision elements in these normative frameworks that will, among other things, minimize implementation problems. This ability to change specific elements within the system of these frameworks eases many practical implementation problems.

It is not felt that the decision methodologies or the information gathering techniques will provide major implementation problems. In general, identification of necessary information, mathematical techniques, computer programs, etc. are available in the literature and to some degree generally accepted. Any one firm that wishes to implement these frameworks may of necessity have to develop the methodology and details for themselves, and hence may have start-up costs, but in general the methods are widely enough available and used so that major implementation problems are not anticipated.

Summary

Thus, the two main uses for these normative frameworks are as bases for future research and for practical R&D project selection in industry. While specific areas for theoretical research are identified, these frameworks can be implemented either as decision systems or as components in other systems without major problems.

Notes

Chapter 1

1. "R&D Scoreboard," *Business Week* (July 8, 1985):86–87.

2. "R&D Research Money," *Business Week* (January 13, 1986):125.

3. Earl L. Bailey and Roger M. Pegram, "The Marketing Executive Looks Ahead," *Experiences in Marketing Management Number 13* (New York: National Industrial Conference Board, 1967), pp. 41–42.

4. Norman R. Baker and William H. Pound, "R&D Project Selection: Where We Stand," *IEEE Transactions on Engineering Management* EM-11 (December 1964):124–34; William E. Sounder, "Analytical Effectiveness of Mathematical Models for R&D Project Selection," *Management Science* 19 (April 1973):907–23; Saul Disman, "Selection R&D Projects for Profit," *Chemical Engineering* (December 1962):87–92.

5. Jay Lorsch, *Product Innovation and Organization* (New York: Macmillan, 1964), pp. 37–51; Thomas J. Allen, "Sources of Ideas and Their Effectiveness in Parallel R&D Projects," in M.C. Yovits et al., *Research Program Effectiveness* (New York: Gordon & Breach, 1966), pp. 351–71; David Ashton, Russell Gotham, and Gordon Wills, "Conditions Favorable to Product Innovation," *Scientific Business* 2, no.1:13–28.

6. Mark E. Stern, *Marketing Planning* (New York: McGraw-Hill, 1986), pp. 153–54; Edgar Pessemier, *New Product Decisions* (New York: McGraw-Hill, 1984), pp. 36–42.

7. William E. Hill and Charles H. Granger, "Management Objectives and Bases for Evaluation," in Carl Heyel, editor, *Handbook of Industrial Research Management* (New York: Reinhold, 1968), pp. 37–39.

8. Booz, Allen & Hamilton, *Management of New Products* (New York: Booz, Allen & Hamilton, 1968), p. 6.

9. Burton V. Dean, *Evaluating, Selecting, and Controlling R&D Projects* (New York: American Management Association, 1968), p. 11.

Chapter 2

1. Robert Bowie, "The Interplay of Corporate and Research Objectives," in Cyril O'Donnell, *The Strategy of Corporate Research* (San Francisco: Chandler, 1967), p. 1.

2. Ibid.

3. Charles Granger, "The Hierarchy of Objectives," *Harvard Business Review* 42 (May-June 1964):63–74.

4. Lyndall Urwick, *Notes on the Theory of Organizations* (New York: American Management Association, 1952), p. 18.

5. Ibid., p. 19.

6. Granger, "Hierarchy of Objectives," p. 64.

7. James B. Quinn, "Budgeting for Research," in Heyel, *Handbook of Industrial Research Management*, p. 281.

8. George Steiner, *Top Management Planning* (New York: Macmillan, 1969), p. 666.

9. Otto Poensgen and Helmut Hort, "R&D Management and Financial Performance," *IEEE Transactions on Engineering Management* 30 (November 1983), pp. 212–22; Roman, *Research and Development Management*, pp. 1–15; Lewis N. Goslin, *The Product Planning System* (Homewood, IL: Irwin, 1967); Yovits, *Research Program Effectiveness* (New York: Gordon and Breach).

10. Villiers, *Research and Development Planning and Control*; Warren C. Lothrop, *Management Uses of R&D* (New York: Harper & Row, 1964).

11. Albert Rubenstein, "Setting Criteria for R&D," *Harvard Business Review* 35 (January-February 1957):95–104.

12. Bowie, "The Interplay of Corporate and Research Objectives," p. 4.

13. Poensgen and Hort, "R&D Management and Financial Performance," pp. 218–19.

14. Baker and Pound, "R&D Project Selection: Where We Stand," pp. 124–34; Sounder, "Analytical Effectiveness of Mathematical Models for R&D Project Selection," pp. 907–23; C.J. Beatie and R.D. Reader, *Quantitative Management in R&D* (London: Chapman and Hall, 1971); M.J. Centron, J. Martino, and L.L. Roepcke, "The Selection of R&D Program Content," *IEEE Transactions on Engineering Management* EM-14 (December 1967):4–13

15. H. Igor Ansoff, *Corporate Strategy* (New York: McGraw-Hill, 1965); Brandenburg, *Research and Development Project Seletion*, pp. 185–96; James Bright, *Technological Planning on the Corporate Level* (Boston: Harvard Graduate School of Business Administration, 1962); Betrand Taylor and Gordon Wills, *Long Range Planning for Marketing and Diversification* (London: Bradford University Press, 1971).

16. Booz, Allen & Hamilton, *Management of New Products*, pp. 9–10.

17. Alan A. Smith, *Technology and Your New Product*, Small Business Series #19 (Washington: United States Government Printing Office, 1956), pp. 19–20.

18. Arthur Gerstenfeld, Charles D. Turk, Raymond L. Farrow, and Ronald Spicer, "Marketing and R&D," *Research Management* 12 (1979):409–12.

19. Edwin Mansfield et al., *Research and Innovation in the Modern Corporation* (New York: Norton, 1971), pp. 98–100.

20. See for example, John E. Bujake, Jr., "Ten Myths about New Product Development," *Research Management* 15 (1972):33; Philip Marvin, "Why New Products Fail," *Machine Design* (November 23, 1961):109–11; Keith W. Bennett, "Poor Management Makes Poor R&D," *Iron Age* (August 30, 1983):32.

Chapter 3

1. Robert J. Mockler, "The Systems Approach to Business Organization and Decision Making," *California Management Review* 11 (Winter 1968):54.

2. Ibid.

3. Peter Drucker, *The Practice of Management* (New York: Harper and Row, 1954), pp. 5–11.

4. Ansoff, *Corporate Strategy*, pp. 29–64.

5. Herbert A. Simon, *Administrative Behavior* (New York: Macmillan, 1957), p. xxv.

6. Richard M. Cyert and James G. March, *A Behavorial Theory of the Firm* (Englewood Cliffs, NJ: Prentice-Hall, 1963), pp. 29–40.

7. Urwick, *Notes on the Theory of Organizations*, p. 18.

8. Ansoff, *Corporate Strategy*, pp. 5–6; Richard G. Brandenburg, *Role of Decision Sciences in Business Policy*, 1972 Northeast Conference, American Institute of Decision Sciences, May 12, 1972, pp. 3–4.

9. Norton Paley, "Corporate Objectives and Marketing Aim," *California Management Review* 11 (Winter 1968):59–64.

10. Ibid., p. 60.

11. Stern, *Marketing Planning*, pp. 61–65.

12. Goslin, *The Product Planning System*.

13. Charles H. Kline, "The Strategy of Product Policy," *Harvard Business Review* 33 (July-August 1955):91–100.

14. Moreno, *Top Management Long Range Planning*, pp. 11–15.

15. Pessemier, *New Product Decisions*, p. 41.

16. David B. Uman, *New Product Programs* (New York: American Management Association, 1969), pp. 19–51.

17. C. Merle Crawford, "Strategies for New Product Development," *Business Horizons* 15 (December 1972):49–58.

18. Aubrey Wilson, "Selecting New Products for Development," in Taylor and Wills, *Long Range Planning for Marketing and Diversification*, pp. 112–25.

19. H. Igor Ansoff and Richard G. Brandenburg, "A Program of Research in Business Planning," *Management Science* 13 (February 1967):B-222.

20. Herbert A. Simon and A. Newell, "Heuristic Problem Solving," *Operations Research* 6 (January 1958):1–10.

21. Baker and Pound, "R&D Project Selection: Where We Stand," pp. 124–34.

22. Hans-Horst Schroder, "R&D Project Evaluation and Selection Models for Development," *Socio-Economic Planning Science* 5 (1971):25–39.

23. Thomas Marschak, "Models, Rules of Thumb, and Development Decisions," in Dean, *Operations Research in Research and Development*, p. 247.

24. A.G. Lockett and A.E. Gear, "Representation and Analysis of Multi-Stage Problems in R&D," *Management Science* 19 (April 1973):947-60.

25. Ibid., p. 959.

26. Schroder, "R&D Project Evaluation."

27. C.M. Mottley and R.D. Newton, "The Selection of Projects for Industrial Research," *Operations Research* 7 (November-December 1959):740-51; Disman, "Selecting R&D Projects for Profit," pp. 87-90; S.W. Hess, "A Dynamic Programming Approach to R&D Budgeting and Project Selection," *IEEE Transactions on Engineering Management* EM-9 (December 1962):170-79; Dean, *Operations Research in R&D*; William E. Souder, "Utility and Perceived Acceptability of R&D Projection Selection Models," *Management Science* 19 (August 1973):1384-94; Lockett and Gear, "Multistage Problems in R&D"; Souder, "Analytical Effectiveness of Mathematical Models for R&D Project Selections," pp. 907-23; Robert G. Cooper, "An Empirically Derived New Product Project Selection Model," *IEEE Transactions on Engineering Management* EM-28 (August 1981):54-61; Tomislav Mandakovic and William E. Souder, "A Flexible Hierarchial Model for Project Selection and Budget Allocation," *R&D Management* 51 (January 1985):23-29.

28. Beattie and Reader, *Quantitative Management in R&D*, pp. 39-56.

29. David B. Hertz and Philip G. Carlson, "Selection, Evaluation, and Control of Research and Development Projects," in Dean, *Operations Research in R&D*, pp. 170-71.

30. Ibid., p. 173.

31. Thomas W. Jackson and Jack M. Spurlock, *Research and Development Management* (Homewood, IL: Irwin, 1966), p. 75.

32. William L. Swager, "Planned Research and Development," *Systems and Procedures* 10 (May 1959):2-7.

33. Ibid., p. 3.

34. Peter F. Drucker, "Twelve Fables of Research Management," *Harvard Business Review* 41 (January-February 1963):103-8.

35. Lauren B. Hitchcock, "Selection and Evaluation of R&D Projects," *Research Management* 6 (1963):235.

36. O'Donnell, *The Strategy of Corporate Research*, pp. 167-76.

37. Albert H. Rubenstein, "Organization and Research and Development Decision Making within the Decentralized Firm," in National Bureau of Economic Research, *The Rate and Direction of Inventive Activity* (Princeton: Princeton University Press, 1962), pp. 385-93.

38. Otto H. Poensgen and Helmut Hort, "R&D Management and Financial Performance," *IEEE Transactions on Engineering Management* EM-30 (November 1983):212-22.

39. Brandenburg, *R&D Project Selection*, pp. 185-91.

40. C. Wilson Randle, "Selecting the Research Program: A Top Management Function," *California Management Review* 2 (Winter 1960):9-15.

41. Bowie, "The Interplay of Corporate and Research Objectives," pp. 1-29.

42. W.C. Asbury, "Establishing Research Projects," in Heyel, *Handbook of Industrial Research Management*, pp. 183-205.

43. Hill and Granger, "Management Objectives and Bases for Evaluation," pp. 33–64.

44. James B. Quinn, "Long Range Planning of Industrial Research," *Harvard Business Review* 39 (July-August 1961):88–102; James B. Quinn, "Top Management Guides for Research Planning," in Bright, *Technological Planning on the Corporate Level*, pp. 169–224; James B. Quinn and Robert M. Cavanaugh, "Fundamental Research Can Be Planned," *Harvard Business Review* 42 (January-February 1964):11–124; James B. Quinn and James A. Mueller, "Transferring Research Results to Operations," *Harvard Business Review* 41 (January-February 1963):49–66.

45. Quinn and Cavanaugh, "Fundamental Research Can Be Planned," p. 115.

46. Robert L. Katz, *Cases and Concepts in Corporate Strategy* (Englewood Cliffs, NJ: Prentice-Hall, 1970); William H. Newman and James P. Logan, *Strategy, Policy, and Central Management* (Cincinnati: Southwestern Publishing, 1983); James M. Higgins and Julian W. Vincze, *Strategic Management and Organizational Policy* (Chicago: Dryden Press, 1986); Lester A. Digman, *Strategic Management* (Plano, TX: Business Publications Inc., 1986); Arthur A. Thompson, Jr. and A. J. Strickland III, *Strategy Formulation and Implementation* (Plano, TX: Business Publications Inc., 1986).

47. Alfred D. Chandler, Jr., *Strategy and Structure* (Cambridge: The M.I.T. Press, 1962), p. 13.

48. Seymour Tilles, "How to Evaluate Corporate Strategy," *Harvard Business Review* 41 (July-August 1963):111–21.

49. Quinn, "Top Management Guides for Research Planning," pp. 184–85.

50. Cannon, *Business Strategy and Policy,* pp. xxi-xxviii.

51. Ansoff, *Corporate Strategy.*

52. Ibid., pp. 25–27.

53. Arnold C. Cooper and Dan E. Schendel, "Strategy Determination in Manufacturing Firms: Concepts and Research Findings," *American Marketing Association Combined Proceedings-Series Number 33* (Spring-Fall 1971):205–9.

54. Ansoff, *Corporate Strategy,* pp. 108–12.

55. James R. Collier, *Effective Long Range Business Planning* (Englewood Cliffs, NJ: Prentice-Hall 1968), pp. 151–56.

56. Granger, "The Hierarchy of Objectives," pp. 63–74.

57. Steiner, *Top Management Planning,* pp. 658–93.

58. Ibid., p. 666.

59. Hill and Granger, "Management Objectives and Bases for Evaluation," pp. 33–37.

60. Ansoff, *Corporate Strategy,* pp. 25–27.

61. O'Donnell, *Strategy of Corporate Research,* pp. 167–70.

62. Ansoff, *Corporate Strategy*; Ansoff and Brandenburg, *Research in Business Planning*; H. Igor Ansoff, "A Quasi-Analytical Approach to the Business Strategy Problem," *Management Technology* 4 (June 1964):66–67; H. Igor Ansoff and John M. Stewart, "Strategies for a Technology Based Business," *Harvard Business Review* 45 (November-December 1967):71–83.

63. Ansoff, *Corporate Strategy*, pp. 4-5.

64. Hill and Granger, "Management Objectives and Bases for Evaluation," p. 39.

65. Ansoff, *Corporate Strategy*, pp. 44-52.

66. Ibid., pp. 22-24.

67. Ibid., pp. 49-57.

68. H. Igor Ansoff, "A Model for Diversification," *Management Science* 4 (July 1958):392-414; H. Igor Ansoff, "Strategies for Diversification," *Harvard Business Review* 35 (September-October 1957):113-24.

69. Louis V. Gerstner, Jr., "Can Strategic Planning Pay Off?" *Business Horizons* 15 (December 1972):5-16.

70. R. W. Dalzell, "Diversification," *Iron Age* (August 16, 1956):22-26.

71. Theodore A. Andersen, "Coordinating Strategic and Operational Planning," *Business Horizons* (Summer 1965):49-55.

72. F.F. Gilmore and R.G. Brandenburg, "Anatomy of Corporate Planning," *Harvard Business Review* 40 (November-December 1962):61-69.

73. Peter M. Gutmann, "Strategies for Growth," *California Management Review* (Summer 1964):31-36.

74. William F. Christopher, "Marketing Planning that Gets Things Done," *Harvard Business Review* 48 (September-October 1970):56-64.

75. Hill and Granger, "Management Objectives and Bases for Evaluation," pp. 33-64.

76. Ansoff, *Corporate Strategy*, pp. 29-43.

Chapter 4

1. Lothrop, *Management Uses of Research and Development*, p. 96.

2. Booz, Allen & Hamilton, *Management of New Products*, pp. 9-10.

3. Ibid.

4. Carl R. Gloskey, "Research on a Research Department: An Analysis of Economic Decisions on Projects," *IEEE Transactions on Engineering Management* 11 (1960):166-73.

5. Randle, "Selecting the Research Program: A Top Management Function," pp. 9-15.

6. "Optimizing the Relationship between Research and Marketing," *Research Management* 4 (1961):133-46.

7. Gerstenfeld, "Marketing and R&D," pp. 409-12.

8. Ibid., p. 410.

9. R.F. Moore, "Five Ways to Bridge the Gap between R&D and Production," *Research Management* 13 (1970):367-73.

10. "Expediting the Transition from Research to Production," *Research Management* 5 (1962):33-47.

11. Bennett, "Poor Management Makes Poor R&D," p. 52.

12. Samuel C. Johnson and Conrad Jones, "How to Organize for New Products," *Harvard Business Review* 35 (1957):49–62.

13. See for example, Quinn and Mueller, "Transferring Research Results to Operations," pp. 49–66; Gerstenfeld, "Marketing and R&D"; Moore, "Five Ways," pp. 372–73; Roman, *Research and Development Management*, pp. 81–128.

14. Booz, Allen & Hamilton, *Management of New Products.*

15. Giovanni B. Giglioni and Arthur G. Bedeian, "A Conspectus of Management and Control Theory," *Academy of Management Journal* 17 (1974):292–306.

16. Booz, Allen & Hamilton, *Management of New Products.*

17. Edwin M. Lindsay, "Financial Management of R&D," *Research Management* 14 (1971):58–66.

18. Whitman and Landau, "Project Selection in the Chemical Industry," pp. 56–61.

19. See for example, Lindsay, "Financial Management of R&D," pp. 58–66; Villers, *Research and Development Planning and Control*, pp. 35–42; Robert N. Anthony, *Management Controls in Industrial Research Organizations* (Boston: Harvard Graduate School of Business Administration, 1962).

20. Ansoff and Stewart, "Strategies for a Technology Based Business," pp. 71–72.

21. C. Wilson Randle, "Problems of R&D Management," *Harvard Business Review* 37 (1959):128–31.

22. William E. Souder, "Autonomy, Gratification, and R&D Outputs," *Management Science* 20 (1974):1147–56.

23. Booz, Allen & Hamilton, *Management of New Products,* p. 13.

24. William F. Ashley and Milton T. Austin, "Case Studies in Network Planning, Scheduling, and Controlling of Research and Development Projects," in Dean, *Operations Research in Research and Development.*

25. Asbury, "Establishing Research Projects," pp. 195–96.

26. Villers, *R&D Planning and Control,* pp. 90–104.

27. Phillip Marvin, "Projecting the Profitability of New Products," in Heyel, *Handbook of Industrial Research Management,* p. 90.

28. Moreno, *Top Management Long Range Planning,* pp. 180–84.

29. Robert M. Bowie, "Top Management Reports and Controls," in Heyel, *Handbook of Industrial Research Management,* pp. 338–71; Villers, *R&D Planning and Control,* pp. 80–96.

30. William E. Souder, "The Validity of Subjective Probability of Success Forecasts by R&D Project Managers," *IEEE Transactions on Engineering Management* EM-16 (February 1969):35–49.

31. Gloskey, "Research on a Research Department," pp. 166–73.

32. "The New Rules for R&D Accounting," *Business Week* (June 15, 1974):34–35.

33. Quinn, "Long Range Planning of Industrial Research," pp. 90–94.

34. Brandenburg, *Research and Development Project Selection,* p. 25.

35. Rubenstein, "Organization and Research and Development Decision Making within the Decentralized Firm," pp. 385–93.

36. Villers, *R&D Planning and Control,* pp. 35–42.

37. Cetron, Martino, and Roepcke, "The Selection of R&D Program Content-Survey of Quantitative Methods," pp. 4–13.

38. Brandenburg, *R&D Project Selection,* pp. 196–226.

39. A.W. Marschal and W.H. Meckling, "Predictability of Costs, Time and Success of Development," in *The Rate and Direction of Inventive Activity.*

40. Donald S. Tull, "The Relationship of Actual and Predicted Sales and Profits in New Product Introductions," *Journal of Business* 40 (1967):233–50.

41. Ibid.

42. James B. Quinn, "Budgeting for Research," in Heyel, *Handbook of Industrial Research Management,* pp. 281–321.

43. B. Jackson, "Decision Models for Evaluating R&D Projects," *Research Management* 26 (July/August 1983):16–22.

44. Edwin Mansfield and Richard Brandenburg, "The Allocation, Characteristics, and Outcome of the Firm's Research and Development Portfolio: A Case Study," *Journal of Business* 39 (1966):447–64.

45. Brandenburg, *R&D Project Selection,* pp. 173–257.

46. Pessemier, *New Product Decisions,* pp. 40–71.

47. H. Igor Ansoff, "Evaluation of Applied Research in a Business Firm," in Bright, *Technological Planning on the Corporate Level.*

48. David B. Hertz, "Risk Analysis in Capital Investment," *Harvard Business Review* 42 (January-February 1964):95–106.

49. Ibid., p. 98.

50. Seymour Tilles, "Strategies for Allocating Funds," *Harvard Business Review* 44 (January-February 1966):72–80.

51. Robert W. Mayer, "Analysis of Internal Risk in the Individual Firm," *Financial Analysts Journal* (November 1959):91.

52. Harry Markowitz, "Portfolio Selection," *Journal of Finance* 7 (March 1952):77–91.

53. Gary G. Schlarbaum, and George A. Racette, "Measuring Risk: Some Theoretical and Empirical Issues," *Journal of Business Research* 2 (July 1974):349–68.

54. Walter A. Morton, "Risk and Return: Instability of Earnings as a Measure of Risk," *Land Economics* 65 (May 1969):229–61.

55. Jon M. Joyce and Robert C. Vogel, "The Uncertainty in Risk: Is Variance Unambiguous?" *Journal of Finance* 25 (March 1970):127–34.

56. Schlarbaum and Racette, "Measuring Risk," p. 362.

57. Robert E. Machol and Eugene M. Lerner, "Risk, Ruin, and Investment Analysis," *Journal of Financial and Quantitative Analysis* 4 (1969):473–92.

58. Ibid.

59. Robert H. Litzenberger and C.V. Rao, "Portfolio Theory and Industry Cost of Capital Estimates," *Journal of Finance and Quantitative Analysis* 7 (1972):1443–60.

60. Marcus C. Bogue and Richard Roll, "Capital Budgeting of Risky Projects with Imperfect Markets for Physical Capital," *Journal of Finance* 29 (May 1974):601–16.

61. Tilles, "Strategies for Allocating Risks."

62. Mayer, "Analysis of Internal Risk," p. 91.

63. J. Fred Weston, "ROI Planning and Control," *Business Horizons* 15 (August 1972):35–42.

64. Ansoff, *Corporate Strategy,* pp. 180–86.

65. Richard S. Bower and Donald R. Lassard, "An Operational Approach to Risk Screening," *Journal of Finance* 27 (May 1973):321–37.

66. E. Eugene Carter, "What Are the Risks in Risk Analysis," *Harvard Business Review* 50 (July-August 1972):72–82.

67. Richard M. Cyert, James G. March and William H. Starbuck, "Two Experiments on Bias and Conflict in Organizational Estimation," *Management Science* 7 (April 1961):254–64.

68. Bogue and Roll, "Capital Budgeting of Risky Projects," pp. 613–14.

69. Marschak, "Models, Rules of Thumb, and Development Decisions," in Dean, *Operations Research in Research and Development,* pp. 247–51.

70. Hertz, "Risk Analysis," pp. 99–106.

71. Weston, "ROI Planning and Control," pp. 35–42; Ansoff, *Corporate Strategy,* pp. 180–86.

72. Sidney W. Hess and Harry A. Quigley, "Analysis of Risk in Investments Using Monte Carlo Techniques," *Chemical Engineering Progress Symposium Series 42: Statistics and Numerical Methods in Chemical Engineering* (New York: American Institute of Chemical Engineering, 1963):55–63; Hertz, "Risk Analysis in Capital Investment."

73. C. Carl Pegels, "A Comparison of Decision Criteria for Capital Investment Decisions," *The Engineering Economist* 13 (1968):211–20; Robert H. Baldwin, "How to Assess Investment Proposals," *Harvard Business Review* 37 (May-June 1959):98–104.

74. Ibid., p. 213.

75. Ibid.

76. Ansoff, "A Quasi-Analytical Approach to the Business Strategy Problem," pp. 69–70; Simon and Newell, "Heuristic Problem Solving," pp. 1–10.

77. Bower and Lassard, "An Operational Approach," pp. 323–24.

78. Wilbur G. Lewellen and Michael S. Long, "Simulation versus Single-Value Estimates in Capital Expenditure Analysis," *Decision Sciences* 3 (October 1972):19–33.

79. Brandenburg, *Research and Development Project Selection,* p. 25.

80. Marvin, "Projecting the Profitability of New Products," p. 90.

81. Philip A. Roussel, "Cutting Down the Guesswork in R&D," *Harvard Business Review* (September-October 1983):154.

82. Brandenburg, *Research and Development Project Selection,* p. 219.

83. Ibid., p. 55.

84. Roman, *Research and Development Management,* p. 333.

85. Beattie and Reader, *Quantitative Management in Research and Development,* p. 124.

86. Weston, "ROI Planning and Control," pp. 35-42; Ansoff, *Corporate Strategy,* pp. 180-86.

87. Hertz, "Risk Analysis," pp. 95-106.

88. Smith, *Technology and Your New Product,* pp. 33-47.

89. Tull, "The Relationship of Actual..."

90. Pessemier, *New Product Decisions;* Burt Schorr, "Many New Products Fizzle Despite Careful Planning, Publicity," in Berg and Schuchman, *Product Strategy and Management,* pp. 196-201; Uman, *New Product Programs.*

91. Pessemier, *New Product Decisions,* pp. 141-82.

92. Schorr, "Many New Products Fizzle"; Uman, *New Product Programs,* pp. 26-27, 68-76.

93. Marschak, Glennan, and Summer, *Strategy for R&D,* pp. 16-18.

94. Booz, Allen & Hamilton, *Management of New Products,* p. 10; Collier, *Effective Long Range Business Planning,* p. 13.

95. Randle, "Problems of R&D Management," pp. 128-36.

96. Dean, *Evaluating, Selecting, and Controlling R&D Projects,* pp. 10-12, 40-42; Johnson and Jones, "How to Organize for New Products."

97. Lauren B. Hitchcock, "Selection and Evaluation of R&D Projects," *Research Management* 6 (1963):259-75.

98. Dean, *Evaluating, Selecting, and Controlling.*

99. Baker and Pound, "R&D Project Selection: Where We Stand," pp. 124-34.

100. Ibid., p. 128.

101. Brandenburg, *R&D Project Selection,* p. 26.

102. Michael A. Cochran, Edmund B. Pyle III, Leon C. Greene, Harold A. Clymer, and Douglas Bender, "Investment Model for R&D Project Evaluation and Selection," *IEEE Transactions on Engineering Management* EM-18 (August 1971):89-100.

103. Robert G. Cooper, "An Empirically Derived New Product Project Selection Model," *IEEE Transactions on Engineering Management* 28 (August 1981):54-61.

104. Souder, "Utility and Perceived Acceptability of R&D Project Selection Models," pp. 1384-94.

105. Ibid., p. 1393.

106. Souder, "Analytical Effectivenes of Mathematical Models for R&D Project Selection," pp. 907-23.

107. Herbert Moskowitz, "An Experimental Investigation of Decision Making in a Simulated Research and Development Environment," *Management Science* 19 (1973):676-87.

108. Dean, *Evaluating, Selecting, and Controlling*; Wilson, "Selecting New Products for Development," pp. 113-25.

109. Souder, "Utility and Perceived Acceptability."

Chapter 5

1. Simon and Newell, "Heuristic Problem Solving," p. 7; Ansoff, "A Quasi-Analytical Approach to the Business Strategy Problem," pp. 69-70.

2. Ansoff, "A Quasi-Analytical Approach to the Business Strategy Problem," pp. 67-75.

3. Ibid., p. 74.

4. Melvin Anshen and William Guth, "Strategies for Research in Policy Formulation," *Journal of Business* 46 (October 1973):499-511.

5. Ibid., p. 499.

6. Ibid., p. 502.

7. Ansoff, "A Quasi-Analytical Approach to the Business Strategy Problem," pp. 74-76.

8. Ansoff, *Corporate Strategy*, pp. 18-22.

9. Brandenburg, *Research and Development Project Selection*, p. 77.

10. Ibid., pp. 77-82.

11. Ansoff, *Corporate Strategy*, pp. 43-60.

Chapter 6

1. Ansoff, *Corporate Strategy*, p. 23

2. Ibid., pp. 29-43.

3. Ibid.

4. Theodore Levitt, "Marketing Myopia," *Harvard Business Review* (July-August 1960):45.

5. Ansoff, *Corporate Strategy*, pp. 25-28.

6. Ibid., pp. 139-71; Katz, *Cases and Concepts in Corporate Strategy*, pp. 205-17, 268-79.

7. Ansoff, *Corporate Strategy*, pp. 25-28.

8. Ibid., pp. 29-43.

9. Simon and Newell, "Heuristic Problem Solving," pp. 1-10.

10. G.A. Smith, Jr., and C.R. Christiansen, *Policy Formulation and Administration* (Homewood, IL: Irwin, 1962), p. xvi.

11. Simon and Newell, "Heuristic Problem Solving," pp. 1-10.

12. Ansoff, "A Quasi-Analytical Approach to the Business Strategy Problem," pp. 69-70.

13. Hill and Granger, "Management Objectives and Bases for Evaluation," pp. 33-64.

14. Quinn, "Long Range Planning of Industrial Research," pp. 88–102, especially p. 91; Quinn and Mueller, "Transferring Research Results to Operations," pp. 49–66.

15. Ansoff, *Corporate Strategy*, p. 6.

Chapter 7

1. Booz, Allen & Hamilton, *Management of New Products*, p. 13.

2. Ibid., p. 10.

3. Collier, *Effective Long Range Business Planning*, pp. 152–53.

4. Mansfield, *Research and Innovation in the Modern Corporation*, pp. 118–20

5. Brandenburg, *Research and Development Project Selection*, pp. 204–6, 240–47.

6. Marschak, "Models, Rules of Thumb, and Development Decisions," pp. 250–54.

7. Tull, "The Relationship of Actual and Predicted Sales and Profits in New Product Introductions," pp. 233–50.

8. James C. Emery, *Organizational Planning and Control Systems* (New York: Macmillan, 1969), p. 117.

9. See, for example, Dean, *Evaluating, Selecting, and Controlling R&D Projects*, pp. 11–12, 23–40; Pessemier, *New Product Decisions*, pp. 39–71.

10. Simon and Newell, "Heuristic Problem Solving," pp. 1–10.

11. Ansoff, "A Quasi-Analytical Approach to the Business Strategy Problem," pp. 69–70.

12. Brandenburg, *Research and Development Project Selection*, p. 26.

13. Souder, "Utility and Perceived Acceptability of R&D Project Selection Models," p. 1393.

14. Maynard W. Shelly, II, and Glenn L. Bryan, *Human Judgments and Optimality* (New York: Wiley, 1964), pp. 32–33.

15. Ansoff, *Corporate Strategy*, pp. 39–42.

16. See, for example, Dean, *Evaluating, Selecting, and Controlling R&D*; Wilson, "Selecting New Products for Development," pp. 113–25.

17. Villers, *Research and Development Planning and Control*, pp. 35–71; Hitchcock, "Selection and Evaluation of Research and Development Projects," pp. 231–44; Philip A. Scheuble, Jr., "ROI for New Product Policy," *Harvard Business Review* 42 (November–December 1964):110–20; Weston, "ROI Planning and Control," pp. 35–42.

18. Baldwin, "How to Assess Investment Proposals," pp. 98–104; Pegels, "A Comparison of Decision Criteria for Capital Investment Decisions," pp. 212–13.

19. See, for example, Roman, *Research and Development Management*, pp. 302–30; Villers, *Research and Development Planning and Control*, pp. 35–71.

20. Hertz, "Risk Analysis in Capital Investment," pp. 95–106; Hess and Quigley, "Analysis of Risk in Investments Using Monte Carlo Techniques," pp. 55–63; Pegels, "A Comparison of Decision Criteria for Capital Investment Decisions," pp. 215–17.

21. Emery, *Organizational Planning and Control*, p. 112.

22. Ibid.

23. Bruce D. Henderson, *Cost of Capital* (Boston: Boston Consulting Group, 1972).

24. Ansoff, *Corporate Strategy*, pp. 19–54.

25. See, for example, Goslin, *The Product Planning System;* Pessemier, *New Product Decisions;* Uman, *New Product Programs*, pp. 25–51.

26. Wilson, "Selecting New Products for Development," pp. 113–20; Heyel, *Handbook of Industrial Research Management*, pp. 233–35; Christopher, "Marketing Planning that Gets Things Done," pp. 57–60.

27. Stern, *Marketing Planning*, pp. 53–55; Christopher, "Marketing Planning that Gets Things Done," pp. 57–60; Wilson, "Selecting New Products for Development," pp. 113–14.

28. Crawford, "Strategies for New Product Development," p. 57; Hitchcock, "Selection and Evaluation of R&D Projects," pp. 240–42.

29. Stern, *Marketing Planning*, pp. 54–58.

30. Heyel, *Handbook of Industrial Research Management*, pp. 233–35; Christopher, "Marketing Planning that Gets Things Done," pp. 57–59; Hitchcock, "Selection and Evaluation of R&D Projects," pp. 240–44.

31. Wilson, "Selecting New Products for Development," pp. 113–17; Heyel, *Handbook of Industrial Research Management*, pp. 233–35; Christopher, "Marketing Planning that Gets Things Done," pp. 57–59; Hitchcock, "Selection and Evaluation of R&D Projects," pp. 240–44.

32. Tilles, "Strategies for Allocating Funds," pp. 76–78.

33. Ansoff, *Corporate Strategy*, pp. 29–43; Hitchcock, "Selection and Evaluation of R&D Projects," pp. 240–42; Stern, *Marketing Planning*, pp. 54–56; Crawford, "Strategies for New Product Development," pp. 49–57.

34. Edward L. Wallace, letter, August 1, 1975.

35. Brandenburg, *Research and Development Project Selection*, p. 167.

36. Ansoff, *Corporate Strategy*, pp. 18–22.

37. Brandenburg, *Research and Development Project Selection*, p. 77.

38. Ibid., pp. 5–7.

39. Booz, Allen & Hamilton, *Management of New Products*, p. 10; Collier, *Effective Long Range Business Planning*, pp. 152–53; Mansfield, *Research and Innovation in the Modern Corporation*, pp. 118–20.

40. Booz, Allen & Hamilton, *Management of New Products*, pp. 11–18.

41. Tull, "The Relationship of Actual and Predicted Sales and Profits in New Product Introductions," pp. 233–50.

42. Booz, Allen & Hamilton, *Management of New Products*, p. 10.

43. Brandenburg, *Research and Development Project Selection*, pp. 5–7.

44. Pessemier, *New Product Decisions*, pp. 4–13; Booz, Allen & Hamilton, *Management of New Products*, pp. 20–22; Johnson and Jones, "How to Organize for New Products," pp. 49–62.

45. Frank E. Harrison, *The Managerial Decision-Making Process* (Boston: Houghton Mifflin, 1975), pp. 198–211.

46. Charles Hampden-Turner, "Synergy as the Optimization of Differentiation and Integration by the Human Personality," in Jay W. Lorsch and Paul R. Lawrence, *Studies in Organization Design* (Homewood, IL: Irwin, 1970), p. 187.

47. Johnson and Jones, "How to Organize for New Products," pp. 49–62; Randle, "Problems of R&D Management," pp. 130–35.

48. Dean, *Evaluating... R&D Projects,* pp. 10–12, 40–42.

49. Ansoff, *Corporate Strategy.*

50. See, for example, Johnson and Jones, "How to Organize for New Products," pp. 59–62; Dan Cordita, "Bringing the Laboratory Down to Earth," Fortune (January 1971):106–23; Bowie, "Top Management Reports and Controls," pp. 137–41.

51. Johnson and Jones, "How to Organize for New Products," pp. 43–62; "Expediting the Transition from Research to Production," pp. 33–47; "Optimizing the Relationship between Research and Marketing," pp. 133–46; Christopher, "Marketing Planning that Gets Things Done," pp. 60–64; Disman, "Selecting Research and Development Projects for Profits," pp. 87–92; Gerstenfeld et al., "Marketing and Research and Development," pp. 409–12.

52. Johnson and Jones, "How to Organize for New Products," pp. 49–52; Wilson, "Selecting New Products for Development," pp. 112, 123–25; Randle, "Problems of Research and Development Management," pp. 128–36.

Chapter 8

1. Booz, Allen & Hamilton, *Management of New Products,* pp. 16–22.

2. Hertz, "Risk Analysis in Capital Investment," pp. 95–106; Hess and Quigley, "Analysis of Risks in Investments Using Monte Carlo Techniques," pp. 55–63.

3. Ibid.

4. Booz, Allen & Hamilton, *Management of New Products,* pp. 3–14.

5. Ansoff, "A Quasi-Analytical Approach to the Business Strategy Problem," pp. 69–70; Simon and Newell, "Heuristic Problem Solving," pp. 1–10.

6. See, for example, Harold J. Leavitt, *New Perspectives in Organizational Research* (New York: Wiley, 1964); Gener W. Dalton, Paul R. Lawrence, and Larry E. Greiner, *Organizatinal Change and Development* (Reading, MA: Addison-Wesley, 1969); Roger Harrison, "Choosing the Depth of Organizational Intervention," *Journal of Applied Behavorial Sciences* 2 (1970):181–202; Warren Bennis, *Changing Organizations* (New York: McGraw-Hill, 1966).

7. Cyert and March, *A Behavorial Theory of the Firm,* p. 26.

8. See, for example, William Kornhauser, *Scientists in Industry* (Berkeley: University of California Press, 1962); Howard M. Vollmer and Donald L. Mills, *Professionalism* (Englewood Cliffs, NJ: Prentice-Hall, 1966).

Bibliography

Books

Ackoff, Russell L. *A Concept of Corporate Planning.* New York: Vantage Press, 1963.
_____. *Scientific Method.* New York: Wiley, 1962.
Anderson, Richard C. *Management Strategies.* New York: McGraw-Hill, 1965. 237 pp.
Andrews, Kenneth R. *The Concept of Corporate Strategy.* Homewood, IL: Irwin, 1971.
Ansoff, H. Igor. *Business Strategy.* Baltimore: Penguin Books, 1969.
_____. *Corporate Strategy.* New York: McGraw-Hill, 1965.
Anthony, Robert N. *Management Controls in Industrial Research Organizations.* Boston: Graduate School of Business Administration, Harvard University, 1962. 537 pp.
Bachman, Paul W. *Research for Profit.* New York: Ronald Press, 1969. 196 pp.
Bailey, Earl L., and Pegran, Roger M. "The Marketing Executive Looks Ahead," *Experiences in Marketing Management,* no. 13, New York: National Industrial Conference Board, 1967.
Beattie, C.J., and Reader, R.D. *Quantitative Management in Research and Development.* London: Chapman and Hall, 1971. 347 pp.
Beckhard, Richard. *Organizational Development.* Reading, MA: Addison-Wesley, 1969.
Bennis, Warren. *Changing Organizations.* New York: McGraw-Hill, 1966.
Berg, Thomas L., and Schuchman, Abe. *Product Strategy and Management.* New York: Holt, Rinehart and Winston, 1963. 610 pp.
Bonge, John W., and Coleman, Bruce P. *Concepts for Corporate Strategy.* New York: Macmillan, 1972.
Booz, Allen and Hamilton. *Management of New Products.* New York: Booz, Allen, and Hamilton, 1968.
Boston Consulting Group, The. *Perspectives on Experience.* Boston: Boston Consulting Group, 1972.
Brandenburg, Richard G. "Research and Development Project Selection." Ph.D. dissertation, Cornell University, 1964.
Bright, James R. *Technological Planning on the Corporate Level.* Boston: Graduate School of Business Administration, Harvard University, 1962. 253 pp.
Burns, Thomas, and Stalker, G.M. *The Management of Innovation.* Chicago: Quadrangle Books, 1962.
Cannon, J. Thomas. *Business Strategy and Policy.* New York: Harcourt, Brace and World, 1968.
Chandler, Alfred D., Jr. *Strategy and Structure.* Cambridge, MA: The MIT Press, 1962.
Churchman, C. West. *The Systems Approach.* New York: Dell Publishers, 1968.
Clarkson, G.P.E. *Portfolio Selection: A Simulation of Trust Investment.* Englewood Cliffs, NJ: Prentice-Hall, 1962.

Cleland, David I., and Kocaoglu, Dundar F. *Engineering Management.* New York: McGraw-Hill, 1981.

Cole, Ralph I. *Improving Effectiveness in Research and Development.* Washington, DC: Thompson, 1967. 270 pp.

Collier, James R. *Effective Long Range Business Planning.* Englewood Cliffs, NJ: Prentice-Hall, 1968. 188 pp.

Conley, Patrick. *Experience Curves as a Planning Tool.* Boston: Boston Consulting Group, 1970.

Costello, Dennis R. *New Venture Analysis.* Homewood, IL: Dow Jones-Irwin, 1985.

Cyert, Richard M., and March, James G. *A Behaviorial Theory of the Firm.* Englewood Cliffs, NJ: Prentice-Hall, 1963.

Dalton, Gene W.; Lawrence, Paul R.; and Greiner, Larry E. *Organizational Change and Development.* Homewood, IL: Irwin, 1965.

Dean, Burton V. *Evaluating, Selecting and Controlling Research and Development Projects.* New York: American Management Association, 1968.

———. *Operations Research in Research and Development.* New York: Wiley, 1963.

Digman, Lester A. *Strategic Management.* Plano, TX: Business Publications, Inc., 1986.

Drucker, Peter. *The Practice of Management.* New York: Harper and Row, 1954.

Ellis, Lynn W. *The Financial Side of Industrial Research Management.* New York: Wiley, 1984.

Emery, James C. *Organizational Planning and Control Systems.* New York: Macmillan, 1969.

Galbraith, Jay R., and Kazanjian, Robert K. *Strategy Implementation.* St. Paul: West, 1986.

Goslin, Lewis N. *The Product Planning System.* Homewood, IL: Irwin, 1967. 159 pp.

Greenwood, William T. *Business Policy.* New York: Macmillan, 1967.

Haines, Raymond M., et al. *Uncertainty in Research, Management, and New Product Development.* New York: Reinhold, 1967.

Hamberg, Daniel. *Essays on the Economics of Research and Development.* New York: Random House, 1966. 170 pp.

Harrison, E. Frank. *The Managerial Decision-Making Process.* Boston: Houghton Mifflin, 1975.

Henderson, Bruce D. *Cost of Capital.* Boston: Boston Consulting Group, 1972.

Heyel, Carl. *Handbook of Industrial Research Management.* New York: Reinhold, 1968.

Higgins, James M., and Vincze, Julian W. *Strategic Management and Organizational Policy.* Chicago: Dryden Press, 1986.

Hofer, Charles W.; Murray, Edwin A., Jr.; Charan, Ram; and Pitts, Robert A. *Strategic Management.* St. Paul: West, 1984.

Hutchinson, John G. *Management Strategy and Tactics.* New York: Holt, Rinehart and Winston, 1971.

Jackson, Thomas W., and Spurlock, Jack M. *Research and Development Management.* Homewood, IL: Irwin, 1966.

Karger, Delmar W., and Murdick, Robert G. *Managing Engineering and Research.* New York: Industrial Press, 1980.

Katz, Robert L. *Cases and Concepts in Corporate Strategy.* Englewood Cliffs, NJ: Prentice-Hall, 1970.

Kornhauser, William. *Scientists in Industry.* Berkley: University of California Press, 1962.

Learned, Edmund P.; Christensen, C. Roland; Andrews, Kenneth R.; and Guth, William D. *Business Policy.* Homewood, IL: Irwin, 1969.

Leavitt, Harold J. *New Perspectives in Organizational Research.* New York: Wiley, 1964.

Lorsch, Jay W. *Product Innovation and Organization.* New York: Macmillan, 1964.

Lorsch, Jay W., and Lawrence, Paul R. *Studies in Organization Design.* Homewood, IL: Irwin, 1970.

Lothrop, Warren C. *Management Uses of Research and Development.* New York: Harper and Row, 1964. 148 pp.

Lynden, Fremont J., and Miller, Earnest G. *Planning, Programming, Budgeting.* Chicago: Markham, 1972. 423 pp.

MacMillan, Ian C., and Jones, Patricia E. *Strategy Formulation.* St. Paul: West, 1986.

Mansfield, Edwin. *Industrial Research and Technical Innovation.* New York: Norton, 1968.

_____. *The Rate and Direction of Inventive Activity.* National Bureau of Economic Research. Princeton: Princeton University Press, 1962.

Mansfield, Edwin; Schnee, Jerome; and Wagner, Samuel. *Overruns and Errors in Estimating Development Cost, Time, and Outcome.* Arlington, VA: Ida Press, 1971.

Mansfield, Edwin; Rapaport, John; Schnee, Jerome; Wagner, Samuel; and Hamburger, Michael. *Research and Innovation in the Modern Corporation.* New York: Norton, 1971.

Marschak, Thomas; Glennan, Thomas K., Jr.; and Summers, Robert. *Strategy for Research and Development.* Berlin: Springer-Verlag, 1967. 330 pp.

Miller, David W., and Starr, Martin K. *The Structure of Human Decisions.* Englewood Cliffs, NJ: Prentice-Hall, 1967.

Miller, Earnest C. *Advanced Techniques for Strategic Planning.* No. 104. New York: American Management Association, 1971. 174 pp.

Moreno, Ignacio Garcia. *Top Management Long Range Planning.* New York: Vantage Press, 1963. 300 pp.

National Bureau of Economic Research. *The Rate and Direction of Inventive Activity.* Princeton: Princeton University Press, 1962.

Newman, William H., and Logan, James P. *Strategy, Policy, and Central Management.* Cincinnati: Southwestern Publishing, 1984.

O'Donnell, Cyril. *The Strategy of Corporate Research.* San Francisco: Chandler, 1967. 202 pp.

Orth, Charles D.; Bailey, Joseph C.; and Wolch, Francis W. *Administering Research and Development.* Homewood, IL: Irwin, 1964.

Pessemier, Edgar. *New Product Decisions.* New York: McGraw-Hill, 1966. 214 pp.

Richards, Max D. *Setting Strategic Goals and Objectives.* St. Paul: West, 1986.

Roberts, Edward B. *The Dynamics of Research and Development.* New York: Harper and Row, 1964. 352 pp.

Roman, Daniel D. *Research and Development Management.* New York: Appleton-Century Crofts, 1968. 450 pp.

Rue, Leslie W. and Holland, Phyllis G. *Strategic Management.* New York: McGraw-Hill, 1986.

Schoner, Bertam. "The Selection of Research and Development Projects." Ph.D. dissertation, Stanford University, 1965.

Seiler, Robert E. *Improving the Effectiveness of Research and Development.* New York: McGraw-Hill, 1965.

Shelly, Maynard W., II, and Bryan, Glen L. *Human Judgments and Optimality.* New York: Wiley, 1964.

Silk, Leonard S. *The Research Revolution.* New York: McGraw-Hill, 1960. 244 pp.

Simon, Herbert A. *Administrative Behavior.* New York: Macmillan, 1957.

Smith, Alan A. *Technology and Your New Product.* Small Business Series #13. Washington: United States Government Printing Office, 1956.

Smith, George Albert, Jr.; Christensen, C. Roland; Berg, Norman A.; and Salter, Malcolm S. *Policy Formulation and Administration.* Homewood, IL: Irwin, 1962.

Steiner, George A. *Managerial Long Range Planning.* New York: McGraw-Hill, 1963. 334 pp.

_____. *Top Management Planning.* London: Macmillan, 1969. 795 pp.

Steiner, George A.; Miner, John B.; and Gray, Edmund R. *Management Policy and Strategy.* New York: Macmillan, 1982.

Stern, Mark E. *Marketing Planning, A Systems Approach.* New York: McGraw-Hill, 1966. 153 pp.

Taylor, Bernard, and Wills, Gordon. *Long Range Planning for Marketing and Diversification.* London: Bradford University Press, 1971. 464 pp.

Terlechyj, N. E. *Research and Development—Its Growth and Competition.* New York: National Industrial Conference Board, 1963.

Theil, Henri. *Optimal Decision Rules for Government and Industry.* Amsterdam: North-Holland, 1961.

Thomason, G.F. *The Management of Research and Development.* London: B.T. Batsford, 1970.

Thompson, Arthur A., Jr., and Strickland, A.J., III. *Strategy Formulation and Implementation.* Plano, TX: Business Publications, Inc., 1986.

Tilles, Seymour. *Strategic Planning in the Multi-Dimensional Company.* Boston: Boston Consulting Group, 1968.

―――. *Strategy Formulation and Evaluation.* Boston: Boston Consulting Group, 1970.

Trumbull, Richard. *Research and Its Management: A Perspective and Critique.* New York: Vantage, 1984.

Uman, David B. *New Product Programs.* New York: American Management Association, 1969. 158 pp.

Urwick, Lyndall. *Notes on the Theory of Organizations.* New York: American Management Association, 1952.

Villers, Raymond. *Research and Development Planning and Control.* New York: Financial Executives Research Foundations, Inc., 1966. 185 pp.

Vollmer, Howard M., and Mills, Donald L. *Professionalism.* Englewood Cliffs, NJ: Prentice-Hall, 1966.

Vorsteeg, Joseph V., Jr. "The Selection, Periodic Review, and Post-Appraisal of Research and Development Projects in the American Industry." Ph.D. dissertation, Ohio State University, 1966.

Warren, C. Kirby. *Long Range Planning.* Englewood Cliffs, NJ: Prentice-Hall, 1966. 108 pp.

Wills, Gordon; Ashton, David; and Taylor, Bernard. *Technological Forecasting and Corporate Strategy.* New York: American Elsevier, 1969. 270 pp.

Yovits, M.C., et al. *Research Program Effectiveness.* New York: Gordon and Breach, 1966. 542 pp.

Zahon, Alan J. *Growth and Financial Strategies.* Boston: Boston Consulting Group, 1971.

Articles

Allen, Thomas J. "Sources of Ideas and Their Effectiveness in Parallel R&D Projects." *Research Program Effectiveness.* Edited by M.C. Yovits et al. New York: Gordon and Breach, 1966.

Andersen, Theodore A. "Coordinating Strategic and Operational Planning." *Financial Analysts Journal* (Summer 1965):49–55.

Anshen, Melvin, and Guth, William D. "Strategies for Research in Policy Formulation." *Journal of Business* 46, no. 4 (October 1973):500–511.

Ansoff, H. Igor. "Evaluation of Applied Research in a Business Firm." *Technological Planning on the Corporate Level.* Edited by James Bright. Boston: Harvard Graduate School of Business Administration, 1962.

―――. "A Model for Diversification." *Management Science* 4, no. 4 (July 1958):392–414.

―――. "A Quasi-Analytical Approach to the Business Strategy Problem." *Management Technology* 4, no. 1 (June 1964):67–77.

―――. "Strategies for Diversification." *Harvard Business Review* 35, no. 5 (September-October 1957):113–24.

Ansoff, H. Igor, and Brandenburg, Richard. "A Program of Research in Business Planning." *Management Science* 13, no. 6 (February 1967):B219–39.

Ansoff, H. Igor, and Stewart, John. "Strategies for a Technology Based Business." *Harvard Business Review* 45, no. 6 (November-December 1967):71–83.

Asbury, W.C. "Establishing Research Projects." *Handbook of Industrial Research Management.* Edited by Carl Heyel. New York: Reinhold, 1968.

Ashley, William F. and Austin, Milton T. "Case Studies in Network Planning, Scheduling, and Controlling of Research and Development Projects." *Operations Research in Research and Development.* Edited by Burton V. Dean. New York: Wiley, 1963.

Ashton, David; Gotham, Russell; and Wills, Gordon. "Conditions Favorable to Product Innovation." *Scientific Business* 2, no. 1:13–28.

Badawy, M. K. "Towards Better Management of Research Organizations." *Journal of the Society of Research Administrators* 8, no. 2 (Fall 1976):9–15.

Baker, Norman R., and Pound, William H. "Research and Development Project Selection: Where We Stand." *IEEE Transactions on Engineering Management,* EM 15 (December 1964):124–34.

Balachandra, R., and Raelin, J. A. "How to Decide When to Abandon a Project." *Research Management* 23, no. 4 (July 1980):24–29.

Baldwin, Robert H. "How to Assess Investment Proposals." *Harvard Business Review* 37, no. 3 (May-June 1959):98–104.

Bard, Jonathan F. "Parallel Funding of R&D Tasks with Probabilistic Outcomes." *Management Science* 31, no. 7 (July 1985):814–28.

Barry, Christopher B. "Portfolio Analysis under Uncertain Means, Variances, and Covariances." *Journal of Finance* XXIX, no. 2 (May 1974):515–26.

Barry, Christopher B., and Winkler, Robert L. "Portfolio Analysis: A Bayesian Approach." *Proceedings of the Fourth Annual Meeting of the American Institute of Decision Sciences.* November 1–4, 1972.

Becher, Selwyn W., and Whisler, Thomas L. "The Innovative Organization." *Journal of Business* 40, no. 4 (October, 1967):462–69.

Becker, Robert H. "Project Selection Checklists for Research, Product Development, Process Development." *Research Management* 23, no. 5 (September 1980):34–36.

Bedell, R. J. "Terminating R&D Projects Prematurely." *Research Management* 26, no. 4 (July 1983):32–35.

Beja, Avraham. "On Systematic and Unsystematic Components of Financial Risk." *Journal of Finance* XXVII, no. 1 (March 1972):37–45.

Bender, A. D.; Pyle, E. B.; Westlake, W.J.; and Douglas, B. "Simulation of R&D Investment Strategies." *Omega* 4, no. 1 (February 1976):67–77.

Bennett, Keith W. "Poor Management Makes Poor Research and Development." *Iron Age* (August 30, 1973):37–39.

Berg, Claus C. "Individual Decisions Concerning the Allocation of Resources for Projects with Uncertain Consequences." *Management Science* 21, no. 1 (September 1974):98–105.

Berg, Norman. "Strategic Planning in Conglomerate Companies." *Harvard Business Review* 43, no. 3 (May-June 1965):79–92.

Bernardo, J. J. "An Assignment Approach to Choosing R&D Experiments." *Decision Sciences* 8, no. 2 (April 1977):489–501.

Bhaneja, Balwant. "Criteria for Effective R&D Management within Government Science Organizations." *Journal of the Society of Research Administrators* 1, no. 3 (Winter 1980):41–46.

Bierman, Harold, Jr., and Hass, Jerome E. "Capital Budgeting under Uncertainty: A Reformulation." *Journal of Finance* XXVIII, no. 1 (March 1973):119–29.

Blanning, Robert W. "Variable Based Budgeting for R&D." *Management Science* 27, no. 5 (May 1981):547–58.

Blume, Marshall E. "On the Assessment of Risk." *Journal of Finance* XXVI, no. 1 (March 1971):1–10.

Bobis, A.H.; Cooke, T.F.; and Paden, J.H. "A Funds Allocation Method to Improve the Odds for Research Success." *Research Management* 14 (March 1971):34–49.

Bogue, Marcus C., and Roll, Richard. "Capital Budgeting of Risky Projects with Imperfect Markets for Physical Capital." *Journal of Finance* XXIX, no. 2 (May 1974):601–16.

Bower, Richard S., and Lassard, Donald R. "An Operational Approach to Risk Screening." *Journal of Finance* XXVII, no. 2 (May 1973):321–37.

Bowie, Robert. "The Interplay of Corporate and Research Objectives." *The Strategy of Corporate Research.* Edited by Cyril O'Donnell. San Francisco: Chandler, 1967.

―――. "Top Management Reports and Controls." *Handbook of Industrial Research Management.* Edited by Carl Heyel. New York: Reinhold, 1968.

Boyer, C.D., and Krayes, R.S. "Evaluating Research Progress." *Chemical Engineering Progress* 59 (March 1963):24–26.

Brandenburg, Richard G. "Characteristics of Strategic Planning." Speech given at the American Institute of Decision Sciences Annual Meeting, May 12, 1972.

―――. "Role of Decision Sciences in Business Policy." 1972 Northeast Conference, American Institute of Decision Sciences. May 12, 1972.

Breen, William J., and Lerner, Eugene M. "Corporate Financial Strategies and Market Measures of Risk and Return." *Journal of Finance* XXVIII, no. 2 (May 1973):339–51.

Brennan, M.J. "An Approach to the Valuation of Uncertain Income Streams." *Journal of Finance* XXVIII, no. 3 (June 1973):661–74.

Bujake, John E., Jr. "Ten Myths about New Product Management." *Research Management* XV, no. 1 (January 1972):33–42.

Cantrall, Edward W., Manly, Donald G., et al. "The Dual Ladder—Successes and Failures." *Research Management* 20, no. 4 (July 1977):30–33.

Carlson, Joseph M. "Needed: A Government Relations Strategy for Research Management." *Research Management* 27, no. 3 (May 1984):6–7.

Carter, E. Eugene. "What Are the Risks in Risk Analysis?" *Harvard Business Review* 50, no. 4 (July-August 1972):72–82.

Cetron, Marvin J.; Martino, Joseph; and Roepcke Lewis. "The Selection of Research and Development Program Content—Survey of Quantitative Methods." *IEEE Transactions on Engineering Management* EM-14 (March 1967):4–13.

Chen, Andrew; Jen, Frank C.; and Zionts, Stanley. "The Optimal Portfolio Revision Policy." *Journal of Business* 44, no. 1 (January 1971):51–61.

Christopher, William F. "Marketing Planning that Gets Things Done." *Harvard Business Review* 48, no. 5 (September-October, 1970):56–64.

Cochran, Michael A.; Pyle, Edmund B.; Greene, Leon C.; Clymer, Harold A.; and Bender, A. Douglas. "Investment Models for Research and Development Project Evaluation and Selection." *IEEE Transactions on Engineering Management* EM-18 (August 1971):89–100.

Cohen, Kalman J., and Cyert, Richard M. "Strategy: Formulation, Implementation, and Monitoring." *Journal of Business* 46, no. 3 (July 1973):349–67.

Collier, Donald W. "Measuring the Performance of R&D Departments." *Research Management* 20, no. 2 (March, 1977):30–34.

Conrad, Gordon R., and Plotkin, Irving H. "Risk/Return: U.S. Industry Pattern." *Harvard Business Review* 46, no. 2 (March-April 1968):90–99.

Cook, W. D. and Seiford, L. M. "R&D Project Selection in a Multidimensional Environment: A Practical Approach." *Journal of the Operational Research Society* 33, no. 5 (May 1982):397–405.

Cooper, Arnold C., and Schendel, Dan E. "Strategy Determination in Manufacturing Firms: Concepts and Research Findings." *Combined Proceedings of the American Marketing Association* Series 33 (Spring-Fall 1971):205-9.

Cooper, Martin J. "An Evaluation System for Project Selection." *Research Management* 21, no. 4 (July 1978):29-33.

Cooper, Robert B. "The Components of Risk in New Product Development." *R&D Management* 11, no. 2 (April 1981):47-54.

———. "An Empirically Derived New Product Project Selection Model." *IEEE Transactions on Engineering Management* EM-28, no. 3 (August 1981):54-61.

Corbin, Richard. "A New Structure for Developing New Products." *Advanced Management Journal* 47, no. 3 (Summer 1982):4-11.

Cord, Joel. "A Method of Allocating Funds to Investment Projects When Returns are Subject to Uncertainty." *Management Science* 10, no. 1 (January 1964):335-41.

Cordita, Dan. "Bringing the Laboratory Down to Earth." *Fortune* (January 1971):106-23.

Cozzolina, John M. "Portfolios of Risky Projects." *Decision Sciences* 5, no. 4 (October 1974):575-86.

Crawford, C. Merle. "Strategies for New Product Development." *Business Horizons* XV, no. 6 (December 1972):49-58.

Cyert, Richard M.; March, James G.; and Starbuck, William H. "Two Experiments on Bias and Conflict in Organizational Estimation." *Management Science* 7, no. 3 (April 1961):254-64.

Dalzell, R.W. "Diversification." *Iron Age* (August 16, 1956):22-26.

Dancy, Albert G. "Department of Defense Research and Development Management." *Public Administration Review* 37, no. 4 (July 1977):247-356.

Davies, George B. and Pearson, Alan W. "The Application of Some Group Problem Solving Techniques to Project Selection in Research and Development." *IEEE Transactions on Engineering Management* EM-27, no. 3 (August 1980):66-73.

Dean, Barton V., Sengupta, S.S., et al. "Research Budget and Project Selection." *IEEE Transactions on Engineering Management* EM-9 (December 1962):158-69.

Dearden, John. "The Case Against ROI Control." *Harvard Business Review* 47, no. 3 (May-June 1969):124-35.

de Carbonnel, Francois E., and Dorrance, Roy G. "Information Sources for Planning Decisions." *California Management Review* 15, no. 4 (September 1973):42-53.

Dietz, Peter O. "Components of a Measurement Model: Rate of Return, Risk, and Timing." *Journal of Finance* XXIII, no. 2 (May 1968):267-75.

Disman, Saul. "Selecting Research and Development Projects for Profit." *Chemical Engineering* (December 1962):87-92.

Dougherty, D. M.; Stephens, D. B.; and Ezell, D. E. "The Lasting Qualities of PERT: Preferences and Perceptions of R&D Project Managers." *R&D Management* 14, no. 1 (January 1984):47-56.

Drucker, Peter F. "Long Range Planning." *Management Science* 5, no. 4 (April 1959):238-43.

———. "Twelve Fables of Research Management." *Harvard Business Review* 41, no. 1 (January-February 1963):103-8.

Dunne, Edward J., Jr., and Klementowski, Lawrence J. "An Investigation of the Use of Network Techniques in Research and Development Management." *IEEE Transactions on Engineering Management* EM-29, no. 3 (August 1982):74-78.

"Expediting the Transition from Research to Production." *Research Management* V, no. 1 (Spring 1962):33-47.

Faust, Richard E. "The Impact of Economic Restraints on R&D Management." *Research Management* 25, no. 8 (November 1982):13-16.

Fisher, Lawrence, and Weil, Roman L. "Coping with the Risk of Interest-Rate Fluctuations: Returns to Bondholders from Naive and Optimal Strategies." *Journal of Business* 44, no. 4 (October 1971):408–31.

Fisk, James B. "Strategy in Industrial Research." *Research Management* VI, no. 5 (1963):325–33.

Flinn, R.A., and Turban, E. "Decision Tree Analysis for Industrial Research." *Research Management* XIII, no. 1 (1970):27–34.

Fox, G. E.; Baker, N. R.; and Bryant, J. L. "Economic Models for R&D Project Selection in the Presence of Project Interactions." *Management Science* 30, no. 7 (July 1984):890–912.

Frankfurter, George M.; Phillips, Herbert E.; and Seagle, John P. "Estimation Risk in the Portfolio Selection Model: A Comment." *Journal of Financial and Quantitative Analysis* XII, no. 1 (January 1972):1423–27.

————. "Portfolio Selection: The Effects of Uncertain Means, Variances, and Covariances." *Journal of Financial and Quantitative Analysis* XI, no. 6 (December 1971):1251–62.

French, Wendell. "Organization Development Objectives, Assumptions, and Straegies." *California Management Review* 12, no. 2 (Winter 1969):23–32.

Gear, Tony E.; Lockett, Alan G.; and Muhlemann, Alan P. "A Unified Approach to the Acquisition of Subjective Data in R&D." *IEEE Transactions on Engineering Management* EM-29, no. 1 (February 1982):11–19.

Gerstenfeld, Arthur; Turk, Charles; Farrow, Raymond; and Spicer, Ronald. "Marketing and Research and Development." *Research Management* XIV, no. 6 (November 1969):409–12

Gerstner, Louis V., Jr. "Can Strategic Planning Pay Off?" *Business Horizons* XV, no. 6 (December 1972):5–16.

Gibson, R.E. "The Strategy of Corporate Research and Development." *California Management Review* 9, no. 1 (Fall 1966):33–42.

————. "A Systems Approach to Research Management." *Research Management* V, no. 4 (Winter 1962):215–28.

Giglioni, Giovanni B., and Bedeian, Arthur G. "A Conspectus of Management Control Theory." *Academy of Management Journal* 17, no. 2 (1974):292–306.

Gilmore, Frank F., and Brandenburg, Richard G. "Anatomy of Corporate Planning." *Harvard Business Review* 40, no. 6 (November-December 1962):61–69.

Gittins, J. C. and Roberts, D. M. "RESPRO—An Interactive Procedure for Planning New Product Chemical Research." *R&D Management* 11, no. 4 (October 1981):139–48.

Glench, William F. "Business Policy Reality and Promise." *Proceedings of the Academy of Management, Thirty-Second Annual Meeting.* August 13–16, 1972:108–11.

Gloskey, Carl R. "Research on a Research Department." *IEEE Transactions on Engineering Management* EM-11 (December 1960):166–73.

Granger, Charles H. "The Hierarchy of Objectives." *Harvard Business Review* 42, no. 3 (May-June 1964):63–74.

Green, Stephen G.; Bean, Alden S.; and Snavely, B. Kay. "Idea Management in R&D as a Human Information Processing Analog." *Human Systems Management* 4, no. 2 (Autumn 1983):98–112.

Gross, Bertram M. "What Are Your Organization's Objectives?" *Human Relations* 18, no. 3 (1965):195–216.

Gupta, A. K.; Raj, S. P.; and Wilemon, D. "R&D and Marketing Managers in High Tech Companies: Are They Different?" *IEEE Transactions on Engineering Management* EM-33, no. 1 (February 1986):25–33.

Gupta, Manak C. "A Model for Optimal Resource Allocation in the Capital Budgeting Market." *Socio-Economic Planning Science* 7 (1973):139–44.

————. "The Optimal Profit Planning Decisions for New Products." *Proceedings of the Fourth Annual Meeting of the American Institute of Decision Sciences* (November 1–4, 1972):283–87.

Gutmann, Peter M. "Strategies for Growth." *California Management Review* 6, no. 4 (Summer 1964):31–36.

Hallenberg, Edward X. "Dual Advancement Ladder Provides Unique Recognition for the Scientist." *Research Management* XIII, no. 3 (May 1970):221–27.

Hampden-Turner, Charles. "Synergy as the Optimization of Differentiation and Integration by the Human Personality." *Studies in Organization Design.* Edited by Jay W. Lorsch and Paul R. Lawrence. Homewood, IL: Irwin, 1970.

Harrison, Roger. "Choosing the Depth of Organizational Intervention." *Journal of Applied Behaviorial Science* 2 (1970):181–202.

Hertz, David B. "Risk Analysis in Capital Investment." *Harvard Business Review* 42, no. 1 (January-February 1964):95–100.

Hertz, David B., and Carlson, Phillip G. "Selection, Evaluation and Control of Research and Development Projects." *Operations Research in R&D.* Edited by Burton V. Dean. New York: Wiley, 1963.

Hess, S.W. "A Dynamic Programming Approach to Research and Development Budgeting and Project Selection." *IEEE Transactions on Engineering Management* EM-9 (December 1962):170–79.

Hess, Sidney W., and Quigley, Harry A. "Analysis of Risk in Investments Using Monte Carlo Techniques." *Chemical Engineering Program Symposium Series 42: Statistics and Numerical Methods in Chemical Engineering.* New York: American Institute of Chemical Engineering, 1963:155–63.

Hill, William E., and Granger, Charles H. "Management Objectives and Bases for Evaluation." *Handbook of Industrial Research Management.* Edited by Carl Heyel. New York: Reinhold, 1968.

Hitchcock, Lauren B. "Selection and Evaluation of Research and Development Projects: Part I." *Research Management* VI, no. 3 (Fall 1963):231–44.

————. "Selection and Evaluation of Research and Development Projects: Part 2." *Research Management* VI, no. 4 (Winter 1963):259–75.

Hodge, Melville H., Jr. "Rate Your Company's Research Productivity." *Harvard Business Review* 42, no. 1 (January-February 1964):109–22.

Hollman, Charles R., and Hendrick, Hal W. "Adequacy of Group Decisions as a Function of the Decision-Making Process." *Academy of Management Journal* 15, no. 2 (June 1972):175–84.

Horesh, Reuven and Raz, Baruch. "Technological Aspects of Project Selection." *R&D Management* 12, no. 2 (July 1982):133–40.

Horovitz, Jacques. "New Perspectives on Strategic Management." *Journal of Business Strategy* 4, no. 3 (Winter 1984):19–33

Horowitz, Ira. "Evaluation of the Results of Research and Development: Where We Stand." *IEEE Transactions on Engineering Management* EM-10 (June 1963):42–51.

"How to Be Happy with Research and Development." *Forbes* (July 1, 1966):25–26.

Hull, Frank M., Hage, Jerald, and Azumi, Koya. "R&D Management Strategies: America versus Japan." *IEEE Transactions on Engineering Management* EM-32, no. 2 (May 1985):78–83.

Jackson, Byron. "Decision Methods for Evaluating R&D Projects." *Research Management* 26, no. 4 (July 1983):16–22.

————. "Decision Methods for Selecting a Portfolio of R&D Projects." *Research Management* 26, no. 5 (September 1983):21–26.

Johnson, Richard M. "Market Segmentation: A Strategic Manasgement Tool." *Journal of Marketing Research* 8 (February 1971):13–18.

Johnson, Samuel C., and Jones, Conrad. "How to Organize for New Products." *Harvard Business Review* 5, no. 3 (May-June 1957):49–62.

Jones, P.M.S. "Determining Priorities and Investment Levels in Scientific Research and Development." *Policy Sciences* 1 (1970):127–34.

Joyce, Jon M., and Vogel, Robert C. "The Uncertainty in Risk: Is Variance Unambiguous?" *Journal of Finance* XXV, no. 1 (March 1970):127–34.

Kalymon, Basil A. "Estimation Risk in the Portfolio Selection Model." *Journal of Financial and Quantitative Analysis* VI, no. 1 (January 1971):559–82.

Kay, Herbert. "Harnessing the Research and Development Monster." *Fortune* (January 1965):160–98.

Keeley, Robert H., and Westerfield, Randolph. "A Problem in Probability Distribution Techniques for Capital Budgeting." *Journal of Finance* XXVII, no. 3 (June 1972):703–9.

Keown, A. J.; Taylor, B. W., III; and Duncan, C. P. "Allocation of Research and Development Funds: A Zero-One Goal Programming Approach." *Omega* 7, no. 4 (1979):345–51.

Kline, Charles H. "The Strategy of Product Policy." *Harvard Business Review* 33, no. 4 (July-August 1955):91–100.

Larsen, F.J. "Initiating and Fulfilling Industrial Research and Development Projects." *Research and Development*. February 1961:19–23.

Lassard, Donald R., and Bowers, Richard S. "An Operational Approach to Risk Screening." *Journal of Finance* XXVIII, no. 2 (May 1973):321–37.

Levitt, Theodore. "Marketing Myopia." *Harvard Business Review* 38, no. 4 (July-August 1960):45–50.

Levy, Haim. "The Demand for Assets under Conditions of Risk." *Journal of Finance* XXVIII, no. 1 (March 1973):79–96.

Lewellen, Wilbur G., and Long, Michael S. "Simulation versus Single Value Estimates in Capital Expenditure Analysis." *Decision Sciences* 3 (October 1972):19–33.

Lindsay, Edwin M. "Financial Management of Research and Development." *Research Management* XIV, no. 4 (July 1972):58–66.

Link, A. N. and Zmud, R. W. "Additional Evidence on the R&D/Marketing Interface." *IEEE Transactions on Engineering Management* EM-33, no. 1 (February 1986):41–45.

Litschert, Robert J. "Some Characteristics of Long Range Planning: An Industry Study." *Academy of Management Journal* 11 (September 1968):315–28.

Litzenberger, Robert H. and Joy, O. M. "Target Rates of Returns and Corporate Asset and Liability Structure under Uncertainty." *Journal of Financial and Quantitative Anaysis* VII, no. 1 (January 1971):675–84.

Litzenberger, Robert H. and Rao, C. U. "Portfolio Theory and Industry Cost of Capital Estimates." *Journal of Financial and Quantitative Analysis* VII, no. 2 (March 1972):1443–60.

Lundberg, Olaf, and Richards, Max D. "A Relationship between Cognitive Style and Complex Decision Making: Implications for Business Policy." *Proceedings of the Academy of Management, Thirty-Second Annual Meeting* (August 13–16, 1972):95–98.

Lusk, Edward J. "A Normative Resource Transfer Model." *Decision Sciences* 5, no. 4 (October 1974):597–613.

Machol, Robert E., and Lerner, Eugene M. "Risk, Ruin, and Investment Analysis." *Journal of Financial and Quantitative Analysis* IV (1969):473–92.

MacQueen, James. "Optimal Policies for a Class of Search and Evaluation Problems." *Management Science* 11, no. 7 (July 1964):746–59.

Maher, P. Michael, and Rubenstein, Albert H. "Factors Affecting Adoption of a Quantitative Method for Research and Development Project Selection." *Management Science* 21, no. 10 (October 1974):119–29.

Maile, Carlton A. and Bialik, Donna M. "New Product Management." *Journal of Small Business Management* 22, no. 3 (July 1984):40–48.

Mandakovic, Tomislav, and Souder, William E. "A Flexible Hierarchial Model for Project Selection and Budget Allocation." *R&D Management* 15, no. 1 (January 1985):23–29.

Manners, George E., Jr., and Steger, Joseph A. "Behavorial Specifications of the R&D Management Role." *IEEE Transactions on Engineering Management* EM-23, no. 3 (August 1976):139–41.

_____. "The Implications of Research on the R&D Manager's Role to the Selection and Training of Scientists and Engineers for Management." *R&D Management* 9, no.2 (February 1979):85–91.

Mansfield, Edwin. "The Process of Technical Change." *Battelle Technical Review* (April 1964): 3–7.

_____. "Rates of Return from Industrial Research and Development." *American Economic Review* (May 1965):95–104.

Mansfield, Edwin, and Brandenburg, Richard. "The Allocation, Characteristics, and Outcome of the Firm's Research and Development Portfolio: A Case Study." *Journal of Business* 39, no. 4 (October 1966):447–64.

Mao, James C.T., and Helliwell, John F. "Investment Decision under Uncertainty: Theory and Practice." *Journal of Finance* XXIV, no. 2 (May 1969):323–38.

Markowitz, Harry. "Portfolio Selection." *Journal of Finance* VII (March 1952):77–91.

Marschak, Thomas. "Models, Rules of Thumb, and Development Decisions." *Operations Research in Research and Development.* Edited by Burton V. Dean. New York: Wiley, 1963.

Marschal, A.W., and Meckling, W.H. "Predictability of Costs, Time and Success of Development." *The Rate and Direction of Inventive Activity.* National Bureau of Economic Research. Princeton: Princeton University Press, 1962.

Martin, Wilfred S. "Research and Development in the 1980s: The Need for Industry-University Cooperation." *Journal of the Society of Research Administrators* 1, no. 3 (Winter 1980):13–21.

Marvin, Phillip. "Projecting the Profitability of New Products." *Handbook of Industrial Research Management.* Edited by Carl Heyel, New York: Reinhold, 1968.

_____. "Why New Products Fail." *Machine Design.* November 23, 1961:11–14.

Mayer, Robert W. "Analysis of Internal Risk in the Individual Firm." *Financial Analysts Journal* (November 1959):91–95.

Meadows, Dennis L., and Marquis, Donald G. "Accuracy of Technical Estimates in Industrial Research Planning." MIT, Cambridge, Mass. Workshop Paper No. 301–67 (November 1967).

Mehrez, A. and Sinuany-Stern, Z. "Resource Allocation to Interrelated Risky Projects Using a Multiattribute Utility Function." *Management Science* 29, no. 4 (April 1983):430–39.

Merrifield, Bruce. "Industrial Project Selection and Management." *Industrial Marketing Management* 7, no. 5 (October 1978):324–30.

_____. "Selecting Projects for Commercial Success." *Research Management* 24, no. 6 (November 1981):13–18.

Merten, Ulrich and Ryu, S. M. "What Does the R&R Function Actually Accomplish?" *Harvard Business Review* (July-August, 1983):24–29.

Minkes, A.L., and Samuels, J.M. "Allocation of Research and Development Expenditures in the Firm." *Journal of Management Studies* 3 (February 1969):62–72.

Mintzberg, Henry. "Research on Strategy Making." *Proceedings of the Academy of Management, Thirty-Second Annual Meeting* (August 13–16, 1972):90–94.

Mockler, Robert J. "The Systems Approach to Business Organization and Decision Making." *California Management Review* 11, no. 2 (Winter 1968):53–58.

Mokkelbost, Per B. "Unsystematic Risk over Time." *Journal of Financial and Quantitative Analysis* VI, no. 2 (March 1971):785–96.

Moore, R.F. "Five Ways to Bridge the Gap between Research and Development and Production." *Research Management* XIII, no. 5 (1970):367–73.

Moreno, Ignacio. "The Significance of New Products." *Product Strategy and Management.* Edited by Thomas L. Berg and Abe Schuchman. New York: Holt, Rinehart, and Winston, 1963.

Morton, Walter A. "Risk and Return: Instability of Earnings as a Measure of Risk." *Land Economics* LXV (May 1969):229–61.

Moskowitz, Herbert. "An Experimental Investigation of Decision Making in a Simulated Research and Development Environment." *Management Science* 12, no. 6 (1973):676–87.

Mottley, C.M., and Newton, R.D. "The Selection of Projects for Industrial Research." *Operations Research* 7 (1959):740–51.

Mumey, Glen A. "Earnings Probabilities and Capital Costs." *Journal of Business* 40, no. 4 (October 1967):450–61.

Muncaster, John W. "Picking New Product Opportunities." *Research Management* 24, no. 4 (July 1981):26–29.

Murdick, R.G. "The Long Range Planning Matrix." *California Management Review* 7, no. 2 (Winter 1964):35–42.

Neave, Edwin H., and Rorke, C. Harvey. "Risk, Ruin, and Investment Analysis: A Comment." *Journal of Financial and Quantitative Analysis* VIII, no. 3 (June 1973):517–26.

"New Rules for Research and Development Accounting." *Business Week* (June 15, 1974):34–35.

O'Donnell, Cyril. "Planning Objectives." *California Management Review* 6, no. 2 (Winter 1963):53–58.

O'Meara, John T., Jr. "Selecting Profitable Products." *Harvard Business Review* 39, no. 1 (January-February 1961):83–89.

"Optimizing the Relationship between Research and Marketing." *Research Management* IV, no. 2 (Summer 1961):133–46.

Paley, Norton. "Corporate Objective and Marketing Aim." *California Management Review* II, no. 2 (Winter 1968):59–64.

Pegels, C. Carl. "A Comparison of Decision Criteria for Capital Investment Decisions." *The Engineering Economist* XIII (1968):211–20.

_____. Personal letter, August 7, 1975.

Peles, Yoram. "A Note on Risk and the Theory of Asset Value." *Journal of Financial and Quantitative Analysis* VI, no. 1 (January 1971):643–47.

Perrakis, Stylianos, and Henin, Claude. "The Evaluation of Risky Investments with Random Timing of Cash Returns." *Management Science* 21, no. 1 (September 1974):79–86.

Petersen, J.W. "New Product Planning." *Product Engineer* 34 (September 1963):96–99.

Petit, Thomas A. "Systems Problems of Organizations and Business Policy." *Proceedings of the Academy of Management, Thirty-Second Annual Meeting* (August 13–16, 1972):103–7.

Poensgen, Otto H. and Hort, Helmut. "R&D Management and Financial Performance." *IEEE Transactions on Engineering Management* EM-30, no. 4 (November 1983):212–22.

Pound, William H. "Research Projection Selection: Testing a Model in the Field." *IEEE Transactions on Engineering Management* EM-11 (March 1964):16–22.

Quinn, James Brian. "Budgeting for Research." *Handbook of Industrial Research Management*. Edited by Carl Heyel. New York: Reinhold, 1968.

_____. "Long Range Planning of Industrial Research." *Harvard Business Review* 39, no. 4 (July-August 1961):88–102.

_____. "Top Management Guides for Research Planning." *Technological Planning on the Corporate Level*. Edited by James Bright. Boston: Harvard Graduate School of Business Administration, 1962.

Quinn, James B., and Cavanaugh, Robert M. "Fundamental Research Can Be Planned." *Harvard Business Review* 42, no. 1 (January-February 1964):111–24.

Quinn, James B., and Mueller, James. "Transferring Research Results to Operations." *Harvard Business Review* 41, no. 1 (January-February 1963):49–66.

"R&D and New Products." *Research Management* 15, no. 4 (July 1982):16–22.

Randle, C. Wilson. "Problems of Research and Development Management." *Harvard Business Review* 37, no. 1 (January-February 1959):128–36.

_____. "Selecting the Research Program: A Top Management Function." *California Management Review* 2, no. 2 (Winter 1960):9–15.

Rao, N. Krishna. "Equivalent Risk Class Hypothesis: An Empirical Study." *Journal of Financial and Quantitative Analysis* VII, no. 3 (June 1972):1763–71.

Ritti, R. Richard. "Dual Management—Does It Work?" *Research Management* XIV, no. 6 (November 1971):19–26.

Roberts, Edward B. "The Myths of Research Management." *Science and Technology* (August 1968):40–46.

Robichek, Alexander A., and Cohn, Richard A. "The Economic Determinants of Systematic Risk." *Journal of Finance* XXIX, no. 2 (May 1974):439–47.

Robichek, Alexander A.; Cohn, Richard A.; and Pringle, John J. "Returns on Alternate Investment Media and Implications for Portfolio Construction." *Journal of Business* 45, no. 3 (July 1972):427–43.

Rogoff, Donald. "Budgeting R&D—A Behavioral Approach." *Managerial Planning* 25, no. 2 (September 1976):4–6.

Roussel, Philip A. "Cutting Down the Guesswork in R&D." *Harvard Business Review* (September-October 1983):154–64.

Rubenstein, Albert H. "Organization and Research and Development Decision Making within the Decentralized Firm." *The Rate and Direction of Inventive Activity.* Edited by National Bureau of Economic Research. Princeton: Princeton University Press, 1962.

_____. "Setting Criteria for Research and Development." *Harvard Business Review* 35, no. 1 (January-February 1957):95–104.

Schendel, D.E., and Hatten, Kenneth J. "Business Policy or Strategic Management: A Broader View for an Emerging Discipline." *Proceedings of the Academy of Management, Thirty-Second Annual Meeting* (August 13–16, 1972):99–102.

Scheuble, Philip A., Jr. "ROI for New Product Policy." *Harvard Business Review* 42, no. 6 (November-December 1964):110–20.

Schlarbaum, Gary G., and Racette, George A. "Measuring Risk: Some Theoretical and Empirical Issues." *Journal of Business Research* 2, no. 3 (July 1974):349–68.

Schoeffler, Sidney; Buzzell, Robert D.; and Heany, Donald F. "Impact of Strategic Planning on Profit Performance." *Harvard Business Review* 52, no. 2 (March-April 1974):137–45.

Schorr, Bert. "Many New Products Fizzle Despite Careful Planning, Publicity." *Product Strategy and Management.* Edited by Thomas L. Berg and Abe Schuchman. New York: Holt, Rinehart and Winston, 1963.

Schroder, Hans-Horst. "Research and Development Project Evaluation and Selection Models for Development: A Survey of the State of the Art." *Socio-Economic Planning Science* 5 (1971):25–39.

Scott, Myrtle. "R&D Management—Some Practical Problems and Possible Solutions." *Journal of the Society of Research Administrators* 7, no. 3 (Winter 1976):27–34.

Severn, Alan K. "Investor Evaluation of Foreign and Domestic Risk." *Journal of Finance* XXIX, no. 2 (May 1974):545–50.

Shepard, Herbert A. "Patterns of Organization for Applied Research and Development." *Journal of Business* 29, no. 1 (January 1956):52–58.

_____. "The Dual Hierarchy in Research." *Research Management* 1 (1958):177–87.

Shepherd, H. "Nine Dilemmas in Industrial Research." *Administrative Science Quarterly* (December 1956):9–18.

Simon, Herbert A. "On the Concept of Organizational Goal." *Administrative Science Quarterly* (June 1964):1–22.

Simon, Herbert A., and Newell, A. "Heuristic Problem Solving." *Operations Research* 6 (January 1958):1–10.

Skinner, Wickham. "Manufacturing—The Missing Link in Corporate Strategy." *Harvard Business Review* 47, no. 3 (May-June 1969):136–46.

Smith, Lee H. "Evaluating Multiple Criteria Models for Two-Criteria Situations." *Decision Sciences* 5, no. 4 (October 1974):587–96.

Solomon, Ezra. "Measuring a Company's Cost of Capital." *Journal of Business* 28, no. 3 (October 1955):240–52.

Sounder, William E. "Analytical Effectiveness of Mathematical Models for Research and Development Selection." *Management Science* 19, no. 8 (April 1973):907–23.

_____. "Autonomy, Gratification, and Research and Development Outputs." *Management Science* 20, no. 8 (1974):1147–56.

_____. "Utility and Perceived Acceptability of Research and Development Project Selection Models." *Management Science* 19, no. 12 (August 1973):1384–94.

_____. "The Validity of Subjective Probability of Success Forecasts by Research and Development Project Managers." *IEEE Transactions on Engineering Management* EM-16 (February 1969):35–49.

Spencer, Milton H. "Uncertainty, Expectations, and Foundations of the Theory of Planning." *Academy of Management Journal* 5, no. 3 (December 1962):197–206.

Stapleton, Richard C. "Portfolio Analysis, Stock Valuation and Capital Budgeting Decision Rules for Risky Projects." *Journal of Finance* XXVI, no. 1 (March 1971):95–117.

Stineback, G. C. "Transition from Research to Production and Sales." *Research Management* VI, no. 2 (March 1965):125–35.

Swager, William L. "Planned Research and Development." *Systems and Procedures* 10, no. 2 (May 1959):2–7.

Tauber, Edward M. "The Emerging New Product Development Industry." *Business Horizons* XVI, no. 2 (April 1973):5–10.

Taylor, Bernard W., III; Moore, R. J.; and Clayton, E. R. "R&D Project Selection and Manpower Allocation with Integer Nonlinear Goal Programming." *Management Science* 28, no. 10 (October 1982):1149–58.

Tilles, Seymour. "How to Evaluate Corporate Strategy." *Harvard Business Review* 41, no. 4 (July-August 1963):111–21.

_____. "Strategies for Allocating Funds." *Harvard Business Review* 44, no. 1 (January-February 1966):72–80.

Treynor, Jack L., and Black, Fischer. "How to Use Security Analysis to Improve Portfolio Selection." *Journal of Business* 46, no. 1 (January 1973):66–86.

Truemper, Klaus, and Dean, Burton V. "The OPRAD Research and Development Management Game." *Management Science* 20, no. 6 (February 1974):999–1009.

Tull, Donald S. "The Relationship of Actual and Predicted Sales and Profits in New-Product Introductions." *Journal of Business* 40, no. 3 (July 1967):233–50.

Utterback, James M. "The Process of Technological Innovation within the Firm." *Academy of Management Journal* 14, no. 1 (March 1971):75–88.

Vance, Jack O. "The Anatomy of Corporate Strategy." *California Management Review* 13, no. 1 (Fall 1970):5–11.

Van Horn, James. "The Analysis of Uncertainty Resolution in Capital Budgeting for New Products." *Management Science* 15 (1969):376–86.

Webster, Frederick A. "A Model of Vertical Integration Strategy." *California Management Review* 10, no. 2 (Winter 1967):49–58.

Weston, J. Fred. "ROI Planning and Control." *Business Horizons* XV, no. 4 (August 1972):35–42.

Whitman, Eric S., and Landau, Edward. "Product Selection in the Chemical Industry." *Research Management* XIV, no. 5 (September 1971):56–61.

Whitmore, G.A., and Amey, Lloyd R. "Capital Budgeting under Rationing: Comments on the Lustig and Schwab Procedure." *Journal of Financial and Quantitative Analysis* VIII, no. 1 (January 1973):127–35.

Wilson, Aubrey. "Selecting New Products for Development." *Long Range Planning for Marketing and Diversification.* Edited by Bernard Taylor and Gordon Wills. London: Bradford University Press, 1971.

Wilson, Charles F., and Alexis, Marcus. "Basic Framework for Decisions." *Academy of Management Journal* 5, no. 2 (August 1962):150–64.

Winkofsky, E. P.; Baker, N. R.; and Sweeny, D. J. "A Decision Process Model of R&R Resource Allocation in Hierarchial Organizations." *Management Science* 27, no. 3 (March 1981):268–83.

Wissema, J. G. "Industrial R&D Prepares for the Eighties." *Research Management* 22, no. 5 (September 1979):22–26.

Wolff, Michael F. "When Projects Select You." *Research Management* 26, no. 3 (May 1983):8–11.

Index